Sustaining Indigenous Songs

SUSTAINING INDIGENOUS SONGS
Contemporary Warlpiri Ceremonial Life in Central Australia

Georgia Curran

berghahn
NEW YORK · OXFORD
www.berghahnbooks.com

First published in 2020 by
Berghahn Books
www.berghahnbooks.com

© 2020, 2026 Georgia Curran
First paperback edition published in 2026

All rights reserved. Except for the quotation of short passages for the purposes of criticism and review, no part of this book may be reproduced in any form or by any means, electronic or mechanical, including photocopying, recording, or any information storage and retrieval system now known or to be invented, without written permission of the publisher.

Library of Congress Cataloging-in-Publication Data

Names: Curran, Georgia, author.
Title: Sustaining Indigenous Songs: Contemporary Warlpiri Ceremonial Life in Central Australia / Georgia Curran.
Description: First edition. | New York: Berghahn, 2020. | Includes bibliographical references and index.
Identifiers: LCCN 2019042434 (print) | LCCN 2019042435 (ebook) | ISBN 9781789206074 (hardback) | ISBN 9781789206081 (ebook)
Subjects: LCSH: Warlpiri (Australian people)–Social life and customs. | Indigenous peoples–Central Australia–Social life and customs. | Oral tradition–Central Australia. | Aboriginal Australians–History.
Classification: LCC DU125.W3 C87 2020 (print) | LCC DU125.W3 (ebook) | DDC 299/.9215–dc23
LC record available at https://lccn.loc.gov/2019042434
LC ebook record available at https://lccn.loc.gov/2019042435

British Library Cataloguing in Publication Data

A catalogue record for this book is available from the British Library

EU GPSR Authorized Representative

LOGOS EUROPE, 9 rue Nicolas Poussin, 17000, LA ROCHELLE, France
Email: Contact@logoseurope.eu

ISBN 978-1-78920-607-4 hardback
ISBN 978-1-83695-405-7 paperback
ISBN 978-1-83695-406-4 epub
ISBN 978-1-78920-608-1 web pdf

https://doi.org/10.3167/9781789206074

Ngajuku kapirdiki
(For my big sister)

This book is dedicated to Jeannie Nungarrayi Egan who worked so hard to help me understand the songs and ceremonies discussed in this book.

Contents

List of Illustrations, Maps, and Figures	viii
Foreword *Otto Jungarrayi Sims*	x
Acknowledgments	xii
Notes on Text	xv
Introduction	1
Chapter 1. Song and Ceremony in Indigenous Australia	11
Chapter 2. Yuendumu: A Brief Social History	26
Chapter 3. Warlpiri Songs: Rights, Genres, and Ceremonial Contexts	43
Chapter 4. *Kurdiji*, a Ceremony for "Making Young Men"	79
Chapter 5. Holding Warlpiri Songs: Addressing Musical Endangerment	122
Conclusion	138
Appendix. Song Verses from the *Kurdiji* Ceremony	144
Glossary	171
References	175
Index	185

Illustrations, Maps, and Figures

ILLUSTRATIONS

3.1	Warlpiri men perform the Easter *purlapa* with boomerang clapsticks	72
4.1	Peggy Nampijinpa Brown with *Watiyawarnu yawulyu* designs	88
4.2	Ruth Napaljarri Oldfield with *Warlukurlangu yawulyu* designs	90
4.3	The *kurdiji* "shields" painted for ceremonies in 2007	92
5.1	Warlpiri men sing *kurdiji* songs at Milpirri, 2016	125
5.2	Warlpiri women dance *yawulyu* for Milpirri, 2016	126
5.3	Warlpiri women dance *Ngapa yawulyu* as part of Unbroken Land in September 2018	137

MAPS

1.1	Central Australia	10
2.1	Central Australia region surrounding Yuendumu	34
4.1	Places along the *Karntakarnta* "traveling ancestral women" *Jukurrpa*	96

FIGURES

2.1	Warlpiri in the Australian language family tree	27
2.2	Subsection system of social organization	35
3.1	Patrimoieties and patricouples	50
3.2–3.4	A song verse sung as three "song items"	56–57
3.5	Musical assertions of ownership	63
4.1	Temporal overview of the *Kurdiji* ceremony	81
4.2	Genealogy of the family of Jampijinpa and Jampijinpa/Japangardi	82
4.3	Genealogy of the family of Japangardi	83
4.4	Co-initiate kin reference terms	84
4.5	Ground plan for the afternoon *yawulyu* and *parnpa*	91
4.6	Ground plan for *parnpa* just after sunset	93
4.7	Ground plan for all-night phase of *Marnakurrawarnu*	94
4.8	Dance movements for *Kurdiji*	98
4.9	Seating arrangements prior to *Warawata*	117
4.10	Ground plan for *Warawata*	119

Foreword

Otto Jungarrayi Sims

Our stories and our songs haven't been written down, they haven't been documented. They were given to us by our ancestors. From the day Warlpiri people are conceived, we are born in the dust of our earth and we feel the elements of the earth that embody us. Our grandmothers and our grandfathers teach us [about] our *Jukurrpa* (Dreaming). We inherit that *Jukurrpa*, that totem. We immediately have the spirit of that ancestor within us. We sing to avoid homesickness, in our ancestors' voices. They look after us, so we can't be lost. Songs keep us safe—we are lost without them. They make our faces glow, and you can see it inside other Indigenous people.

When we listen to our grandfathers singing the songs, our ears, and our subconscious mind, open up. As we grow older, we realize that this is what they (the elders) were talking about. *Yapa* culture hasn't been written about or documented since time began. Now those ancestral beings have turned into stones, into sacred rocks, scared trees or sacred engravings. For *yapa* (Indigenous people), for me to interpret the rock or the tree . . . it is not through a physical mind. I have to switch my mind off to read it with a spiritual mind.

We can only share the outer layers, the top layers of meaning. The first layer consists of the stories that we tell our kids. The second layer is about the family groups. The third layer is where you come from, your totem, where you inherit your *Jukurrpa* from. It is the fourth layer that is very sensitive. If we reveal that layer, we are nothing as an Indigenous person. We only share the outer layers. We warn Indigenous persons, the *yapa* communities around Australia, that we don't want to reveal the hidden mystery of how we survived. If we reveal that, whitefellas will come in and manipulate us. We have to think, and we have to balance it. This is how they did it in the old days too. The *Jukurrpa* is from the beginning.

Some parts of *Kurdiji* (ceremonies for making young men) can be a bit sensitive. Some layers the women listen to. It's about ancestral beings who criss-crossed our country in the *Jukurrpa*. Some stuff we can't reveal; some stuff is open to the public. Some parts of *Kurdiji* are open, some are not open. The duration of the song, the tempo, the timing of the song, when to begin, when to stop, when to dance, when not to dance, and what time. All of these things have been recorded. The older people know what we're singing about, but not the young ones. They are still unskilled. Some are learning as they grow older and they get mature. This is when their way of thinking opens. It's a way of preserving language. It's an old language. I can't even understand it. It's really old.

We do this as it's a new way of preserving language and songs. Then we can make arguments with the government. We have language. It was given by the ancestral beings. It's about keeping our stories strong in a time when the world is changing really rapidly. With technology we can do this. If we want to make an argument with a mining company, we can [show] we have the songs within us and we've recorded them. *Ngurrju nyampu piya* [it's good like that]. Young people today… they can make an argument. Only the top layer though. One day we'll tell the story, we'll go somewhere, to big festivals overseas and tell them about the beauty of what makes our great land Australia. It is forever, it won't cease. We hold on. We go to the elders. [Books] like this will boost us to hold on, our family, our way of life through songs, our *Jukurrpa*, holding the totems, and holding the culture religiously. *Ngurrju-nyayirni* (It's really good). It's about all this, and it has been forever.

Otto Jungarrayi Sims is a senior Warlpiri elder who has grown up and lived all his life in Central Australia. He is an internationally acclaimed artist and through his work advocates for Warlpiri cultural traditions to remain strong in the future. Sims is the chairperson for Warlukurlangu Artists Aboriginal Corporation.

Acknowledgments

First and foremost, I sincerely thank the many people from Yuendumu who have at various times over the last fourteen years incorporated me into their world and shared with me the rich experience of their lives. Certain people I particularly acknowledge for their contribution. Jeannie Nungarrayi Egan (who sadly passed away in 2009) and her husband, Thomas Jangala Rice, were key collaborators in the Warlpiri Songlines Project, through which I undertook my PhD research from 2005 to 2008. Their hard work, patience and passion for teaching me about Warlpiri songs and ceremonies could not have been surpassed. Jangala, with his knowledge of Warlpiri songs, their religious significance, and the country with which they are associated, and Nungarrayi, with her passion for documentation, made for a truly remarkable team. Other Warlpiri people that were key to this project include especially Coral Napangardi Gallagher and Ruth Napaljarri Oldfield, both very dear friends whose warmth, patience, and love of life have provided me with continual encouragement over many years.

I also want to thank a large group of senior women with whom I spent a great deal of time recording songs, talking about associated stories, visiting the country, going hunting, camping out, and attending business meetings. Their good nature in often hard conditions will always be an inspiration. I thank them all for looking after me—Maggie Napaljarri Ross, Mary Nangala Ross, Judy Nampijinpa Granites, Ruby Napurrurla Williams, Ruby Nakamarra Collins, Lucky Nampijinpa Langton, Nelly Nangala Wayne, Peggy Nampijinpa Brown, Pamela Nangala Sampson, Dora Napaljarri Kitson, Liddy Napanangka Walker, Long Maggie Nakamarra White, Lucy Nakamarra White, Biddy Napaljarri White, Ena Napaljarri Spencer, Ruth Napaljarri Oldfield, Lucy Napaljarri Kennedy, Coral Napangardi Gallagher, Freda Napaljarri, Lena Nungarrayi, Gracie Napangardi Johnson, Rosie Napangardi Johnson, Lynette Nampijinpa Granites, Yuni Nampijinpa Martin, Rosie Nangala Fleming, Lorraine Nungarrayi Granites, Emma Nungarrayi

Granites, Maisy Napurrurla Wayne, Bessie Nakamarra Sims, Daisy Nangala, Mavis Nampijinpa, and Topsy Napaljarri.

I also thank a core group of senior men with whom I worked at various stages—I am honored to have been taught about their songs and ceremonies: Harry Jakamarra Nelson, Tommy Jangala Watson, Warren Japanangka Williams, Gary Jakamarra White, Shorty Jangala Robertson, Paddy Japaljarri Simms, Paddy Japaljarri Stewart, Ted Jangala Egan, Johnny Japanangka Williams, Harry Japanangka Dixon, Neville ("Cobra") Japangardi Poulson, Warren Japanangka Williams and Thomas Jangala Rice.

Special thanks must go to Nancy Napurrurla Oldfield, who not only let me stay in her house for well over a year but continues to be a wonderful friend. Thanks to Perry, Ashley, Zyanne, Kara, and the many other people who lived with us at various stages during my fieldwork, in particular Leanne, Bess, Julie, Katherine, Janet, and Isabelle. Thanks also to Barbara, Edgar, Mildred, Maxie, Glenda, Leon, Fay, Luke, Fianca, Leroy, Carlos, Lulu, Troydon, and many others for being a secondary family next door and sharing my day-to-day life with me. Thanks to Coral Gallagher, Maggie Ross, Marlette Ross, Louanna Williams, Kamen Cook, Ruth Oldfield, Ena Spencer, Lucy Kennedy, Erica Ross, Enid Gallagher, Reilly Oldfield, Ormay Gallagher, Otto Simms, Lucy Dixon, and Harry Dixon for looking after me as part of their mob during countless business trips and throughout day-to-day life in Yuendumu. To many, many others in Yuendumu, who I have not had a chance to list here, thank you all for your friendship. It is sad how many have now passed away.

Thanks to the mob at the Mt Theo Program (WYDAC), particularly Suzie Lowe, Brett Badger, and Talitha Lowe, for their support of our project and for providing an office for Jeannie and Thomas, in which we worked for many months. Thanks also to the Warlpiri Media mob, particularly Rita Cattoni, Susan Locke, Trevor Edmond, Anna Cadden, Simon Japangardi Fisher Sr., and more recently Jeff Bruer. Frank and Wendy Baarda, Pam and Peter Malden, Gloria Morales, Cecilia Alfonso, Bob Gosford, Sam McKell, Liam Campbell, Claire Pocock, Lee Williams, Karissa Preuss, Anna Meltzer, and Frances Claffey have all provided support at various points. Nicole Lee and Jonno Raveney—thank you both for your hospitality during visits to Alice Springs. There are countless other people across Central Australia who provided me with friendship and support who are far too numerous to list here.

I especially wish to acknowledge the outstanding support of Nicolas Peterson. Nic initially got me involved in the Warlpiri Songlines Project, helped me organize my fieldwork, spent time with me in Yuendumu, gave me ideas and had lengthy discussions with me, read numerous drafts of this book, and provided continual practical support and friendship. Thanks also to Ros Peterson for her warmth and hospitality and for looking after Warlpiri visitors in Canberra. Another special thanks must go to my other supervisor Mary Laughren. Mary initially suggested that I apply to be a part of this project, and she has given me continued support over many years. She has shared with me her rich knowledge of Warlpiri culture and language through time spent together in Yuendumu and other places. Her intimate knowledge of details of Warlpiri culture and language, in particular through the invaluable resource of her Warlpiri dictionary and her insightful comments on my thesis drafts have enriched this book. I thank Yasmine Musharbash and Françoise Dussart for their companionship and loyalty during periods of fieldwork. Insightful comments by Françoise Dussart and Sylvie Poirier have been crucial in shaping the ideas presented in this book. More recently, I am grateful for the support and collaboration of Linda Barwick and Myfany Turpin and their assistance in creating opportunities that have allowed me to continue working with Warlpiri people and engaging in research on their musical culture.

Finally, I would like to thank my family for their support over the years. My mother and father, Suzanne and Bertram Curran, my partner Ben Palmer, and our children Lachlan, Louis, and Maia. I am grateful for their practical and emotional support, for sharing in the adventures, and for their acceptance and tolerance of the personal demands that go along with my unconventional career choices.

Notes on Text

In consultation with Warlpiri families, the decision to include the names of deceased people in this book has been made so as to recognize their contribution to this research. In all other parts, Warlpiri "skin" names have been used rather than personal names.

Introduction

NEW YEAR'S EVE 2005

I sat protectively encased by a group of women on the cement veranda in front of their house—our eyes looking outward to the streets. Our day was just beginning. The campfire smoldered nearby—it was no longer needed as it had already provided us with tea for the morning. The lethargy that would be brought on by the heat of the coming day hung close, but it had not yet hit. Cars cruised past. From the windows, people shouted to their families with a kind of urgency that for some reason did not seem to require any kind of immediate attention. A battered red sedan pulled up to the fence that surrounded the house's yard. Jupurrurla slowly emerged from the car, his wife Nangala following behind with a paper bag full of food. In his characteristically soft but assured manner, Jupurrurla informed us that two more boys had been "caught" last night and had been taken to a nearby bush location to be looked after by a group of senior men until ceremonies began. This news was fresh from his and Nangala's recent visit to the Big shop, one of Yuendumu's two grocery stores, which had opened only an hour earlier but to which the majority of the settlement's residents had already visited for breakfast supplies. Our group began to murmur among itself. Having only come to live in Yuendumu just over a month earlier, I was unsure of what this meant for the coming days.

§

I was grateful to have such an encompassing group of women take me under their wing. As a twenty-three-year-old student having lived in and traveled independently to various cities and towns in my short adult life, I was used to looking after myself. But in Yuendumu it was different. Here, one had to have family. Napaljarri was close to one of my PhD supervisors, Mary, and had been one of the first people I had met in Yuendumu. She gave me my skin name, Nungarrayi, which made her my *pimirdi* (father's sister)—and therefore directly responsible for my learning.[1] Napaljarri was also intimately involved with Yasmine, who was doing postdoctoral research in Yuendumu during this period. I did not know Yasmine before I arrived in Yuendumu, but she met me at the arch over the road when I first drove into the settlement and looked after me in those early days. Napaljarri knew that it was her responsibility to care for me—a duty she did not question due to her relationship with both Mary and Yasmine.

I had a Toyota, which allowed us to go out hunting every afternoon, get firewood when we needed it, and drive around Yuendumu whenever necessary. Unlike most other *kardiya* (non-Indigenous people) in Yuendumu, I had no job—other than to be an anthropologist. I was still figuring out what that meant in this new context. I had some money that I had received as a stipend from the university, but after my monthly car repayment, there wasn't much left, which allowed me to genuinely enter into relationships of equality. Demands were made of me, I obliged when I could, and I was looked after knowing I always had somewhere to go and people to be with. I was incorporated into the extended families of these women, the children and their mothers who spent their days with us, and the young men, who haphazardly visited whenever they needed something.

§

By lunchtime, my Toyota was sinking under the weight of blankets, billycans, swags, drums of flour, and many other items that we would supposedly need over the following weeks. Napaljarri told me to go on the "short-cut road." By afternoon, we would be in the nearby settlement of Wariyiwariyi. If it rained, it would wash out the short-cut road, making it impassable, and we would have to drive along the "main road" instead. But there hadn't been any rain for a while.

We formed a convoy with several other vehicles. Three Napaljarri sisters traveled in my car. All were elderly women who had grown up walking around the bush between Wariyiwariyi and Yuendumu—Anmatyerr and Warlpiri country. Napangardi came with us too. Over the next few years, I came to love Napangardi's gregarious personality and wit. One of the Napaljarris who I traveled with had once been a big businesswoman, and I had read about her in Françoise Dussart's ethnography of ritual life in

Yuendumu in the 1980s. Now she was *warungka* (mad/senile). Some of the family had not wanted her to come as she'd be too difficult to look after and would get confused. But we also couldn't leave her alone in Yuendumu. Another Napaljarri required a lot of physical help. She had suffered a stroke when she was only in her forties and had never received proper rehabilitation, so she had trouble walking and using one of her arms. I soon learned techniques for helping her in and out of my car, making her bed so she could easily get into it, and setting things up so that she could manage to look after herself.

We left in convoy with several other vehicles also packed to bursting, their roof racks swaying as we drove out through Yuendumu's north camp, the visible dust rising from our cars signaling to others that we had left. After driving eastward for about an hour and a half along a dirt track, we pulled up a short distance from a few makeshift shelters. To our immediate north was the settlement of Mt Allan, spoken of more often by Warlpiri people as Wariyiwariyi; a hill divided the settlement into two sides. I quickly picked up the twofold ego-centered directional language, by which one referred to the opposite side of the hill they were on as the "otherside." To the south of the settlement was a cleared area that had recently been graded in preparation for the upcoming ceremonies. The whole area was buzzing with people who had set up camps nearby. I gathered under the shade of a large tree with the group from Yuendumu, hiding from the intense afternoon desert heat typical at this time of year. Various people came over to talk to us, many of whom I already knew from Yuendumu, many of whom I was meeting for the first time.

In the late afternoon, we put our swags in a long line, forming the camp in which single women would sleep for the next few weeks. Our heads faced to the east. My swag was snugly wedged in the midst of this line, which protected me as a vulnerable outsider in this world. Another Napaljarri who had traveled in one of the other cars from Yuendumu slept next to me. She had known my other PhD supervisor, Nic, from when Nic had worked closely with her late husband in the 1970s. Other married couples and families who had come from Yuendumu camped in their own small groups a short distance away around their own fires. As the day and the year ended, the dry heat slowly became less intense. The setting sun in the distance provided a warm light that brought on an overwhelming feeling of communality. I felt relaxed and at home as I sat on my swag drinking a large pannikin of tea. People sat talking into the night in a language that I had yet to understand. Occasionally a car engine backfired. We heard the shouts of drunks in the distance as one year passed into the next.

NEW YEAR'S DAY 2006

Over breakfast, the women in our camp chatted about needing *yurlpa* (red ochre). Napaljarri produced a hunk of white rock from her bag to emphasize that they still needed the shiny red version of that type of rock for painting designs on the women's chests while singing *yawulyu* (women's songs) later that day. There was a place where we could get it nearby. When I had finished my tea, several women gathered their crowbars and billycans, and we piled back into my Toyota. We spent an exhausting day in the hot sun. There weren't many trees around, and I could feel my skin burning—heat exhaustion began to overwhelm me. These elderly women kept at it, hacking away at the dry, hard earth with their crowbars. In the end, they had a few large chunks of reddish rock. Napaljarri rubbed some onto her hand and whispered to me that when it was ground into powder and mixed with oil, it would shine.

When we returned to our camp, we heard that two more boys had been "caught" during the day. Their mothers were sitting near an area that had recently been cleared for the upcoming ceremonies. They were crying out in an ongoing high-pitched wail, a look of helplessness and despair on their faces. In the late afternoon, as the sun sank closer toward the western horizon, a crowd clustered on the edge of the cleared business area, women sitting on the far western side and men on the far eastern side, around one hundred meters from each other. The women were rubbing oil and some of the crushed red ochre onto their arms and legs, and they encouraged me to do the same. Two teenage boys sat among the women, looking down in what appeared to be intense shame. Silence fell over the group as two men in their twenties walked solemnly over to the women and took the boys' hands, firmly leading them over to sit with the men. Their mothers, with whom they had been sitting, wailed helplessly, hysterically trying to grasp hold of their sons, though intentionally missing as they were escorted away. These women threw themselves against the red earth in despair and sat sobbing dramatically until after sunset. The rest of us went back to our camp. I collapsed into my swag, exhausted from the intensity of the day's events: the heat, the physical labor, and the emotion of the afternoon overcame me.

2 JANUARY 2006

After lunch, groups of women began to gather under a large shaded area that they had built on the western side of the business ground. The *yurlpa* we had collected the day before and the white version, called *ngunjungunju*, which someone produced from their bag, were applied to women's chests in beautiful designs. As they painted one another, the women sang *yawulyu* associated with the same Dreamings as the designs. As these women were painted they became infused with a special quality—they shone with beauty as a magical feeling overcame the group.

On the eastern side of the business ground, the men were dancing. I could see Napangardi's brother, a Japangardi I knew from Yuendumu. He was painted with white ochre to which fluff was attached, and feathers protruded from his hair. Napangardi saw me looking at him and whispered, "That's goanna from Mt Theo—he's looking for Nungarrayi." She smiled mischievously but hushed me when I began to question further. Months later, reminding me of this dance, Napangardi told me the story of an anthropomorphized goanna, Japangardi, from Mt Theo, who was a "loverboy" for his mother-in-law, Nungarrayi, a taboo love match for Warlpiri people. This is who Japangardi had become in his dance.

Three separate groups of women had formed under the shade. Each group was singing different *yawulyu* and smaller groups of women were painting one another independently. The effect of these groups sitting in close proximity was that the singing turned in to a mélange of sound, and it was difficult to make out the individual songs. The women in these groups were thus leaning in close together so they could hear each other. This continued until sunset, and afterward I headed back to our camp to get something to eat and have a rest before the big ceremony, which was to be held that night. Again exhausted from the activities of the last few days, I lay down in my swag and fell, unknowingly into a deep sleep.

A few hours later, I awoke to the sound of a heavy beat and singing in the distance. I jumped up, alarmed that I had missed the start of the ceremony. No one was at our camp, so I hesitantly made my way over to the business ground. Aware that there were probably places I should and should not be but completely ignorant as to where these were, I desperately searched for someone I knew. Finally, a Napaljarri noticed me and called out to come and sit with her. She told me that her husband, Japangardi, had been looking for me, and she went to get him. The three of us went to the side of the business area—a place for both men and women to meet. Japangardi told me sternly that it was important that I record this ceremony. He seemed annoyed that I was late and had missed the beginning. I was aware that I had already used up a substantial amount of space on the SD cards I had for my audio recording device earlier in the day. As Japangardi matter-of-factly explained, they would be singing until sunrise, and it was very important that I record *all* the songs. I realized that it would not be possible to record another eight hours of singing while still adhering to the recording quality of current international best practice. I contemplated how to explain this to Japangardi. As I began, his eyes glazed over, and he firmly told me that I would just have to do it somehow before disappearing back to sit with the male singers. I sat down with the women, deflated, and experimented with different settings on my recording machine to see which ones might allow more space to document these events. Eventually I set it to the poorest quality MP3 recording, realizing that this was the only way I could capture the spectacular singing from this all-night event. I imagined the criticism I would later receive for recording such a brilliant ceremonial performance at such low quality. Fortunately I had a long lead, so I could set up the microphone within the group of male singers while still operating the recording machine from my position on the edge of the group of women a few meters behind to the west. In the space between the singers and the larger group of women, a line of dancers formed in a long row—behind some of the women, several others held their waists lightly as they danced. I set the machine to record and monitored it throughout the night—dogs knocked it constantly, and men tripped on the lead as they regularly went for toilet breaks or yelled to their wives for tea or food. I was called upon many times to dance with the other Nungarrayi women. I followed their movements as best as I could, shuffling forward with arms slumped. Occasionally certain women would hold a firestick, of which several were circulating, before placing it back into the fire to keep it burning. On two occasions, a firestick was passed to me, and I danced at the front of the line to the delighted shouts and encouragement from women behind me. The night was long, and the men frequently yelled out for the time, calculating how many more hours until the sun would rise and bring an end to their all-night effort.

Six teenage boys sat crouched at the back of the business ground. They were the ones who had been "caught" in the days beforehand—two just that afternoon, two the night before we had left Yuendumu, and two in the days before that. For the duration of the night, the women focused their attention to the east, to the female dancers in front of them and to the group of male singers further to the east again. At several points I stole a glance back westward to see the spectacular vision of the boys as they stood up to stretch their legs, their bodies decorated in white fluff and glowing in the firelight bounded on their western side by a windbreak made of thick leaves. Throughout the night, their slightly older and much more physically mature brothers-in-law looked after them. The same men who had taken them from their mothers earlier in the afternoon in ritualized drama were looking after them during this long and arduous night. Dawn began to encroach. The eastern sky slowly became orange. Quite suddenly I was told to pack up, as we had to leave quickly. The microphone was swept up in a frenzy of blankets and billycans, and we raced back to our camp. A dominant whirring sound came from behind us, and I dared not look back as the men finished up their business. At our camp, all the women buried their heads in their swags, clearly indicating to me that I was not to look over to the business ground. I lay down at first, making a point "not to look" at what was audibly a grand event happening nearby. It wasn't long though before I was asleep.

§

This book tells the story of the way I learned about Warlpiri ceremonies. My first time at *Kurdiji* I felt like I understood little of what was going on. At the time, I was overwhelmed in many ways by new faces, a new language, and new experiences. Over the following years, as I worked in Yuendumu recording and documenting many different genres of Warlpiri songs, my learning took a more formalized approach, involving an analytical aspect that simply did not exist in the performance contexts. During this time, Warlpiri people would often say to me in response to questions I had about *Kurdiji*, "You know, you were there, and you danced." During these years, I went to many more *Kurdiji* in various communities—Yuendumu, Mt Allan, and Willowra—and came to know what to expect. This book presents my understanding of Warlpiri songs and ceremonial practices, including *Kurdiji*, which I have learned through a different process to most Warlpiri people. Similarities exist, however: learning cannot be rushed, and the only way to truly learn is through embodied participation.

When I lived in Yuendumu between 2005 and 2007, as a PhD student on the Warlpiri Songlines project under the guidance of Warlpiri elders and academics with longstanding connections to Warlpiri people, my job largely centered on recording songs and transcribing and translating them with the assistance of elders and literate Warlpiri people. On top of this, I would obtain as much exegesis as possible about these songs. In some ways, this is a sort of documentary project instigated by Warlpiri people keen on recording the rich detail encoded in songs—something that was no longer being learned by younger generations. This project was popular among Warlpiri people in Yuendumu, and I never had a shortage of people wishing to work with me. The research we were doing was regarded as important not only because it created a record of cultural heritage that Warlpiri people were deeply proud of but also because older people who had this knowledge were dying and younger generations were not learning these songs, at least not with the same depth of knowledge or detail as previous generations had learned them. Academically, however, I felt vulnerable. This type of work was in some ways regarded as an old-fashioned "salvage" project, obsessed with "tradition" and steeped in past practices that hold little relevance in the contemporary world.

In this book, I take a performative approach to the study of songs and their place in ritual, concerning myself with the process of continuity and change to ceremonial life for the Warlpiri people of Yuendumu. My primary aim is to analyze these songs in their contemporary ritual context. I hope that this approach does not undermine the profound significance of the religious knowledge encoded in Warlpiri songs, often in fascinatingly esoteric ways. In 1984, the great scholar of Warlpiri language Ken Hale wrote of the intellectual joy that comes from understanding a Warlpiri song verse (1984: 259). Being privileged enough to have experienced this is a gift for which I am eternally thankful to the many Warlpiri people who have worked with me over the last fourteen years. I hope that this book demonstrates the profound intellectual substance of these songs and their complex systems of interrelated knowledge. While these songs may be sung by older generations, this book aims to illustrate their importance and vitality for all generations of Warlpiri people, even those who may have very little knowledge of the content of the songs.

OUTLINE OF THIS BOOK

This book centers on understanding the changing contexts for Warlpiri songs and ceremonies. As many Indigenous Australian[2] musical practices are considered endangered, this book aims to illustrate that, despite this extreme fragility, songs and their associated ceremonies maintain social vitality and purpose in the contemporary Warlpiri world. Chapter 1 provides an overview of how to understand the continuity and change of the songs and ceremonial lives of Central Australian Aboriginal people and sets out the fieldwork practices that have underpinned the analyses presented in this book. Chapter 2 follows by providing a brief social history of the settlement of Yuendumu and the populations of Warlpiri people who live there. Chapter 3 sets forth the features of various genres of Warlpiri song and introduces the ways in which these songs link Warlpiri people to owned Dreamings and country and broader kinship networks. The central case study is presented in chapter 4, which provides a detailed description of a *Kurdiji* ceremony and highlights both the performance of ritualized actions and the context-specific emergent features of the ceremony; these contribute to its vitality in the contemporary Warlpiri world. Chapter 5 illustrates that, despite the socially imperative nature of contemporary ceremonial life in settlements like Yuendumu and its function in carrying forward many core cultural values, it exists in contexts of extreme vulnerability in the modern world. In this book's conclusion, I further consider the tensions that arise from this context.

NOTES

1. For a Warlpiri woman, paternal aunts (fathers' sisters, FZ) are responsible for teaching their nieces (brothers' daughters, BD) their Dreaming, country, and songs as ownership is inherited patrilineally.
2. Throughout this book, I use the term "Indigenous Australians" when referring to broader issues faced by Aboriginal and Torres Strait Island Australians. I use the term "Aboriginal" when referring to people from mainland Australia. Wherever possible, I specifically refer to the Warlpiri groups of Central Australia, as this is where the ethnography is based, and I do not wish to make generalizations about other Aboriginal groups.

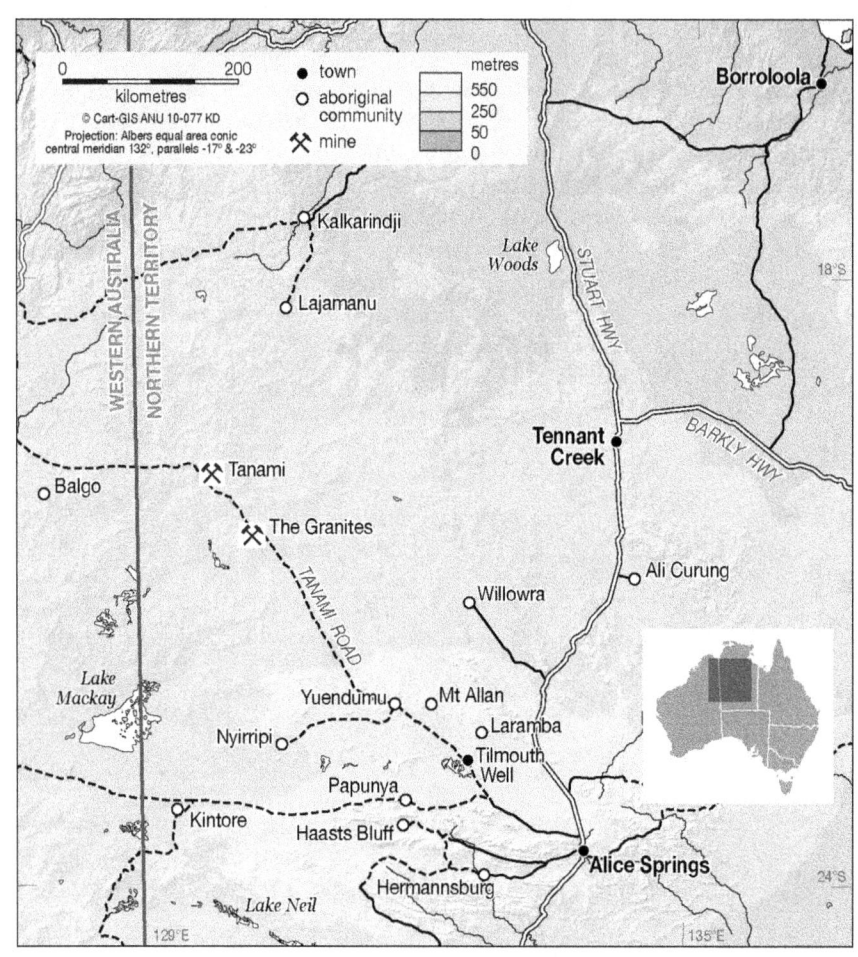

Map 1.1 Central Australia. Created by CartoGIS Services, CAP, Australian National University.

Chapter 1

Song and Ceremony in Indigenous Australia

This book is an ethnography of the contemporary world of singing and ceremony for Warlpiri people living in the settlement of Yuendumu, located in the Central Australian Tanami Desert (see map 1.1). For Indigenous peoples across Australia, songs and ceremonies are core components of cultural heritage that encapsulate the cosmological beliefs, understandings of land, and kinship systems fundamental to cultural and social well-being. As they have in many areas of Australia, dramatic changes to Aboriginal ways of living have occurred since colonization. In Central Australia, it was not until well into the 1900s that Aboriginal people began living in settlements, eating introduced diets, and, much later again, structuring their lives around a westernized workday. Yet how exactly have these historical factors impacted the status of songs and ceremonies? Are songs merely components of "traditional" life that are only known and appreciated by older generations—mementos of a past that are irrelevant in today's world? Has the powerful role that ceremonies once held in Aboriginal religious life lost some of its significance? And if these ceremonies are still central to aspects of Aboriginal sociality, what will happen when the generation that knows these songs passes on? Who will sing these songs that are at the core of the ceremonies' performance? In this book, I explore the tensions that surround the decline of the knowledge and practices required to continue these deeply valued singing traditions and ceremonial practices.

Early Australian anthropology has centered on analyzing how rituals adapt to the particular contexts and circumstances of surrounding social worlds. Indigenous knowledge and songs are well known to manifest in new forms and contexts as the surrounding circumstances change. In the north of Australia, contemporary, popular musical styles incorporate elements of more "traditional" songs, carrying into the future the knowledge of country, kinship, and stories. In Central Australia, this is less the case due to greater conservatism and restrictions on the sharing of some knowledge in certain public contexts. Despite this, there have been many responses to the declining opportunities for performance, with Aboriginal people making efforts to set up new contexts in which to nurture songs, their knowledge, and associated practices. Future cultural reproduction of these cherished aspects of cultural heritage is, however, considered by Indigenous people to be under threat, and it is common to hear people talk of the "loss of culture." Documenting and preserving Indigenous cultural heritage, set against this backdrop, is seen as valuable and as having the potential to ensure that Indigenous people will have access to these fundamental aspects of their cultural identities at a future point when the knowledgeable elders may have all passed away. For many Indigenous peoples living in the regions of coastal and southern Australia, which were settled earlier, the records of early ethnographers are some of the only details they have of their languages, music, and distinct cultural practices from a period prior to and during early colonization. Efforts in cultural maintenance often prioritize these aspects of "culture" over the less consciously absorbed but still identifiably distinct Indigenous modes of being that continue to the present day. Nicolas Peterson has, problematized this kind of understanding of the maintenance of a "Culture" in noting that it is

> now associated with a completely objectified and thing-like understanding that bears little resemblance to any nuanced anthropological view in which much culture is implicit, taken for granted, and embedded in sedimented dispositions. (2017: 237)

Nonetheless, fixed understandings of culture still receive significant attention in Australia, with federal governments emphasizing through policy and funding avenues the importance of maintaining this "Aboriginal culture," a view also supported by Aboriginal people and their nationwide organizations (Merlan 1989). For Indigenous people, whose lived everyday experience is within these cultural worlds, confusion arises as views of well-being are increasingly framed by connections to a "culture" that is increasingly difficult to maintain into the neocolonial present (and future).

Despite these more nuanced scholarly understandings, it is a widely held rhetoric among the broader Australian population and the Aboriginal people themselves that singing and ceremonial life are aspects of a "traditional" or "authentic" Aboriginal culture. Pervasive pan-Aboriginal representations include symbolic references to music, including didgeridoos, clapsticks, body paint, and iconic dance styles. In the southeast of Australia, many people of Aboriginal descent have lost a great deal of knowledge of their ceremonial practices due to enforced settlement and the imposition of new ways of living since the beginnings of British colonization in 1788. Social problems such as drug and alcohol abuse, unemployment, and family welfare issues are often attributed to a loss of a cultural identity that is intimately associated with songs and related ceremonial practices. These views recognize the connection between a strong Aboriginal culture and peoples' capacity for meaningful lives, even if they do fix an understanding of this Aboriginal form of identity. Many programs that seek to deal with social and health problems initiate cultural heritage maintenance projects. In Yuendumu, the highly successful Mt Theo Program (now Warlpiri Youth Development Aboriginal Corporation), which works to positively engage Warlpiri youths, runs a program called Jaru Pirrjirdi (which translates as "strong culture"). This initially began as a diversionary program in which older Warlpiri people would take their younger family members out into the bush and teach them about the stories and songs relating to particular locations in Warlpiri country. The Warlpiri Milpirri Festival, a spectacular one-night event held every two years in the northern Warlpiri community of Lajamanu, also addresses these challenges by innovatively setting performances of traditional genres of song side-by-side with composed hip-hop performances by younger school children (see Biddle 2019). Warlpiri elders participate in these initiatives enthusiastically, holding a similar view that if young people could only know about these "traditionalized" aspects of their culture, they would have more fulfilling lives and would no longer resort to antisocial behaviors.

This book aims to provide ethnographic understanding of the place of songs and ceremonies in modern Warlpiri lives, centered predominantly in Yuendumu. It is based largely on fieldwork undertaken between 2005 and 2008, but it includes reflections over the subsequent ten years as I have continued to visit and spend time with Warlpiri people and participate in ceremonial activities when possible. I approach Warlpiri song and ceremony through broader ethnographic descriptions of Warlpiri musical lives and a detailed case study of the *Kurdiji* ceremony, which is held several times in Yuendumu every summer. *Kurdiji* has increased in size in recent decades and involves participants across generations, and it is considered essential for Warlpiri sociality. In this book, I explore this apparent vitality against the background rhetoric of the endangerment of ceremonial knowledge and practices.

UNDERSTANDING MUSICAL CHANGE IN CENTRAL AUSTRALIA

Musical change is normal and necessary. Bruno Nettl explains that "if there is anything really stable in the musics of the world, it is the constant existence of change" (1983: 275). In Australia, where songs hold together Indigenous cosmological beliefs of an ongoing period of creation, known widely in Aboriginal English as "the Dreaming" or "Dreamtime," westernized concepts of time and history are conflated. Stanner writes that "although . . . the Dreaming conjures up the notion of a sacred, heroic time of the indefinitely remote past, such a time is also, in a sense, still part of the present" (1979: 24). Songs and stories in Central Australia link places together. This notion, central to Aboriginal worldviews, is often commonly referred to as a "songline" in Aboriginal English (Moore et al. 2016). For Warlpiri people, songs are considered to be the voices of ancestral beings as they traveled through sites in Warlpiri country in this creational period. Fred Myers writes of Pintupi notions of the Dreaming, noting that

> it represents all that exists as deriving from a single, unchanging, timeless source. All things have been the same forever deriving from the same basic pattern. The Dreaming, which cannot be altered by human action, is the very image of self-direction and the source of a given autonomy in human life. (1986: 52)

This view, one often portrayed by Aboriginal people themselves, describes an overarching dominant structure that shapes the events of people's lives. In T. G. H. Strehlow's *Songs of Central Australia* (1971), one of the earliest comprehensive documentations of song in this region, he reiterates the Aboriginal belief that songs are given to people from Dreaming ancestors, thus giving people little control over the ways in which they are performed. Despite these many bold comments about the unchanging nature of Aboriginal songs, some of Strehlow's observations indicate that he may have suspected otherwise. For example, in discussing the learning process involved when teaching ceremonies to initiates, he writes,

> Most of the verses of these songs are learned by the young men at a time when the correct explanations of the archaic and poetic words have not yet been given to them. (Strehlow 1971: 203)

This suggests that Strehlow recognized that the knowledgeable elders were controlling the ways in which songs were being learned and understood so as to slowly reveal knowledge as their junior counterparts became ready. Thus, the older men maintain a degree of control over when and how songs are learned, and which bits of this powerful information particular people know. Another early scholar of Central Australian Aboriginal beliefs, Geza Roheim (1945: 3) describes instances of unconscious mislearning of a song, such as incorporating a misheard word, leading to a transformation in tradition. Hale explores these kinds of changes to songs as creative acts, illustrating the ways in which people actively control which songs are sung rather than learn verbatim passages. He refers to this phenomenon as "slippage" and describes purposeful "mislearning" in which people make small changes to songs to make aesthetic improvements (1984). Hale demonstrates this through an example of the Warlpiri and Arandic contexts of the honey ant song, using the differences to illustrate how changes can be incorporated to provide avenues for creativity. He puts forth the idea, that "the *learning* of a song is a creative act" (1984: 260). This idea is necessary to understand musical change in the Central Aboriginal Australian context. Geoff O'Grady was possibly the first to point out "the unity of the actual and the potential," drawn from his observations of lexical items that were shared for "fire" and "firewood" or "animal" and "meat" (1960). Change is thus incorporated easily in to an Aboriginal worldview, and, I argue, it is a necessary component of any tradition, as evidenced in other literature of Aboriginal Australia.

Dussart discusses songs that are dreamed by Warlpiri people in Yuendumu, noting that

> they consider the material to be retrieved or re-remembered—reclaimed from the Dreaming after an unspecified time of neglect or amnesia. (2000: 147)

Similarly, with reference to the Kukatja from around the Balgo area, northwest of Yuendumu, Sylvie Poirier (2005) emphasizes understandings of the "openness" and "flexibility" of the Dreaming also illustrated through the processes of being given new ceremonies in nocturnal dreams. The late Warlpiri elder Lucy Napaljarri Kennedy reiterated these ways of knowing "new" stories from other places: she told of *milarlpa* (spirits) from her country that brought the Dreaming from another place to where she was in Yuendumu, informing her of it in a dream which she was then able to share with others.

Ian Keen (1994) comments on the restriction of religious knowledge in northeast Arnhem Land to ritually senior Yolngu men and women. He highlights the ambiguous meanings of songs and suggests that such ambiguity is a way to control access to and use of this valuable and powerful knowledge (Keen 1994: 42). Also taking up this point, Francesca Merlan notes that the "the textual opacity of Aboriginal songs forces the learner (whether outside analyst or local person) to rely largely, even entirely, upon knowledgeable interpreters . . ." (1987: 146). This puts those ritually knowledgeable people in a powerful position, as they are relied upon for an understanding of ritual matters. In Keen's discussion, titled "The Same but Different," he shows that there is agreement among Yolngu about the general stories and symbols used in myth but the interpretations of them can be quite different (1994: 61).

In Yuendumu, broader social systems undoubtedly set up contexts for many of the events of individual lives, yet social actors shape their world within this organized society, adhering to the accepted customs, broader structures, and systems (including the Laws determined by the Dreaming). In some ways Pierre Bourdieu's notion of *habitus* can be useful for understanding this way of living, as the Aboriginal understandings of the Dreaming reflect a deeply buried structure that shapes people's dispositions to act in the world in ways that accept the dominance of "the system" (1977). I will return to this notion in chapter 5, where I discuss the ways in which the participants of a *Kurdiji* ceremony absorb broader themes surrounding the ceremony without being "taught" in any formalized way. While still maintaining an interest in human practice, Marshall Sahlins's ideas differ somewhat from Bourdieu's, emphasizing that human beings are not passively living their lives according to the dictums of particular cultural rules but are in fact active in controlling what happens (1985). I draw on both of these ideas, underscoring that rituals and ceremonies are practices in which the participants actively shape what happens but do so within deeply embedded traditional structures. The *Kurdiji* ceremony presented as a case study in chapter 4 illustrates how cultural values and orientations of Warlpiri society are made real through the performance of this ceremony. Edmund Leach explains that "ritual is a medium for the expression of cultural ideas and models that, in turn, serves to orient, though not prescribe, other forms of social behaviour" (1976: 40). I demonstrate through this case study that Warlpiri *Kurdiji* ceremonies are not understood by the participants through objective analyses of what the words or actions mean but rather through the experience of singing, dancing, and performing the ritual in its contemporary social context. Michael Jackson has argued that "human experience is grounded in bodily movement within a social and material environment and examining at the level of event the interplay between habitual patterns of body use and conventional ideas about the world" (1983: 327). In chapter 5, I argue that Warlpiri people through collective participation as dancers, singers, and actors adopt the values and core themes central to the *Kurdiji* ceremony, which focuses on social maturity for many different family members.

Several scholars provide good examples of Aboriginal songs and ceremonies enduring through time by adapting to changing circumstances in people's worlds. Dussart has written about the changes that have occurred to the performance of public rituals for Warlpiri people living in Yuendumu (Dussart 2004: 276), explaining that after settlement in 1946, public performances were dominated by the men's genres of *purlapa*, which were held in the settlement for a predominantly Aboriginal audience.[1] With the onset of the Aboriginal Land Rights (Northern Territory) Act 1976 and the subsequent need to perform public ceremonies as proof of legal rights to land, women began to be included in these public performances, and the audience extended to include non-Aboriginal viewers. Dussart explains that when the acrylic art movement began in the 1980s, there were demands for public performances at the openings of art exhibitions all over the world for international, mostly non-Indigenous audiences. She demonstrates that these modifications in gendered roles and performance contexts have resulted in clear changes to purposes for performance of these ceremonies.

With similar concern to shifting gendered positions, Elizabeth Mackinlay has discussed how ceremonial contexts have adapted to post-settlement changes in Borroloola, in the Gulf of Carpentaria region (2000). She demonstrates through an example of a particular song how a genre of restricted women's performance became unrestricted as male/female roles changed over the last fifty years. She attributes the employment of men in the cattle industry in the 1950s to the creation of a gender imbalance among the Yanyuwa living in Borroloola. As the men were often away for long periods working, the women were employed as domestic help on homesteads, giving them a greater opportunity to expand their ceremonial responsibilities. The opening up of a particular genre of women's performance to incorporate men was a way in which women redressed the gender imbalance that had been created in this period.

Both the examples from Dussart and Mackinlay demonstrate that performance genres are flexible and open to negotiation according to the performers' changing life experiences. It is evident that in analyses of contemporary songs and ceremonies, there is much to be learned about the changes occurring within a society. Scholars such as Anthony Seeger (1987) have suggested that musical practices create and define many aspects of social life. He describes this type of analysis as "musical anthropology" and contrasts it with Alan Merriam's (1964) earlier "anthropology of music," which emphasized the study of music in culture. Thus Seeger argues that,

> rather than assuming that there is a pre-existing and logically prior social and cultural matrix within which music is performed, it examines the way music is part of the very construction and interpretation of social and conceptual relationships and processes. (Seeger 1987: xiv)

While historical and cultural structures clearly have deep influences on the values and beliefs carried forward by individuals, I also aim to illustrate in this book that Warlpiri people are manipulating, controlling, adapting to, negotiating creatively with, and choosing how they engage with the components of their lives that reinforce the value systems underpinning traditional worldviews. Songs and ceremonies are practice-based modes for ensuring that Aboriginal value systems are carried forward into a modernized world. Confidence in this system can be seen in the words of the late Warlpiri elder Rex Japanangka Granites. When asked about the decline of contexts for younger Warlpiri people to learn songs, he responded by emphasizing that the "country doesn't change"—knowledge of *Jukurrpa* and ceremonial practices remain deep in the country, such that if they are forgotten or neglected by people, they are nonetheless always there, ready to be reactivated.[2] This viewpoint has also been put forward by Otto Jungarrayi Sims in his foreword to this book.

POWERFUL ABORIGINAL SONGS

Songs in Aboriginal Australia are powerful instruments in shaping the world (Ellis 1984; Marett 1994). Songs make things happen, and their purpose is to transform something so that it is in some way different after the song is sung. Examples of this are songs that make boys into men, songs that summon rain, songs that make people fall in love, and songs that cure the sick. Allan Marett emphasizes this point in saying,

> How much more care must be exercised when we understand that the power of songs is believed to reside in their capacity to tap into the very sources of creativity and to influence the way in which the universe comes into being. (Marett 1994: 71)

Ritual symbols have the capacity to give deep insight into the worldview of groups of people, often far more so than the insights of the individual participants. In this book, I draw on the ideas developed over the last few decades that ritual performances are powerful because of what they do rather than what they mean. In chapter 4 I set forth the events surrounding a *Kurdiji* ceremony with a theoretical focus on performance. I also analyze in detail the songs sung during this ceremony, as they are vital in guiding the ritualized events and actions.

John Austin (1975 [1962]) has distinguished in his work between the performative act of speaking and the actual content of what is being said.

He outlines examples of words that are performative in themselves, such as "I thee wed . . .," in which the act of saying these words is what is meaningful, resulting in an anthropological tendency to de-emphasize analyses of the content of uses of ritual language, emphasizing instead its performative function. Many people studying rituals have ignored uses of ritualized language, regarding them as verbatim recitals with little actually being understood and therefore having little relevance to the meaning of the overall performance. Maurice Bloch (1974: 67) has suggested how the meaning potential of language is lost by the kind of formalization that occurs in a ritual context, drawing on Austin's (1975 [1962]) ideas of the "illocutionary act" in which the purpose of language is to influence people, not to explain things. Among Warlpiri people, songs may only be known by a small group of elderly people, and the content and symbolic associations are not widely understood by the majority of the participants. This would not have been the case several decades ago when more people understood the associations of these songs. Other men who sit with these singers are "just humming" (Peterson 2008) the tune of these songs, a factor Peterson reflects on as a decline in learning, but which may equally be seen as the very beginnings of learning in which younger singers first master the tune of a song before learning the words. The language of Warlpiri songs in these contexts may be paralleled to uses of Latin in Catholic church services, in which passages are recited as they have been categorized over time as being essential to achieve particular social purposes. While the individual words may not mean a great deal, they influence people's actions, understandings and feelings regarding the performance when put together in the given context. In this book, I argue, however, that these songs are also crucial in guiding the dancing and actions of other participants of the ceremony. It is hard to imagine the form this ceremony would take if there were no men who knew these songs, not merely because there would be no singing, which is regarded as necessary to achieve the expected purposes, but also because the other participants would have no guide as to what they needed to be doing and when to do it. It is for these reasons that, despite my emphasis on performance as the main mode of understanding, I devote significant attention to the function of the songs and their language and provide details of the words and associated stories that enrich the understanding that an outsider can have of these songs. As outlined in the foreword to this book, Warlpiri songs have layers of understandings that are revealed at appropriate ceremonial moments and according to the individual learning efforts of Warlpiri people. The details provided in this book fall under the public layers of meaning. They are provided in multigendered and multigenerational contexts. Warlpiri people desire this layer of meaning to be understood by a wider audience in order to promote and foster respect for the religious significance of Warlpiri ceremonial lives. In aspiring for documentation of these broader public understandings of Indigenous musical practices many Warlpiri elders hope to create a future in which appropriate community members may still further enrich their learning through engagement with ceremonial practices.

Among participants, there is an implicit knowledge of how a ceremony will take place, as they have attended similar ceremonies throughout their lives. Edward Schieffelin explains that, in rituals, "meanings are formulated in a social rather than cognitive space, and the participants are engaged with the symbols in the interactional creation of a performance reality" (1985: 707). In the analysis of the *Kurdiji* ceremony, I emphasize the way in which the symbolic material (in the song language, dances, and other movements) is being performed. I also aim to show that there is a cognitive dimension to these ceremonies that should not be ignored due to this emphasis on performance. Here I show that there is an understanding by the participants that they are relating to the *Jukurrpa* and that this is important in their minds for linking songs to actions and for defining social and ritual roles. The associations that are made between particular songs, dances, and actions among the participants make the songs meaningful in a way that has little to do with an intellectual analysis of their symbolic meanings yet is ultimately linked. Therefore, while the meaning of these songs for the participants is not based on analyses of song content, there is a requirement that there be people in attendance who understand the more esoteric interpretations of songs well enough to be able to pass on these associations to other participants.

WRITING CULTURE

Despite significant emphasis on Aboriginal ritual lives in the early to mid-twentieth century, anthropological interest in ceremonial life has declined in recent decades, particularly research with an ethnographic focus in Central Australia. Consequently, there are few ethnographic descriptions of contemporary Central Australian ceremonial life. This is the case for many reasons; of particular note are the negative assumptions of the era of salvage ethnography and tensions that arose in the self-determination era, which emphasized the importance of Indigenous self-representation. This historical background has also led to widespread assumptions and many misunderstandings surrounding divisions between men's and women's ritual worlds and the boundaries of restricted, sensitive, and highly powerful aspects of men's knowledge and other more publicly open aspects of Aboriginal rituals. While some feminist writers (Kaberry 1939, Bell 1983, and Dussart 2000) have done much to rectify the prior emphasis on men's ritual lives of the early 1900s, showing that women too have powerful and complex ritual lives and significant contributions to this aspect of society, misconceptions still widely exist. As such, the "sensitive" nature of some men's songs and ceremonies is often emphasized, resulting in nervous negotiation of the research worlds surrounding Central Australian songs, ceremonies, and rituals. I entered my fieldwork with many of these reservations. The reality of this situation is that senior Warlpiri men and women have systems through which they have controlled access to knowledge for millennia, both within their own societies and in encounters with outsiders. The senior Warlpiri men who live in Yuendumu are assertive and clear about the ceremonial contexts that are appropriate for recording and publication. As I spent more time in Yuendumu, I realized that Warlpiri people are in fact deeply enthusiastic about recording songs and ceremonies, and, in many ways, they saw this effort as my contribution to these contexts. By the end of my initial fifteen-month stay in the settlement, the boss of *Kurdiji* ceremonies held over the summer of 2006–7 would make sure that I knew ahead of time that I had a commitment to record and would call out for me at the appropriate moment to turn on the sound recording machine.

Richard Bauman, in "Verbal Art as Performance" (1975), gives significant attention to the emergent quality of performance, emphasizing that

> the ethnographic construction of the structured, conventionalised performance system standardises and homogenises description, but all performances are not the same, and one wants to be able to appreciate the individuality of each, as well as the community-wide patterning of the overall domain. (1975: 37)

With this in mind, I present in this book a focal case study of a particular *Kurdiji* ceremony that was performed in February 2007. More generalizing ethnographic descriptions of Warlpiri ceremonies exist in Mervyn Meggitt's classic ethnography *Desert People* (1966), as well as in theses by Stephen Wild (1975) and Megan Dail-Jones (1984), but these do not take into account the emergent nature of rituals. In focusing on a particular ceremony, I aim to show that while Warlpiri people may make idealized versions of this ceremony in their minds, what actually happens at any one particular ceremony is dependent on the contingencies of the particular situations and the dynamics of the lives of the participants at that time. This reinforces the idea that the performance of rituals does not follow rigid structures; the practices are being negotiated in the moment according to the interests of the participants (see Shieffelin 1985).

I have chosen the *Kurdiji* ceremony as a focal case study because the ritual was held several times each summer in Yuendumu, and also many times in other Central Australian settlements, from the beginning of my fieldwork in 2005. Variations of this ceremony are held across the Central Desert and considered an essential "rite of passage" (Van Gennep 1960 [1909]) for boys of prepubescent age to turn into men, thus making it a particularly interesting case study when exploring the importance of ritual to contemporary Warlpiri lives. *Kurdiji* is a public ceremony in which a large majority of the Yuendumu population participates at various stages. Because ceremonies like *Kurdiji* are often referred to as "male initiation" rituals, there is an outsider misconception that they are somehow restricted to men, particularly senior men who have a great deal of knowledge of Aboriginal religious life, and that the knowledge contained in these ceremonies should not be discussed in the presence of women or the general public. While there are some stages of *Kurdiji* ceremonies that are restricted to men only (as recorded in Meggitt 1962: 281–316), I did not attend these nor was I even aware that they were happening. I write only about the public sections of this ceremony that are viewed by all people and to which outsiders are frequently invited. Warlpiri people were keen for me to participate and record details of this ceremony, and my research was eased by their enthusiasm and the large numbers of people wanting to be involved. The *Kurdiji* ceremony marks an important stage in the life cycle of the boys involved, and it is highly significant for their fathers, brothers, and circumcisers, as well as for a range of their female kin, including their mothers, sisters, future mothers-in-law, and future wives. The male and female realms of ceremony mix together in many ways. Dussart has taken up this point, emphasizing that "women know about what is not proprietarily (in a ritual sense) 'theirs,' and that while much of this knowledge cannot be performed by women formally, they nevertheless exert influence in performative domains technically off-limits to them" (Dussart 2000: 59). *Kurdiji* is probably best described as a "maturity rite," which is as important for women as it is for men. It is through this ceremony that lifelong relationships between many participants, both male and female, are forged.

As I have emphasized above, rituals are socially emergent, and participants do not all experience them in the same way. The analysis presented in this book is not intended to be a "correct" version, but one that exists in a set cultural frame. Thomas Jangala Rice and Jeannie Nungarrayi Egan, with whom I worked closely to form the understandings presented in this book, were perhaps somewhat unusual in their willingness, ability, and desire to articulate the meanings of this ritual and the details of the symbolism used in the song texts (see Curran 2013 for a detailed overview of our collaborative research approach). Transcribing songs was somewhat more difficult than transcribing spoken Warlpiri. Often whole songs were labeled with generalized meanings, whereas for others, individual words could be detected and glossed. Some songs were in other languages (often Anmatyerr or Luritja), and many words were in a special kind of song language or a kind of skewed pronunciation of spoken Warlpiri. For many songs, even Jeannie and Thomas were reluctant to give me an articulated explanation, preferring to allude to the meaning of the words through metaphoric association until I eventually caught on. I came to appreciate this method as a central part of learning about songs. The longer I spent in Yuendumu and the better my knowledge of Warlpiri ways of life and environment became, the more interesting I found this way of learning, in which proving my prior understanding became a prerequisite for deep teaching. While I present many of the ethnographic descriptions in this book in narrative form, I emphasize that they are written based on my own experience, understandings of the world, and historical fieldwork contexts, which necessarily cannot be the same for others.

FIELDWORK

My initial period of fieldwork was undertaken for a total of seventeen months between late 2005 and early 2008. I lived in Yuendumu permanently from November 2005 until February 2007, and then I undertook two month-long visits in May 2007 and January/February 2008. In the years since this time, I have visited Yuendumu several times a year and collaborated in many research projects. I have used similar methodological techniques throughout these periods of fieldwork. My primary methodology has been participant-observation, immersing myself in Warlpiri people's lives. Not only did this mean that I was always aware of ceremonial or other events but also that I got to see things from a Warlpiri perspective, gain an understanding of their shared values (as well as people's individual eccentricities), and participate in everyday discussions surrounding these.

    I took detailed notes after all ceremonial events—it was often difficult for me to take notes during the ceremonies, as many were held at night and I simply did not have any light by which I could write. Often I was preoccupied with monitoring the sound levels on the recording machine, and my participatory roles in these ceremonies meant that I was required to dance at certain times and move around to different areas of the ceremony ground. While I could set up the recording machine and still participate, carrying a notebook around and writing was not only a burden but would likely have been inappropriate. Indeed, because of this I may not have remembered some of the subtleties of what happened, but in many other ways my understanding of the social negotiations that occurred during ceremonies and the ways people "experienced" the rituals were greatly enhanced. Warlpiri people emphasized to me that my understanding of ceremonies came much more from my participation than from my transcription of the recordings or questions during later interviews. For the *Kurdiji* ceremony that I have written about in this book, I also went over what happened with several key participants and incorporated the details into the descriptions.

Additionally, and as part of my involvement with the Warlpiri Songlines Project, I used a Marantz solid state digital recording machine to make elicited recordings with many senior singers and non-elicited recordings of ceremonies for which I had gained prior consent. This task was undertaken in intense collaboration with Thomas and Jeannie. Thomas, being one of only a small group of senior men who were still alive and healthy, shared the extraordinary depth of his religious knowledge by singing many public men's songs and providing detailed exegesis. He also facilitated my work with other senior men and guided me in how to appropriately record ceremonial events. Thomas is also one of the senior men who sang the *Kurdiji* songs that are the focus of the central case study. He is widely respected for his knowledge of traditional law and culture. Jeannie, having been a teacher at the Yuendumu School for over thirty years as part of the bilingual education program, was literate in both English and Warlpiri. She assisted my work with Thomas, transcribing the words of the songs and ensuring that I understood the subtleties of the exegesis Thomas provided. She also attended recording sessions that we organized with senior women, later transcribing the words of these songs and working with these women to write down as much information as possible about the songs and their associated *Jukurrpa* stories. Many older women in Yuendumu also participated in this recording project—I have more recordings and detailed transcriptions of *yawulyu*, a genre of women's song, than any other genre. These recordings are all housed at the Warlpiri Media Archive (PAW) in Yuendumu and at the Australian Institute for Aboriginal and Torres Strait Islander Studies (AIATSIS) in Canberra, and some of them have been produced into songbooks as part of revitalization projects in subsequent years (Gallagher et al. 2014; Warlpiri women from Yuendumu 2017a).

As Yuendumu is a relatively tight-knit community, it is widely accepted that a number of senior people have the authority to discuss ritual knowledge and know the associated songs. On arriving in Yuendumu and explaining my research topic, I was immediately guided to these people. Unfortunately, this had the adverse effect of making it very difficult to discuss the experience of ceremonial performance with those people who were not deemed to be experts yet who were important participants in these ceremonies. I was able to converse with them, however, in several situations where they played a key role in the performance. In many instances where there was no longer a senior person left who knew the songs, a younger "owner" was called upon to attend recording sessions even if they did not know how to sing the songs—their presence as an owner for that song was more important in that situation than their knowledge of the songs. Research projects like this one have allowed younger Warlpiri people to engage in learning centered around songs and ceremonies for which there are today fewer performance contexts.

The next chapter gives some insight into the social history of Yuendumu, the largest Warlpiri settlement in Central Australia and the place where I spent the majority of my time during the fieldwork for this project. This background is important to understand the present-day contexts in which Warlpiri people live and hold the ceremonies that are focal to this book.

NOTES

1. Women, however, were probably holding ceremonies in special women's areas during this time, but only singing and dancing publicly in larger ceremonies such as *Kurdiji* and other aspects of initiation. Mary Laughren (personal communication, 2009) has suggested that the segregation of men and women increased with settlement, as there were many avoidance relationships among people living in a restricted location. This would have significantly limited where women could go in the settlement.
2. From a recorded interview with Granites in 2017. Interview archived with the "Vitality and Change in Warlpiri Songs" research collection at the Australian Institute for Aboriginal and Torres Strait Islander Studies.

Chapter 2

Yuendumu

A Brief Social History

Prior to European colonization of the Australian continent beginning in 1788, Warlpiri speakers occupied a large area of the Tanami Desert area to the northwest of the region that is today the town of Alice Springs (see map 1.1). Non-Aboriginal people did not intrude into the more central parts of Australia until the mid-1800s. The earliest ethnographers in this region, Spencer and Gillen (1899) do not mention the Warlpiri in any detail, and therefore little documentation exists about Warlpiri life before the 1900s. It can be assumed from Warlpiri oral history and documented observations of early explorers that Warlpiri people prior to European colonization lived and traveled within this region in small family groups. These movements were influenced somewhat by the availability of food resources and water, but much more so by the demands and obligations of ritual life. Several archaeological studies date Aboriginal settlement of this area back to the Pleistocene age at the end of the world's last period of repeated glaciations, which finished in 12000 BCE. Smith et al. have shown that the red ochre mine at Karrku (in the south of Warlpiri country), which is still used today, has been mined since 32000 BCE. Examination of the rock art of this region shows that people who inhabited this area have had a ritual life reaching back at least five thousand years (Smith et al. 1998: 276).

O'Grady, Voegelin, and Voegelin (1966), in their groupings of Australian languages, show Warlpiri to be part of the expansive Pama-Nyungan language family, sharing similarities with languages spoken across a large section of the southern part of Australia. They classified Warlpiri in the Ngarrga group, which also incorporates Warlmanpa, a nearly extinct language that was once spoken by people living on the eastern side of the Tanami.

Patrick McConvell and Laughren (2004) show that there are certain shared innovations among the Ngarrga and Ngumpin subgroups within the Pama-Nyungan family, indicating a closer shared ancestor language (which they label proto-Ngumpin-Yapa) (see figure 2.1). The Ngumpin languages are spoken by people living in the region northwest of the Tanami into the south Kimberley region of Western Australia and the Southern Victoria River District. This suggests that the speakers of modern-day Warlpiri have historical connections with speakers of other Ngumpin languages, whether the connections between these language groups are genetic or due to a high degree of borrowing because of extensive social contact.

Linguistic evidence shows more difference between the Warlpiri and Arandic languages spoken in the region surrounding Alice Springs, suggesting that there was little contact between these groups. Later studies concerning Arandic languages show evidence of dropping initial consonants, revealing them to be more similar to Warlpiri than O'Grady, Voegelin, and Voegelin (1966) originally assumed. Birdsell's (1993) genetic data shows a clear division between people living in the western part of Central Australia and those in the geographically neighboring regions of Western Australia, indicating a long-standing separation between these two groups. Keats (1977) suggest that there was certainly intermixing between the Warlpiri and their nearby Central Australian neighbors—the Luritja, Pitjantjatjara, and Arrernte, and perhaps even further afield with groups to the east around Mornington Island. Certainly today, the Warlpiri living in Yuendumu associate more with their eastern and southern neighbors, particularly Anmatyerr- and Luritja-speaking groups. Peterson has noted that when

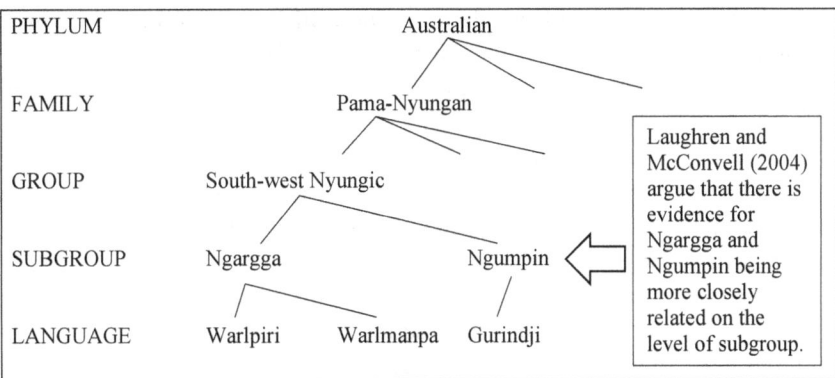

Figure 2.1. Warlpiri in the Australian language family tree. Created by the author. Based on O'Grady, Voegelin, and Voegelin's (1966) classification of the Australian languages (partially represented).

he worked in Yuendumu in the 1970s, everybody was "facing the Tanami," whereas today they are "facing Alice Springs."[1] This shift in emphasis on to the larger township of Alice Springs may have encouraged Warlpiri people who today live in Yuendumu to associate more with other groups who also use Alice Springs as a centralized town. Warlpiri people living in Lajamanu, a more northern settlement, again "look to the north," utilizing the towns of Katherine and Darwin for services. For most Warlpiri people, the creation of the world in the timeless and ever-present *Jukurrpa* provides explanation for the past further back than can be remembered.

Unlike groups in other regions of Australia, Warlpiri people had limited contact with Europeans until the establishment of several permanent pastoral leases on their land in the 1920s. Before this, some early explorers, namely Stuart (1865), Gosse (1874), and Warburton (1875), had explored parts of this region in the late 1800s, but due to the sparseness of the land, they infrequently ran into Aboriginal people—although they did note in their diaries evidence in the form of campsites, wells, and tracks for people living there. Warburton described running into several groups of Aboriginal people on his journey, often kidnapping them and begging them to direct him to water (Warburton 1875: 176, 203-7). He also mentions seeing smoke in the distance but that the people had run away when he arrived at its source (Warburton 1875: 207). Warlpiri people encountered other Europeans, including inland telegraph-line workers from 1870 to 1872 and the large numbers of people who came into the Tanami for the short-lived gold rush in 1909, and later at the Granites in 1932 (Meggitt 1962: 22). Michael Terry explored the area around Mount Denison (just to the north of Yuendumu) and up into the Tanami in the 1920s. In his book *Hidden Wealth and Hiding People,* he gives detailed descriptions of Warlpiri country and the encounters he had with the groups of people throughout his expedition (1931). These encounters were temporary, however, as these visitors were only passing through, although a small number of miners continued to work at the Granites and the Tanami until after World War II.

In the early 1930s, Theodore Strehlow was appointed as an officer for the Department of the Protector of Aborigines (Hill 2002: 235). As the son of Lutheran missionary Carl Strehlow, he had grown up in Hermannsberg and had a good knowledge of Aboriginal languages and ways of life. Strehlow's role was to patrol the largely Aboriginal population "rather than have a policeman patrol the area of 15,000 square miles with a resident white population of less than 30" (Hill 2002: 235). Aside from Strehlow, the first Europeans to have permanent interactions with Warlpiri people were the early pastoralists. The first pastoral lease in the area surrounding Yuendumu was granted at Coniston in 1917 (Hartwig 1960: 3). Leases at Ti-Tree, Napperby and Mount Doreen soon followed. Initially, Warlpiri people avoided contact with European settlers as much as possible by living farther out in the desert in areas where the pastoralists had no interest, only occasionally coming into the occupied areas to access the stations established there. The severe drought of 1924–29 forced Warlpiri people to occupy the same areas and seek food from the station owners, causing tensions and conflict. The most well-known account of these conflicts today is that of the Coniston massacre in 1928, where Frederick Brooks, a dingo trapper who was camped near a soakage named Yurrkuru (Brooks Well) just to the north of Yuendumu, was speared by a Warlpiri man (see *The Northern Standard*, 13 November 1928). Today, Warlpiri people tell this story, often recounting that because Brooks had stolen this man's wife, his punishment was to be speared to death. The result, however, was the massacre of sixty to one hundred Warlpiri and Anmatyerr people by the parties led by Constable George Murray, who were trying to capture the man responsible. The man who had actually killed Brooks managed to hide from the police and lived into old age in Yuendumu. As a consequence of this period of police brutality, the Warlpiri began to develop a distrust of European settlers.

During the 1930s, several stations were established for mining and cattle rearing. Mount Denison station and Mount Doreen were sources of employment for many Warlpiri people. Mount Doreen was established by Mr. W. Braitling in 1926, and during the decades that followed, many Warlpiri men worked there collecting wolfram from the nearby mine, while women were employed as domestic servants. Many men also began to work as stockmen at both Mount Denison and Mount Doreen. Mount Doreen, especially the springs in the Pikilyi area, became the site of a major land-use conflict (Peterson and McConvell 1978) between Braitling, the Aboriginal people, the government, and the Baptist Union of South Australia. The springs are one of the only permanent water sources within a large area—and all these groups had to rely on it if they wanted to live in the area.

While stories of hard times and brutality mark this period of Warlpiri history, there are also many fond memories of a time when Warlpiri people lived in their country and traveled widely, and they were supplied with rationed food and blankets even though they were compensated lightly for their work. Meggitt has suggested that "once the drought of 1924 had forced people to live on cattle stations and nearby mines, they became too accustomed to the new foods, warm clothes, steel axes and the like to wish to return permanently to the rigorous life in the bush" (Meggitt 1962: 27). Many of the oldest generation of Warlpiri people who live in Yuendumu today (i.e. those in their sixties and seventies) worked on these stations as young adults. These rationed foods remain as favored staples in the Warlpiri diet, including tea, sugar, flour, and tobacco. Nowadays, it is the stockmen who used to travel widely around Warlpiri country who maintain a good knowledge of sites central to Dreaming tracks and songlines. Many Warlpiri people continued to live in Warlpiri country until the 1950s and 1960s, trapping dingos to the north of Yuendumu and getting money for their scalps, but only coming into Yuendumu occasionally.

In 1946, the Yuendumu Aboriginal reserve was established. All unemployed Warlpiri were sent to the reserve from the nearby cattle stations. Another of these reserves had been established at Tanami, but after a drought in 1945 all the people living there were sent to the Granites and then later to Yuendumu. Yuendumu (*Yurntumu* in standardized orthography), gets its name from a soakage to the south of the actual settlement that is an important place belonging to the *Yurrampi Jukurrpa* (Honey Ant Dreaming). This *Jukurrpa* also travels through the center of Yuendumu to a soakage called Yakurrukaji just on the northeastern side of the settlement area. Today a large pole erected for the power supply in the center of the settlement is said to be on the path of the Honey Ant Dreaming's travels, this also being called *Yakurrukaji* despite the soakage's actual location several hundred meters farther northeast in the scrub. For these reasons, many of the residents of Yuendumu today refer to their settlement as Yurrampi (Honey Ant).

The Native Affairs Branch initially financed the Yuendumu reserve. Meggitt (1962: 29) estimates that by the end of 1946, about four hundred Warlpiri people were living there. Meggitt (1962) explains that bringing together all these people in one place sparked old feuds, enough that some people were relocated to another recently established settlement at Hooker Creek (today Lajamanu), some six hundred kilometers away on the northern edge of the Tanami. Prior to settlement, Warlpiri people identified with Ngaliya, Warnayaka, Yalpari, or Walmala groups, depending on their location of origin within Warlpiri territory. Dussart (2000: 40–44) has written about how residential patterns in Yuendumu in the 1980s reflected these groups. The patterns, however, no longer exist, as people are allocated housing by the Yuendumu Council in random areas and move often following the death of relatives. Today Warlpiri people identify with the settlement where they grew up: Yuendumu Warlpiri, Lajamanu Warlpiri, Willowra Warlpiri, and Nyirrpi Warlpiri.

Meggitt (1962: 29) estimates that by 1955, two-thirds of all Warlpiri people were living on settlements and the rest were on cattle stations. Frances McGarry was appointed manager of the settlement at Yuendumu in these early days and was responsible for overseeing the distribution of rations each Saturday morning (Steer 1996: 33). He also directed the clearing of an airstrip (for further details see O'Grady 1977). Philip Steer and Laurie

Reece arrived in Yuendumu in 1947 to start a branch of the Baptist Union of Australia, initiating the beginnings of a community store and a school system for the children. The Steers left Yuendumu in late 1949, and Reverend T. J. Fleming arrived with his family in 1950 to continue their duties, staying there for the next twenty-five years. Elspeth Young has noted that "by 1950 they were, in addition to their evangelical duties, running a store, a school (partly staffed by government employed teachers) and a clinic, and teaching skills such as carpentry and dressmaking to adults" (1981b: 61). Melinda Hinkson (1999: 17) describes this situation, noting that "the early period of settlement was a focused exercise in the training of citizens: education in hygiene, routine labour, child care, domestic work, Christianity, [and] European education," but she also notes that

> while regulated work regimes brought people into the settlement during working hours, outside of these times the physical and social separation of Warlpiri people with Europeans was relatively stark. Such segregation was reflected in the physical layout of the town—a central area in which European housing, the mission and ration sheds were built, with Warlpiri humpy camps situated at considerable distance. This separation was apparently mutually maintained by Warlpiri people and Europeans. (1999: 18)[2]

This separation should have made it easier to continue with ceremonial life, as Warlpiri people were not continuously under the scrutinizing eyes of these overseers. However, certain adaptations to traditional ceremonial patterns were clearly being made as they adjusted to the requirements of the workday and the church. In these early days, the missionaries discouraged ceremonies by requiring the activity to be held outside of the enforced daily obligations of school, church, and work. Against the background of segregation, Hinkson suggests that in the self-determination era, these two separate worlds became blurred, and by the 1990s, when she undertook fieldwork in Yuendumu, it was a distinctly "intercultural domain" (1999). Dussart has pointed out, among many other factors, that

> alcohol consumption, sexual liaisons with non-Aboriginal peoples, and nominal economic compensation in the form of rations (in lieu of cash) all contributed to the accelerated transformation of pre-contact Warlpiri social structure. (Dussart 2000: 37)

Following the Australian referendum in 1969, award wages to Aboriginal stockmen, social security payments, including aged and disability pensions but not unemployment benefits, began to be paid directly to Aboriginal people. As of 1959, when Aboriginal people were first included in the social security system and given training wages, their wages had been paid first to the superintendent, who then redistributed them in the form of blankets and rationed food. Following the payment of full wages to Aboriginal stockmen in 1968, cattle station owners dispensed with many of their Aboriginal workers (all of them in some cases), increasing their reliance on white stockmen and upgrading the fencing infrastructure on their properties. This resulted in a further increase in Aboriginal people moving to join their families in settlements like Yuendumu. Yasmine Musharbash notes that "the direct receipt of social security has been singled out by most social scientists as the single most significant factor determining the economic status of Aboriginal people and their relationship to the state to date" (Musharbash 2003: 17). This factor also contributed significantly to changes in Warlpiri ceremonial life, as individuals often put aside large sums of their personal money for these purposes. Peterson (2000) has shown that the direct receipt of cash meant that Aboriginal people could buy their own cars, a fact that has dramatically expanded the ability of Warlpiri people to transport initiates and their guardians to ceremonies. These factors have significantly impacted the geographical breadth of participants and the social networks central to many Warlpiri ceremonies.

In 1973, the Yuendumu Community Council was established to take control of the administrative affairs of and service delivery in the community. In 1974, with the arrival of Frank and Wendy Baarda, the Yuendumu Mining Company was established, and the school started up the bilingual education program. The 1980s saw the beginnings of the Warlpiri Media Association, Warlukurlangu Artists, and Yurrampi Craft, and the 1990s saw the establishment of the Yuendumu Women's Centre, the Tanami Network, and the Yuendumu Old People's Program. All of these organizations (with the exception of Yurrampi Craft, which no longer exists) play an important part in the daily lives of Warlpiri people today.

With the self-determination era, which was inaugurated under the Whitlam Labor government of the early 1970s, Warlpiri people began to have more control over their land and the structure of their lives. In 1978, Warlpiri people lodged a land claim for the parts of their land that were still unalienated, gaining total control of over 100,000 square kilometers of land in the Tanami Desert (Peterson and McConvell 1978). Following this, in the late 1970s and early 1980s, there was a movement to establish outstations in the areas surrounding Yuendumu. Young (1981b: 70) has noted that by 1979 there were six centers established on land that was now under Warlpiri control. Today there are twenty-one outstations in the areas surrounding Yuendumu, although none are permanently occupied. Many of these places have houses or some other form of permanent shelter, while people camp in others with windbreaks made out of sheets of corrugated iron. Today, the vast majority of these facilities are no longer working.

Some outstations were highly successful for a period in the 1980s. Wayililinpa, to the south of Yuendumu, had for example a population of over a hundred people, with a school employing a non-Aboriginal teacher who traveled from Yuendumu each day and an Aboriginal teacher who lived there permanently with her family. Many outstations did not, however, have schools, and as Young (1981b) points out, in the 1980s there were few school-aged and hence parent-aged people living at outstations. This left only older people and young children, who were in a vulnerable state as there were no younger adults who could use rifles to hunt for game or travel into Yuendumu in the case of a medical emergency (1981b: 72). In accordance with the Warlpiri custom of vacating a house after the death of one of its residents, it was no longer feasible for most of the residents to live at Wayililinpa after several people died there. While some outstations are still occupied today, with family groups settling there for periods, there are many that remain mostly vacant and only used occasionally for camping trips. The settlement of Nyirrpi, originally established as one of these outstations in 1974, has been one of the more successful examples, eventually becoming a permanent settlement that is today inhabited by several hundred people.

DAILY LIFE IN YUENDUMU

The population of Yuendumu was 692 people according to the 2006 census, which was compiled while I was undertaking fieldwork. This number included a population of eighty-four non-Aboriginal people (Australian Bureau of Statistics 2006). This large population by desert standards is, like that of many Central Australian Aboriginal settlements, quite mobile, with many people frequently going to Alice Springs or other desert communities to live for periods of time. Also, like many other Aboriginal populations across Australia, Yuendumu's has had a massive birthrate increase in recent decades. Young's estimations of population distribution in 1978 showed a significantly larger proportion of children to older people, a demographic change that she attributes to the decrease in infant mortality rates during this period (1981b: 64). This fact in itself is interesting when considering a study of ritual, as the roles of the different generations shift in significant ways. Peterson has argued that this demographic change has had a marked impact on the size and frequency of initiation ceremonies (2008). Yuendumu is predominantly populated by Warlpiri people, although there is a small minority of people identifying with other Aboriginal groups who have married into the community and have come to live there. Today Warlpiri people live in many settlements around Central Australia, such as Nyirrpi, Lajamanu, Willowra, Alekarenge, and Alice Springs, and also in various places farther afield, such as Melbourne, Bundaberg, Adelaide, Darwin, Katherine, and Port Augusta (Burke 2018). There are also many Warlpiri people who went to work in cattle stations in the Eastern Kimberley who stayed and married Nyininy or Jaru people. These people now live in settlements such as Yaruman (Ringer's Soak) and Balgo. Many older people living in the Eastern Kimberley can speak Warlpiri as well as Walmajarri or Jaru. Warlpiri is also spoken at Balgo, and these families continue to transmit Warlpiri culture and language to their children.

Yuendumu is in some ways very different from other Aboriginal settlements in that, due to its predominantly Warlpiri population, it features more cultural cohesiveness as its inhabitants possess similar worldviews and ways of doing things. The central area shown on Map 2.1 remains the Warl-

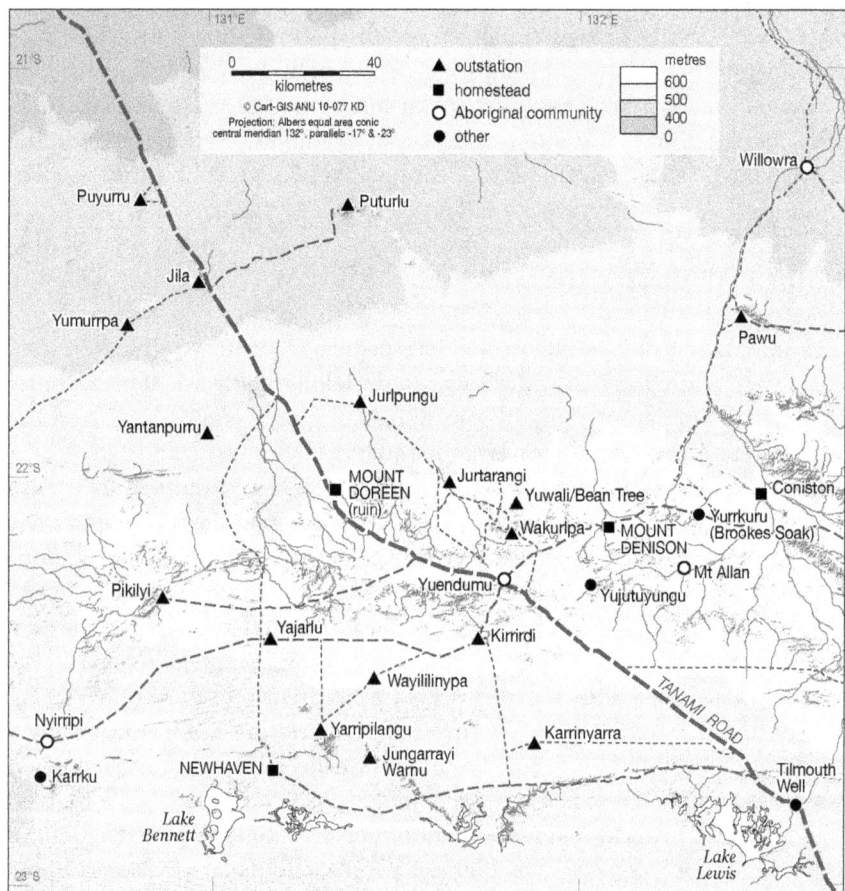

Map 2.1. Central Australia region surrounding Yuendumu. Created by CartoGIS Services, CAP, Australian National University. All Aboriginal settlements, homesteads, and outstations, as well as several smaller sites mentioned in this book, are marked on this map.

piri heartland, which people living in other places call home, with a particular reference for younger Warlpiri people to their settlement of origin. The other Aboriginal people, predominantly Luritja and Anmatyerr, who also come to Yuendumu to live for periods have similar enough ways of doing things that holding joint ceremonies is possible and often influential.

WARLPIRI SOCIAL ORGANIZATION

Warlpiri people distinguish between closely and distantly related kin, considering all people in their immediate world to be related to them through kinship ties. While deeper kinship relations to close family indicate connections to country and Dreamings, these subsection terms, often called "skin names" in an everyday context, are more overarching and create the basis for daily interactions among all people, even those with no prior connections to Warlpiri country or people. This sociocentric system of social organization divides all people into eight subsections so that it is possible to relate to them in daily life.

A similar subsection system is used in a broad area across the central desert area of Australia, albeit with slight language differences for the names of the subsections. A. P. Elkin first suggested that "the subsection system spread from the East Kimberley fan-wise in a general eastern direction to

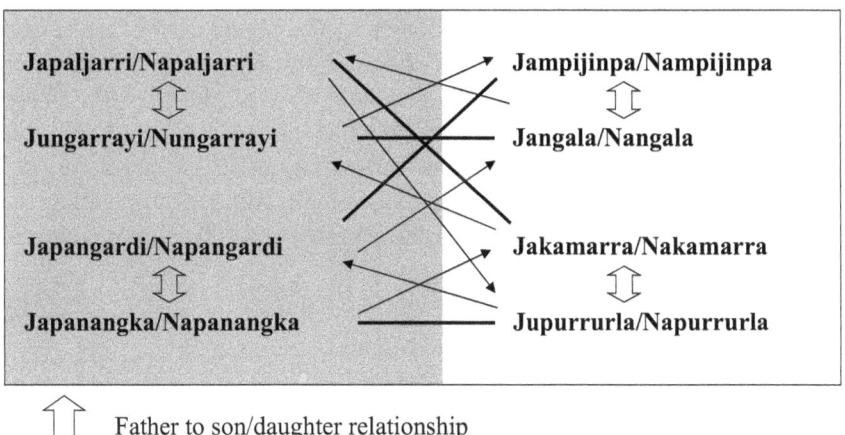

Figure 2.2. Subsection system of social organization. Created by the author.

just inside north-western Queensland; to the south-east it reached the Arandic groups in Central Australia, but not the south-west or south-east corners of the Territory" (Elkin 1970: 709).

The overarching nature of this system summarizes a more complex system of kin classification, including patrimoieties and patricouples, which are discussed in chapter 3 with respect to ownership of *Jukurrpa* and country and the roles in ceremonial performance. The subsection system makes use of eight different terms, of which there are male and female equivalents (male terms beginning with "J" and female terms beginning with "N"), and these encompass all relationships. In day-to-day interaction, the use of these subsection terms to address and refer to people is considered to be more polite than using personal names. Most people refer to me as Nungarrayi, the skin name I was given when I first arrived in Yuendumu. To denote particular affection, the people I am particularly close to and associate with more often call me by the relationship that we are to each other. For example, a Napurrurla woman would call me *jukana* "cousin" (mother's brother's daughter, or father's sister's daughter), a Napanangka calls me *jaja* "granddaughter" (daughter's daughter). Nicknames are also commonly used in daily reference, deriving from prominent physical attributes (people of short stature are often named "Shorty," and tall people often have their name prefaced by the word for "long," Nakamarra), common sayings associated with a person (one man is named "40 dolla" because he is constantly asking people for forty dollars), or places from which they are associated (e.g., Mount Theo-*wardingki* for someone who was born near Mount Theo).[3] Diminutives of subsection terms are often used for children, some of which stick for life (e.g., one old man still goes by "Jakarra," the "baby talk" version of the subsection Jakamarra and his nickname since childhood) (see Laughren 1984 for further details of "Warlpiri baby talk"). When a Warlpiri person dies, their name must not be spoken for a number of years. During this time people with the same name or ones that sounds similar are referred to as *kumunjayi*.

DAILY LIFE

Being only 270 kilometers from the town of Alice Springs—an accessible distance by desert standards—Yuendumu receives many visiting government employees. A large number of organizations—including an art center, a media center, a school, two shops, a mining company, a clinic, a health center, a women's center, the Baptist church, an aged-care program, a Central Land Council office, a council building, a Centrelink office, a community garage, a childcare center, a Community Development Employment Program

(CDEP), a police station, and a youth program—employ non-Aboriginal people living in Yuendumu in some way. As there is a long history of anthropological, linguistic, or other academic research taking place in this settlement, engaging in research work has become an institutionalized activity in which many Warlpiri people participate. The many visits by government workers from Alice Springs result in an endless string of meetings occurring on most weekdays. Munn has described daily life in Yuendumu in the 1950s as "marked by the traditional division between men's and women's daily activities" (1973:12), with women congregating in women's camps and men gathering in shady spots in the bush. These patterns continue today and are more obvious at times when ceremonies are being organized or are taking place.

Many Warlpiri people engage in the activities of these various organizations and receive small amounts of supplemental income on top of government unemployment and pension payments. The art center in particular provides income for some of the population of Yuendumu, as there is a core group of well-known artists who paint there everyday along with others who occasionally go there for supplementary income. There are only a few Warlpiri people who are permanently employed in one or more of these places. There are really only a small number of Warlpiri people in Yuendumu with permanent jobs: five or six people who work at the school as teachers, teaching assistants, and janitors; several people with administrative jobs at the Yuendumu Council; a Central Land Council employee; and a few employees each at the Mt Theo Program, the Warlpiri Media Association, and the Yuendumu Clinic. Other temporary jobs, including many within these same organizations, depend on whether funding needs are met. At any one time, no more than around forty Aboriginal people are employed full time in the settlement.

Nighttime activities include driving around to visit family and friends, gossiping and telling stories in camps, or watching television. Younger people engage in youth activities such as basketball, football, and discos, which are set up and organized by the youth program. There are also frequent gatherings of gospel singers at the Baptist church or at the house of a member of the Pentecostal or Assembly of God churches, and these sessions often last until the early hours of the morning. Weekends are somewhat different, as most non-Aboriginal people stay in their houses and most Aboriginal people engage in popular leisure activities such as hunting, swimming, or simply touring their country. These activities that were essential for survival in the past are now popular recreational pursuits instead. Those who do not have access to vehicles tend to stay at home and play cards and talk or move around the settlement visiting various family members. A small number of Warlpiri people living in Yuendumu regularly attend the Sunday morning services at the Baptist church.[4]

There are, of course, generational differences in the activities that occupy Warlpiri people's days. Young men from their late teens to their early thirties tend to live a life on the road, traveling from their home base of Yuendumu to different settlements or to Alice Springs. Younger women of this age group also travel often, but the responsibilities of motherhood often tie them down. Many younger women leave their children in the hands of parents or grandparents while they go off on frequent trips. Older people tend not to travel much, though many are still considerably mobile. The remoteness of Yuendumu requires travel for health appointments as well as for the mortuary rituals for kin living in others settlements. Homesickness is a powerful emotion for most Warlpiri people; regardless of how much they move around, they are keen to come back to Yuendumu. There is also a football season that lasts throughout the winter months, an important annual event. A large majority of people living in Yuendumu attend the finals, in which the Yuendumu team is often a participant.

Warlpiri life changes dramatically over the period from just before Christmas until the end of January. Because the school shuts down for the holiday and the art center closes for the year, many non-Aboriginal staff take their annual leave. Warlpiri people also hold the *Kurdiji* ceremonies at this time, which are discussed in chapter 4. It is likely due to the schedule and routine of the cattle industry that the Warlpiri began to dedicate this time of year to *Kurdiji*. The summer months would have been a holiday period for many of the workers on cattle stations, and the Aboriginal people would have had ample time to perform these ceremonies in their entirety. The long break from school also allows time for *Kurdiji*. While the young men involved in these ceremonies rarely go back to school after they have been initiated, it is still important to hold *Kurdiji* during this time so that it does not interfere with the schooling of younger family members and the schedules of the teaching staff, allowing all to attend.

This general ebb and flow of daily life is punctuated by certain events. A high death rate is an unfortunate fact of life in Yuendumu today, often meaning that people have to travel long distances to attend mortuary rituals, known as "Sorry" in surrounding settlements. During these rituals the kin of the deceased must stay at a "Sorry camp" for many weeks, sometimes longer, and other aspects of their lives are halted until all family members have finalized these mortuary rituals. Interfamily fighting also interjects into everyday life. Over the fourteen years that I have been working in Yuendumu, several long-running feuds between family groups have encompassed much of the population and involved large-scale fights within and outside of the settlement. Large numbers of people across the desert region attend sports weekends over the winter period, traveling to the various settlements where these events are held.[5] Baptisms, Christian funerals (which occur up to several months after "Sorry rituals"), sing-a-longs, and Bible study groups also interrupt daily life. Most Warlpiri people identify with the Baptist church, though there are a small number of Pentecostals and others still who attend the Assembly of God church. All of these churches hold events within Yuendumu and often host trips to various places around Australia.

HISTORICAL SHIFTS TO WARLPIRI CEREMONIAL LIFE

Ceremonial activities punctuate daily life in ways similar to those described above. These events normally involve relocating from a regular camp to another settlement or a temporary place within Yuendumu. Many ceremonial forms are also showcased to visitors during settlement events, such as the opening of buildings and new infrastructure. Examples of these types of ceremonies will also be outlined in the descriptions of song genres in chapter 3.

Ceremonial life in Yuendumu has undergone significant changes against the historical background and description of contemporary daily life described above. I do not wish to draw a harsh distinction between pre-contact and post-contact times, but I do want to show that there has been a process of change over the last hundred years as Warlpiri people have moved from being self-supporting people living off the land to welfare-dependent settled people. The significant changes that have taken place over this short period have impacted how the ceremonies that were once so essential to Warlpiri life are being held today, if they are at all. Some ceremonies (such as *Kurdiji*) have expanded in size as a consequence of these changes to Warlpiri life. Dussart has pointed out that Warlpiri people today are the most populous group in the Northern Territory, and,

> coupled with their residency on the actual traditional lands associated with Warlpiri patrimony, [that] accounts in measure for the vigour of Warlpiri ritual life as it is undertaken at Yuendumu, compared to that of other groups and other settlements. (Dussart 2000: 40)

As Warlpiri people settled in places like Yuendumu, ceremonial life underwent many changes. Initially structured around the routines surrounding cattle station work, ceremonial life began to follow a western calendar. A significant break during Christmas meant that ceremonial activity intensified during this time. Dussart (2000: 40) also notes that in the early days of the settlement, ceremonial life was frowned upon by the missionaries to such a degree that Warlpiri people had to hold ceremonies at times when they were not under intense scrutiny. Yuendumu still follows this westernized calendar today. The *Jardiwanpa* ceremony, for example, has come to be held during the cooler months of August/September. Over the last few decades, it has occurred directly after the Yuendumu Sports Weekend—a pattern that Warlpiri people now find desirable and have adopted as an established tradition, just as they have come to associate the *Kurdiji* ceremonies with the hot weather of the summer holiday just after Christmas.

The settlement of many different family groups in one place intensified Warlpiri social life. As noted above, this initially caused feuds to flare up, with the close residential associations of these families also having an impact on ceremonial performance. Dussart discusses how settlement has impacted on the performance of the *Jardiwanpa* ceremony:

> Prior to settlement, rights to perform all subsequent *Jardiwanpa* were passed on to descendants of landowners and the ritual participants along the patriline. With the advent of sedentarization, the generational pattern of transmission further complicated these parallel ownership rights by adding the influence of residential association. (Dussart 2000: 33)

With the intensification of social life came an increase in activity as well as an increase in the numbers of people involved. Dussart describes this by saying that "the pool was enlarged to include individuals who had ties based on residential proximity but who often came from different patrilineal descent groups" (2000: 33). She summarized this by saying that "while these ideal relationships are still found at the roots of ritual organization, they have been modified in the wake of sedentarisation" (Dussart 2000: 35).

Wild (1987) examines Warlpiri ceremonies in the light of the history of Lajamanu, considering changing relationships to land, relationships with other settlements, and nontraditional social forces. He discusses the changes that took place when Warlpiri people were taken to Lajamanu, a site outside of Warlpiri country, noting that "songs and dances assisted these changing relationships to land" (Wild 1987: 105). Large-scale ceremonies increased as settlements grew, and new ceremonies from other tribes were adopted by the populations. Songs and song ownership were used to legitimize the rapidly changing social conditions and the ebb and flow of political alignments.

The ceremonies held by contemporary Warlpiri people reflect this history of residential intensification. In the last few decades, sweeping cult-like or large-scale ceremonies that incorporate many people are held more often and with greater participation than the site-specific ceremonies that require detailed knowledge of the places and the song series related to them. Today, these site-specific ceremonies are often incorporated into the larger ceremonies rather than being performed on their own. In the late 1970s and early 1980s, a ceremony came to Yuendumu from Balgo, which the majority of the population of Yuendumu participated in (see Laughren 1981; Wild 1981; and Young 1981). While this ceremony is no longer held today, the idea of inclusiveness it exemplified is still emphasized today as ceremonies such as *Kurdiji* expand—indeed, on many occasions during my fieldwork, *Kurdiji* has incorporated several hundred people from geographically distant places. Peterson (2000) has discussed the reasons for the intensification of these ceremonies, with particular reference to the expansion of *jilkaja*, in which large family groups journey to collect pre-pubescent male youths to bring back to their settlement area for *Kurdiji* ceremonies and other extended parts of male initiation. Mortuary rituals have also expanded in their scale, and today, people travel much longer distances to attend them—a result of the increased social networks (and avenues for increased communication) that people have over larger distances.

Recently, other kinds of ceremonies for which specific knowledge of *Jukurrpa* and country is required have declined. Being settled in one place has had a marked impact on Warlpiri people's knowledge of their country. While people still go on bush trips and regularly visit important locations on their land, this by no means gives them the same knowledge as the older people who lived in this country and had an intimate knowledge of it when they were younger, depending on its resources for their survival. Song series used in ceremonies often depict aspects of esoteric knowledge and evoke emotive responses to particular features of the country; without the experience of these places, it is very hard to understand these concepts. It has been suggested that songs providing rich descriptions of places are more important to Aboriginal people now that they do not frequently visit, and may have never visited, the country, as they provide richly detailed descriptions of places (Toner 2007: 183). With respect to Warlpiri songs, however, it appears that they are not understood as a consequence of this lack of intimate knowledge of landscape. Younger people actively participate in many of the large-scale inclusive ceremonies mentioned above, yet they have little interest either in the site-based ceremonies or in learning the accompanying detailed knowledge of country and religion. This is in large part due to a lack of opportunity, as *Kankarlu*, the secondary phase of male maturity rights during which much of this knowledge was taught, is no longer held.

Against this historical and social backdrop, I next set forth the cosmological understandings of the world that form the basis for Warlpiri worldviews and the kinship systems, connections to lands, and songs that nurture these forms of religious identity. The next chapter also addresses how songs maintain these forms of knowledge in Warlpiri worlds and describes the ceremonial contexts in which they are held, both in the past and today.

NOTES

1. These ideas are based on personal communication with Nicolas Peterson in 2009.
2. See Hinkson (1999) for a discussion of how these two domains became blurred in the self-determination era.
3. The suffix -*wardingki* in Warlpiri typically is added to a place where a person was conceived, indicating that they originated in that particular place. Today, however, it is applied more generally, such as when someone is associated to the building in which they live in Yuendumu—for example, one elderly woman is often referred to as "Mission House-*wardingki*," as she lives at the mission house and has done so for a very long time.
4. This small attendance at the church differs from the 1970s, when the church would be full for services (Laughren, personal communication, 2008).
5. In July and August, sports weekends are held in various settlements across the desert. During the periods when they are taking place, other settlements are virtually deserted, with few people staying behind.

Chapter 3

Warlpiri Songs
Rights, Genres, and Ceremonial Contexts

Napaljarri and her twenty-nine-year-old granddaughter, Napangardi, came rushing along the street toward me. The day before, we had organized to drive to the Mount Allan settlement to visit some relatives and go to the shop there. The pair yelled out that the shop was closing at 11 A.M. that day and would not open again until after 2 P.M. We decided it would be best to wait and go that afternoon. I went to see Napaljarri's two sisters, who had also expressed interest in the trip, and told them what was going on. They both agreed to come and then suggested that we stop at a place called Yujutuyungu on the way. "You know, that *Jukurrpa* we were singing about last week," she explained. The sisters and some other women from Mount Allan had gathered just the week before to record women's songs from the *Yurrampi Jukurrpa* (Honey Ant Dreaming). Napaljarri had said then that she'd wanted to take me to Yujutuyungu so that I could see the *Jukurrpa*–Japangardi and Japanangka—honey ants that had traveled from near Papunya, a southern settlement, up through Yuendumu and toward Mount Allan.

Napangardi sat in the front of the car with me and told me that she owned the place where we were going. Her father, who had died many years earlier, and his siblings had also been owners of this place, as had their father and his siblings before them. When we arrived, the older women started to reminisce. All three of these women had grown up in this place as teenagers. They giggled, as if still that age, reminiscing about how one of them had married her promised husband. They showed me *pardinjalpa*, a plant that can be ground into a mixture and used to massage babies when they have a cold. We could see Mount Wedge further to the south—a few days earlier, a large snake had been found there, and it was rumored that the army had had to come and take it away. There were hills in the distance—I was told that these were honey ants traveling past on their way from Papunya. As we walked further away from the car and began to climb a rock outcrop, they showed me two holes where two ancestral Napangardi and Napanangka women had been digging for honey ants—these holes met in the middle under the ground, and the two women had ended up stabbing each other with their digging sticks. Three vertically erect stones stood nearby—the physical manifestation of three ancestral Japangardi and Japanangka men. Napangardi told me that one of them was her father. As we headed toward a large cave where my three older companions had lived with their father decades before, we heard a loud noise from behind some rocks. The older women, excitedly but somewhat cautiously, went over to explore the area, expecting to find tracks leading them to a large perentie goanna that we could later cook for our lunch. They did not discover any tracks, however, and concluded that it had been *milarlpa*–the spirits of the honey ant Dreaming ancestors.

COSMOLOGICAL NOTIONS OF *JUKURRPA*

The power of Warlpiri songs and ceremonies is, on one level, connected to their functional roles and capacity to achieve certain social purposes. On another level, these songs hold great power, as they are intimately connected to the Warlpiri cosmological concept of the *Jukurrpa*, which is central to Warlpiri identity, social relationships, and connections to country. The *Jukurrpa* permeates contemporary Warlpiri life on many levels as a timeless creational moment in which the world came, and continues to come, into existence. The story that introduces this chapter illustrates the role that *Jukurrpa* stories and places have in everyday life for Warlpiri people living in Central Australian settlements. In this chapter, I consider the concept of the *Jukurrpa* as it has been written about in numerous ethnographic texts and as I have come to understand it through my engagement with Warlpiri people during the time I have spent in Yuendumu. This concept, far from being an abstract aspect of Warlpiri religious life only understood by older generations (as is sometimes assumed), holds important contemporary significance. Here I will discuss the various ways in which individual Warlpiri people are connected to the *Jukurrpa* and related country, songs, and ceremonies. I will then outline distinct genres of Warlpiri song, which are defined around gender and levels of public openness.

The *Jukurrpa* permeates Warlpiri life on many levels. The mundane, everyday activity of going to the shop turned into a trip infused with philosophical significance, connecting people to their past and to kinship networks and reinforcing ownership and knowledge of country and associated stories. The above account reiterates Poirier's observations that, for Aboriginal people, "there are no ontological dichotomies between social, natural and cosmological" (2005: 52). Notions of the *Jukurrpa* are not set aside in Warlpiri lives, nor are they only appreciated by older people who understand its more esoteric aspects. Notions of the *Jukurrpa* are relevant to people's contemporary social lives on a day-to-day basis as well as in ceremonial contexts. Cosmological understandings of the Dreaming have been described in a vast body of literature from across Australia (see for example Stanner 1966, 1979), and *Jukurrpa* is a term shared in various cognate forms across a number of Aboriginal groups in the desert region of Central Australia (see Dussart 2000; Glowczewski 1991; Meggitt 1962; Munn 1973; Myers 1986; and Poirier 2005).

The outline of events surrounding the *Kurdiji* ceremony presented in chapter 4 will demonstrate, through examples of ritual practice, how the *Jukurrpa* is continually negotiated by Warlpiri people living in contemporary Yuendumu. While always present as a guiding force or point of reference to make sense of the world, it is by no means a dictating and inflexible code for how things must play out. This degree of flexibility is an inherent part of this philosophy. Poirier explains that

> not only has the *Tjukurrpa* always existed, but it continues to permeate and animate all matter, to actualise itself and be actualised in the ongoing present, in a world where networks of social relationships and exchanges involve not just humans but also named places and the ancestors, both acting as sentient agents. From an Aboriginal perspective, reality unfolds and reveals itself through the multiple interactions and relations among different constituents of the world, be they human, non- human or ancestral. (2005: 57)

Poirier argues that "the Aboriginal approach to time is relational and process-oriented rather than linear and genealogical, and it cannot be dissociated from place, meaning the landmarks where events occur" (2005: 57–58). While this viewpoint may appear to imply a sense of ahistoricity, it instead emphasizes an interest in history as a continuum. On one level, there does appear to be a kind of sequential order to the journeys of ancestral beings across Warlpiri country, but all events are sung about in songs and spoken about in stories as if they are happening simultaneously. *Jukurrpa* ancestors are ever-present in places, though there is often a reference to a moment of travel in which they made their marks on the landscape. In chapter 4, the songs that are sung in the all-night part of the *Kurdiji* ceremony follow the journey of ancestral women who travel across the country and continually encounter other *Jukurrpa* ancestors, many of whom are sung about at particular points along their journey. All of these individual *Jukurrpa* stories have a kind of logical sequential order in which certain events happen after others. However, all of these ancestral beings are present at particular places at the same moments as others. This indicates that there is more of a focus on their presence in *places* rather than on the temporal relationship that these stories have to each other. Poirier shows that, for Aboriginal people, "their sense of historicity rather is one of a reality that unfolds and reveals itself in places and through dynamic and intricate interplay among events and actions from the *Tjukurrpa*, the human and non-human realms" (Poirier 2005: 59). From this view emerges an understanding of the *Jukurrpa* as a set of rules or a pattern for living that is continually negotiated according to context but which has always existed in the landscape, although it may not have been revealed until a particular point in time.

Contemporary Warlpiri people experience the *Jukurrpa* in many ways within their day-to-day lives. Poirier notes that among the Kukatja, "although they are rarely seen, the ancestral beings are able to make their presence known by a variety of different means and to manifest themselves in a range of different forms" (2005: 61). During my periods of fieldwork, there have been many instances where people felt the presence of ancestral beings. These moments were always interpreted contextually, with consideration to current events and the particular site. In 2007, during the weeklong Women's Law and Culture meeting hosted by the settlement of Haasts Bluff, women from all over the Central Desert gathered to perform songs and dances. As we drove toward the site where we would camp for the week, the women I was traveling with murmured in the back of the car about the two Jangalas, key characters in the *Warlukurlangu Jukurrpa* (Fire Dreaming) story. The chosen place for the meeting, while not associated particularly with a named site, was directly on the path of the *Warlukurlangu Jukurrpa*, in which two Jangalas were fleeing southward from their father who was trying to burn them (see Warlpiri women from Yuendumu 2017a for full story). Throughout the week, rumors abounded concerning the presence of *kurdaitcha* lurking around the boundaries of our camp.[1] Many of the older women would sit up at night calling for the two Jangalas to keep us safe. A friend of mine who was camped next to an older woman associated with the *Warlukurlangu Jukurrpa* told me that in the middle of the night, she woke up as she felt a wisp of wind move across the top of her. The old lady next to her woke at the same time muttering about how the two Jangalas had just walked over the top of them while they were asleep. The *Jukurrpa* is present in Warlpiri lives at all times, and its presence is felt in many ways.

Dussart has identified five distinct meanings surrounding the term *Jukurrpa* that are used in different contexts by Warlpiri (2000: 17–22). First, she highlights its most common usage, which is to designate a moment when "the world was physically and spiritually shaped by Ancestral beings who gave the Warlpiri their moral and ritual order" (2000: 18). In the story that opened this chapter, *Jukurrpa* was referred to as a time when features of the landscape that we can see today were created, such as the holes in the rock outcrop created by the ancestors digging for honey ants. The *Jukurrpa* is also continually spoken of in the present tense, with the hills in the distance being referred to as the *Jukurrpa*, honey ants traveling in the present time. The emphasis in this first meaning of the *Jukurrpa*, however, is on the creation of places in this overarching moment rather than in a continuum of other historical events. Second, Dussart notes the use of the term *Jukurrpa* as a collective noun to designate the ancestral beings themselves and the deceased ancestors of contemporary Warlpiri people. This is also seen in the story at the beginning of this chapter that references honey ants, which are the subject of the *Jukurrpa* story. Napangardi's grandfather is referred to directly as a honey ant, one of the *Jukurrpa* ancestors. Dussart does note however that this does not mean that the deceased relatives are "instantly folded into, or immediately become one with, some larger cosmological force situated in the Dreaming" (2000: 18). Napangardi's father, who everyone present remembered as a living person, was not referred to as *Jukurrpa* but as an owner of this place from whom Napangardi inherited her rights, as his individual identity as a person was still remembered by all present. The third way in which the term *Jukurrpa* is used is to refer to the narrative stories found in songs, objects, designs, and dances associated with ritual. Dussart notes that these stories are also proffered in nonceremonial contexts. Napaljarri's reference to the songs and dances they had sung as being *Jukurrpa* allude to this meaning. The fourth meaning revolves around how gender and kinship play out in ceremonial contexts, meaning that there are segments of narratives that may be gender and age specific and others that may not be. Finally, Dussart reiterates that nocturnal dreams provide much of the mythological knowledge that the Warlpiri possess, and these are also known as *Jukurrpa*. Dussart emphasizes that all these different ways of talking about the *Jukurrpa* are interrelated.

Rituals and ceremonies are performative means for addressing the *Jukurrpa*–drawing its relevance and potency into the contemporary context. The particularities of ritual contexts continue to shape symbolic representations of the *Jukurrpa*, emphasizing its moral codes and their relevance to modern Warlpiri life.

KIRDA AND KURDUNGURLU RIGHTS AND RESPONSIBILITIES

As illustrated in the story at the beginning of this chapter, Warlpiri people relate to places and the associated ancestral events in many ways. The three older Napaljarri women, while not associated with *Yurrampi* "honey ant" *Jukurrpa* in formal ways, which will be outlined shortly, drew their connection with this place from the time they spent living there as young adults. Napangardi, who has spent her whole life growing up in the Yuendumu settlement, related to this place through her ancestors, drawing a particular inherited connection as an owner through her paternal line. She also draws a strong connection to this *jukurrpa* from growing up in the settlement of Yuendumu, located on the path of the honey ant's ancestral journey. All of these women also related to the place through our visit that day—the story of the *milarlpa* moving from behind the rocks is still recounted to this day when we reminisce about visiting Yujutuyungu. This story demonstrates how people living in contemporary Yuendumu take on the visual and acoustic forms of the *Jukurrpa* in both its surface (*kankarlu*) and deeper (*kaninju*) features.

The Yuendumu settlement area is situated on the path of the *Yurrampi Jukurrpa*, meaning that the population that lives there has a connection to this *Jukurrpa* regardless of their inherited rights. Many Yuendumu residents refer to their settlement as *Yurrampi*. For young people who have spent their whole lives growing up in Yuendumu, this forms a central part of their identity. Many women discover that they are pregnant while in Yuendumu, and thus most babies born to women from Yuendumu connect to *Yurrampi Jukurrpa* as their conception *Jukurrpa*. People talk about themselves as being "put" in that place by the *Jukurrpa*, again reiterating the power of the *Jukurrpa* to shape human actions.

Warlpiri people as individuals are connected to particular *Jukurrpa* and associated with their country. The Warlpiri derive the strongest sense of connection to country from their inherited rights, through both their mother's family and their father's. In chapter 2, I described the subsection system that is central to social interactions among Warlpiri people in their daily lives. This system is built upon patricouples, which can also be grouped to form two patrimoieties of Warlpiri social worlds. These patrimoieties are the basis for the transmission of people's affiliations to country, songs, ceremonies, and associated *Jukurrpa*. Warlpiri people have *kirda* rights of ownership for the *Jukurrpa* that they have inherited through their patriline. Napangardi and her brothers derive their ownership rights to the country surrounding Yujutuyungu and the other places associated with *Yurrampi*

Jukurrpa in this way. The complementary role of *kurdungurlu*, glossed variously as "manager," "policeman," and "working man," can be claimed for song series associated with country belonging to their mother and mother's father (*jamirdikipungu*).

It is the *kirda* who claim traditional ownership of particular *Jukurrpa* and associated sites. It is also their responsibility to keep the country healthy by performing the ceremonies associated with these *Jukurrpa*. They have the right to live on that land and use its resources. Glowczewski (1983) too has discussed the differing roles of men and women as *kirda*, noting that while a female child is born into her father's patrilineal line as *kirda* for the same *Jukurrpa* and country, she is taught specifically feminine knowledge by her father's sisters, thus drawing on Dussart's fourth understanding of the *Jukurrpa* outlined above as gender and kinship specific (2000: 18). The complementary role of *kurdungurlu* is also crucial in maintaining the country and *Jukurrpa* associated with particular song series. These people are responsible for providing advice on the singing and dancing that a *kirda* performs. In the practice of looking after country and performing associated ceremonies, the *kirda* and *kurdungurlu* are both crucial. Any major visit to country or any decision about a ceremonial performance must involve both *kirda* and *kurdungurlu*. Dussart has also pointed out that

> *kurdungurlu*-ship can be claimed by the rights associated with the site at which one is "conceived." While claims on the basis of conception site may coincide with inherited rights, there are ample examples of managerial positions being claimed by people whose ties to the associated *Jukurrpa* are only classificatory. (2000: 35)

As Warlpiri people ideally marry into the opposite patrimoiety (and matrimoiety), the *kirda* and *kurdungurlu* automatically belong to opposite patrimoieties. Each of these moieties has two patricouples, within which ownership of country is passed down. These patricouples have egocentric terms. *Kuyuwapirra* (father's father) is one's own patricouple. *Kuyuwurruru* (mother's mother) is one's mother's mother's patricouple, which together forms a patrimoiety with *kuyuwapirra*. The opposite patrimoiety to one's own consists of one's spouse's patricouple, called *kuyukirda* (father's mother), and one's mother's father's patricouple, called *kuyuyarriki* (mother's father).

Generally, Warlpiri people affiliate *Jukurrpa*, country, and songs, through subsection pairs which form patricouples for classificatory purposes, but specific individuals from these classes are considered to be the true *kirda* or *kurdungurlu* through their particular inherited rights. Patriliny is sustained by keeping these associated rights within the patrimoiety. When a man dies,

Patrimoiety 1: NGURRA-YATUJUMPARRA	Patrimoiety 2: NGURRA-KURLARNIYARRA
Kuyuwapirra Jungarrayi/Nungarrayi Japaljarri/Napaljarri	*Kuyukirda* Jampijinpa/Nampijinpa Jangala/Nangala
Kuyuwurruru Japangardi/Napangardi Japanangka/Napanangka	*Kuyuyarriki* Jakamarra/Nakamarra Jupurrurla/Napurrurla

Figure 3.1. Patrimoieties and patricouples. Created by the author. The names for categories are based on ego as J/Nungarrayi (if J/Napaljarri is ego *kuyuwurruru* are the same but the *kuyukirda* are J/Nakamarra and J/Napurrurla, and the *kuyuyarriki* are J/Nampijinpa and J/Nangala).

one of his distant brothers may marry his widow and have children who inherit their rights in ceremony from both of these men, further broadening the rights an individual may have.

Kirda and *kurdungurlu* have distinct performance roles. *Kirda* are responsible for dancing and taking a leading role in singing. *Kurdungurlu* oversee that these are being undertaken correctly and are typically involved in preparation of materials and the ceremonial ground and painting designs on the artefacts that will be used in a ceremony. When the *kirda* for a particular *Jukurrpa* passes away, the associated ceremony is typically "put away" for a period of time (often a few years) before being brought out again by the *kurdungurlu*. As John Bern and Jan Larbalestier have pointed out with respect to the ceremonies associated with Limmen Bight on the western coast of the Gulf of Carpentaria, "Rights in ceremonies, including those parts of the ceremony which celebrate the sites of particular estates, extend beyond the members of a single estate group" (Bern and Larbalestier 1985: 69). It must not be assumed that ownership of country and *Jukurrpa* transposes neatly to ownership roles in related ceremonies. Instead such ceremonies may incorporate more distantly related people—a factor that is most likely based on residency and larger numbers of people available to participate. As discussed with respect to the case study presented in chapter 4, larger, more incorporative ceremonies increasingly dominate the ceremonial lives of Warlpiri people in Yuendumu, and therefore there is an emphasis on inclusivity in performance.

People with no particular inherited association to the particular Dreaming and country were often present, but they were nonetheless incorporated on the basis of their affiliated subsection. Dussart has proposed that this type of incorporation of people is a result of sedentarization, as more people have been implicated in the performances than they would have been prior to settlement (Dussart 2000: 33). This type of incorporation may also have been important prior to sedentarization as a crucial way to maintain alliances and keep social exchange networks relatively open.

Warlpiri people testify that the *Karntakarnta* song series, which follows the journey of a group of ancestral women from the far west of Warlpiri country eastward and is sung for the *Kurdiji* ceremony, "is for everybody," perhaps as the songs are for the maturity rights for all boys regardless of their inherited rights. The journey of the ancestral women focal to these songs winds through different tracts of country belonging to different patricouple groups, starting at Kunajarrayi, which belongs to the J/Napaljarri and J/Nungarrayi patricouple, then moving to country around Warnapiyi, which belongs to members of the J/Nampijinpa and J/Nangala, patricouple, etc.[2] This journey continues until women from many different parts of the country have joined it. This joining up of people and establishment of relationship networks is in fact a core theme emphasized in many aspects of the *Kurdiji* ceremonies. While there is no sense of ownership of the ceremony being associated with ownership of these places, the songs connected to the particular sites are said to belong to the patricouple who are *kirda* for that place. The reason for the lack of emphasis on *kirda* and *kurdungurlu* for the *Karntakarnta* song series, commencing at Kunajarrayi, may be due to the long period of time during which performances of this ceremony have been used for initiating boys in Yuendumu. Other settlements use different but related song series in a similar way. Due to the inclusive nature of this song series and the irrelevance of these *kirda/kurdungurlu* categories in the performance of *Kurdiji* (as discussed in chapter 4), these ownership and managership rights may have become a point of non-emphasis.[3] The senior men who are in charge of *Kurdiji* in both Yuendumu and Mount Allan, however, do maintain individual *kirda* rights for the starting points of these song series.

In the *Kurdiji* ceremony described in chapter 4, it is not the *kirda* and *kurdungurlu* who are focal to the performance but rather the relatives of the boys being initiated. *Kirda* and *kurdungurlu* are present in the *yawulyu* and *parnpa* on the first day. However, the all-night part of the ceremony, in which the *Karntakarnta* song series is sung, is organized around generational moieties resulting in active ceremonial roles for younger participants in particular. This organization emphasizes alternate generations as being of the same group, which naturally leads to the inclusion of more participants. It is desirable to have as many people as possible participating in ceremonies; the events that draw in large numbers of active participants are considered "winners" compared to other ceremonies.

Myers (1986: 203–4) has discussed how Pintupi social organization is structured around generational moieties, indicating that they have borrowed this emphasis from western desert groups. Thomas Rice (personal communication, 2006) also explained that the Pintupi *Warawata* ceremony, which is currently performed on the second day of *Kurdiji*, has replaced a more complex Warlpiri ceremony known as *Kirrirdikirrawarnu*. The *Marnakurrawarnu* ceremony (described in chapter 4), which is Warlpiri in origin, is also structured around generational moieties. Peterson (2000) has argued that this organization system allows for active roles to be given to younger generations and the incorporation of large numbers of people has contributed to the expansion of the *jilkaja* journey associated with initiation. The songs sung in the *Kurdiji* ceremony, however, do relate to a specific country with associated religious significance, and Warlpiri people, through these individual country affiliations, have inherited *kirda* and *kurdungurlu* rights.

The grand scale of ceremonies such as *Kurdiji* in the contemporary Warlpiri world may well be due to their incorporative nature in which people of all generations with all levels of knowledge have important roles. Other large-scale ceremonies have been popular in recent decades for the same reasons, though many are no longer held today. Laughren, Wild, and Young have all independently written about the popular "Balgo business," which was introduced to Warlpiri settlements in the 1970s at a time when local self-government and equality for Aboriginal people were new government policies and when the Warlpiri had just succeeded in a land claim (Laughren 1981; Wild 1981; Young 1981a). Wild argued, that this movement might have been an attempt to reassert power and increase involvement in Warlpiri rituals, which were in a state of decline (1981). "Balgo business" is different from other ceremonies that have been adopted, as the song texts are not understood by Warlpiri people and the dance styles are markedly different from traditional Warlpiri styles. Nonetheless, the popular ceremony, which included the majority of the population, was frequently held during the 1970s and 1980s.

The mortuary rituals held directly after someone dies, known as *Malamala*, also incorporate the majority of the population. Musharbash has noted that these ceremonies are held with such frequency in the contemporary Warlpiri world that they have had marked impacts on Warlpiri sociality (2008b: 22). During my periods of fieldwork, frequent "Sorry business," as it is more regularly known, structured people's lives in significant ways, considering the high death rates in Yuendumu and within the extended relationships networks of the desert settlements.

As the Balgo business is no longer held in Yuendumu, *Malamala* and *Kurdiji* are the only ceremonial practices that are not organized around the *kirda/kurdungurlu* relationship. Instead, both ceremonies incorporate large numbers of participants and are certainly the most frequently held rituals. A high death rate means that *Malamala* or "Sorry business" is a common part of everyday life in Warlpiri settlements (Musharbash 2008b). At the same time, an increase in birth rates, noted initially by Young in 1981(b), continues today resulting in the need for *Kurdiji* ceremonies to be held for many more boys each year. Peterson has argued, however, that because there are fewer older men who know the songs and greater numbers of boys needing to be put through these ceremonies, the senior men are managing the logistics by limiting the number of *Kurdiji* ceremonies each year but incorporating more boys into each ceremony (2008). A few decades ago, only three or four boys would be initiated at once; nowadays, there are commonly around ten and often more (the ceremony described in chapter 4 is an exception to this general trend).

Kurdiji and *Malamala* are connected in many ways, and there are many parallels in their organization and the roles of particular kin. Munn observed that "Warlpiri men associated the metaphor of dying with circumcision" (1973: 189). There are parallels between the *Kurdiji* ceremony *Malamala* ceremony, particularly shared organizational features and shared terminology for the participants, such as an initiand metaphorically dying as a boy and being reborn as a young man. Musharbash has described the organization of *Malamala* in Yuendumu, noting that "people sit in four distinct groups waiting for everyone to arrive: Men on the eastern side of the "Sorry ground" (in two opposing groups, one to the south, one to the north) and women on the western side, mirroring the men" (2008b: 26). This is very similar to the way people sit prior to the *Warawata* ceremony, as will be described in more detail in chapter 4. Myers has shown similarities between mourning and initiation among the Pintupi, noting in particular that people in the generation level above either an initiand or a deceased person can be distinguished behaviorally (1986: 200; refer to his discussion of *yirkapiri*). The kind of symbolic death of a young boy during his initiation is emphasized through these parallels.

Warlpiri lives have undergone significant changes over the last hundred years. This is reflected in the changing functions of individual ceremonies, the contexts in which they are held, how frequently they occur, and attitudes toward their function in modern life. J. Lowell Lewis has suggested that performances are particularly useful with regard to analyzing cultural patterns as they are contained by framing devices, with everyday life being an "unmarked background" against which they are set (1999: 539). Here I focus on defining song and ceremony as a distinct domain, albeit one that influences and reflects upon many other areas of Warlpiri life. Particularly, I emphasize the different aspects that come together to make a song. These include language, music, dance, and the painting of bodies and objects. I will also describe the different genres of Warlpiri song as I saw them sung for a variety of ceremonies. William Foley has noted that "genres do not exist as abstract categories, but only as schemes of interpretation which are enacted in particular performances" (1997: 377). In my descriptions of song genres in this chapter, I give examples of the particular ceremonial contexts in which I experienced the types of song. Following Gregory Bateson's (1972: 128) observations that different forms of human verbal communication have framing devices that clearly mark certain messages as belonging to a certain type, Irvine Goffman (1974) developed the notion of "keying" performances to mark them as particular types or genres. These descriptions aim to outline the different "keys" that mark genres of Warlpiri song as distinct from one other.

WHAT IS A SONG IN THE WARLPIRI CONTEXT?

The Warlpiri language does not have a single word for "song" in the generic, English sense. Rather, it contains terms for specific genres of song. The verb *yunparni*, however, is used to describe the act of "singing" with respect to all genres, indicating that while there is no generic word for "song," a classification exists in Warlpiri minds that all genres are of a similar semantic domain. Songs and the ceremonies in which they are sung are regarded as a domain of Warlpiri "high culture," which is a distinct domain from everyday life. Only those who have had the opportunity and have made the intellectual effort to learn about the specialized religious knowledge have the authority to sing songs. Songs are considered property owned by particular people, and they are seen as powerful and effective means for acting in and on the world. Warlpiri songs are thus clearly recognized as distinct modes of formalized performance where the act of singing particular songs is meaningful and powerful. Margaret Clunies Ross suggests that "the starting point for the determination of formal performances is whether the practicing community ascribes formality to a set of behaviours and places it within an indigenous taxonomy of registers" (1983: 17–18). Other criteria that she uses to identify formal performance include the following:

Firstly, that those who practice them consciously consider them to constitute an entity separable from other behaviour sets; secondly, that the entity possesses consistent structural features over and above those of the communication medium itself; and thirdly, that it is performed in specific contexts that the practitioners recognise as conventional and appropriate. (1983: 18)

In the Warlpiri context, there is certainly an emic classification of song as a mode of formal performance, distinct in purpose from everyday speech and performed in particular accepted contexts. This includes a clear separation from the performance of popular music genres such as rock, country, and reggae. The styles of music being classified very differently in Warlpiri minds, even if they consist of singing, are described with the verb *yunparni*.

Richard Moyle (1979: 17) regards the basic unit for Pintupi and desert music more generally in terms of the song series (sometimes referred to as song cycle or song line) "rather than the individual song." Alice Moyle, in a more general description of Central Australian songs, uses many different terms such as "song styles," "song types," "song forms," and she eventually defines "song items" as being "performed in a sequence or series usually with short breaks in between" (1973: 240). With respect to Arandic songs, Strehlow defines song cycles as "a complete set of verses associated with any ceremonial site and pertaining to the doings of any single mythical being or group of identical totemic ancestors" (1971: xiii). I use the word "song" in a generic sense to discuss this domain of Warlpiri life. More specifically, I follow Linda Barwick's use of the word "song series" when specifically referring to "a collection of songs from a particular country, belonging to a particular group of people and a particular ceremonial genre" (1989: 13). Additionally, Barwick emphasizes that a song series is made up of a series of "small songs" (a term used by Ellis and Barwick 1987), which are the two or three lines of singing that are repeated a number of times in performance. In this book, I use the word "verse" to refer to this concept of a "small song." In Warlpiri singing events, a sung version of a verse consists of a number of song items, each sung repetitively over a thirty- to forty-second period. Each of these song items consists of an identical rhythmic text, but not necessarily the same melodic contour, as the other song items in the verse (see figure 3.2 for an example).

Myfany Turpin refers to a performance of this kind of "song series" as "many small songs performed at one venue, which usually lasts a number of hours" (2005: 92). My definition of ceremonial performance and of song more generally incorporates song texts, music, painting up, dancing, and the ritualized contexts and social negotiations that surround these elements.

Figure 3.2

Figure 3.3

I do not include in this definition the telling of associated narratives, as in my experience these occur outside of the ceremonial context.

Performance context plays an important part in whether an act is regarded as "singing." R. Moyle has noted that "there are some phenomena associated with song performance which, while they may satisfy the technical requirements of music sound in a European sense, are nonetheless not con-

Figure 3.4

Figures 3.2–3.4. A song verse sung as three "song items." *Wapurtarli yawulyu*, recorded in December 2006 by the author with Jeannie Nungarrayi Egan, musical transcription by Calista Yeoh.

sidered 'singing' by the Pintupi" (1979: 13). These include such things as a sung commentary about a song that has just been performed, text rehearsal (when trying to remember the appropriate words), singing "aaaa" over the melody, and calls made during performance. Wild has similarly noticed that

> on rare occasions a Warlbiri individual may sing one or two songs of a Warlbiri song cycle in the course of his normal daily activities, but on these occasions he is not performing for anyone; he is merely reminding himself, or reminiscing, about the rituals in whose contexts the songs are normally performed. (1975: 57)

In my own experience, song verses may also be sung in isolation on various occasions. Such instances of "singing" often occur when a nostalgic memory is evoked of the content of a particular verse when visiting related country, observing geographical features, creating associated items of material culture, or hunting for particular foods.

Ellis's description of what a "song" actually is in the Central Australian context maintains that the "interlocking of all components is the key," and without this the product is not "song" (1983: 142). Turpin has also emphasized that "songs are a multimedia package where particular meanings may be represented in dance patterns, visual designs or in accompanying explanations, as well as in song text" (2005: 90). I too emphasize that a Warlpiri song incorporates language (through song texts), musical features, dancing, painting of designs on bodies and objects, and the social negotiations that continually surround the performance of all these aspects of song in a ceremonial context.

SONG LANGUAGE

The language of Warlpiri songs serves a very different function from that of everyday speech, not being for the communication of meaning so much as it is for ritualized and connotative purposes. It is the *act* of singing particular words within a particular musical and social frame that is meaningful and powerful, reinforcing the feelings associated with a song and the traditional place that it has in a ritual. Often the language is different from everyday speech, but it is also common for it to be similar to spoken Warlpiri but with multiple connotations that add layers of meaning (see Curran 2010). This has been noted across Australia with respect to Aboriginal songs from many different areas. Strehlow observed that Arrernte song language uses prose words from other languages as poetic synonyms in songs (1971). He also notes that there is often an intermingling of two languages but that this did not seem to inconvenience the singers, as many are bilingual. Peter Sutton also observes that many different languages are used in songs, some of which are intelligible to the people singing and some of which are not. He states that "there is no strict identification of the language of a song with the language of a clan whose site is being celebrated in that song" and observes that "there was often some reluctance to identify the language of these sacred songs . . ." (1987: 83). Hale too (in Green 2001: 38) recounts the thrill of discovering that some Warlpiri songs were in Anmatyerr, an Arandic language. Many of the Warlpiri songs that I recorded in Yuendumu also made use of other languages—in particular the languages spoken by neighboring groups from Anmatyerr to the east and Luritja to the south. Normally the songs in these languages are associated with travels of Dreaming ancestors to particular places.

The use of different languages, however, can also indicate that songs have been traded to Warlpiri people, and the particular languages used can give some indication of the places they have come from. In his description of the *Kajirri* ceremony, Meggitt explains that it has been transmitted over a long distance and modified in both form and interpretation (1966). He notes that this ceremony has links to those held by other groups to the east and north. It is evident from descriptions such as this that songs change form as they are traded from one region to the next and adapt into more region-specific ceremonial modes. Yet often they retain some of the elements from their origins or from other influences they have encountered.

Charles Briggs and Richard Bauman have noted that one way of keying a performance to a certain generic type is to use intertextual references (1992: 135). This is common among Warlpiri songs, with references to other *Jukurrpa* stories or songs and their characters clearly grounding a particular song within the realm of "song" rather than "everyday speech." The use of the first-person singular pronoun *-rna* throughout Warlpiri songs frames the singers as having the voice of the Dreaming ancestors, again clearly differentiating performance of song from other everyday activities. The use of this first-person singular form in the example from the Minamina *yawulyu* song series below indicates that the singer is identifying with the Dreaming ancestors focal to the song.

Manitirrpitirrpi	*manitirrpitirrpi*
red bird[4]	red bird
Kanalyurlparna	*kanalyurlparna*
in one group–1SGsubj.	in one group–1SGsubj.

I am the red birds in one group.

Again, in the song from the same song series below, the singers identify themselves as the country through the use of this first-person suffix.

Kurrkara	*kaarla*	*maninya*
Desert Oak	sound of wind	effecting–Pres
Warlurrumpurna		*maninya*
Honey Grevillea–1SGsubj.		effecting–Pres

I am Honey Grevillea country, getting homesick from the sound of the wind in the desert oaks.

Interestingly the first person is only ever used in its singular form regardless of how many singers there may be, perhaps indicating that the *Jukurrpa* is viewed as a singular entity.

Another special grammatical marker used in Warlpiri songs is the common example of the addition of *-nya* on verbs as a kind of presentative suffix. In the example from the *Karntakarnta* song series below, the suffix *-nya* is attach to the verb *nguna-* (to lie).

| *Ngapakurla* | *jurarri* | *jurarri* | *ngunanya* |
| water-DAT-LOC | streaming | redup. | lying-Pres. |

| *Ngapakurla* | *parlawamu* | | *ngunanya* |
| water-DAT-LOC | settled on ground | | lying-Pres. |

There is water running over everything. There is water lying on top of everything.

When this special marker is used in songs, the information encoded in the song is presented as being the way it is, and has always been. This reflects the Warlpiri notion of the *Jukurrpa* dictating the way the world is, with the singers having little control. The use of the present tense in most Warlpiri songs alongside this presentative suffix also indicates that the Warlpiri notion of the *Jukurrpa* is not of a past moment but of one that continues and encompasses all time periods.

As Sutton notes, "Mythic references in songs are far more oblique than in the words of spoken narratives" (1987: 86). The use of metaphor and symbolism is abundant in the language of Aboriginal songs. Strehlow has also noticed the use of archaic and poetic words used in Arrernte songs, describing it as "the curse of absolute unintelligibility" (Strehlow 1971: 202–3). An example of this type of esoteric gloss is using it to describe the features of the landscape or the *Jukurrpa* of a certain place instead of actually naming it. Sutton states that

> songs are usually ... cryptic. A song will very frequently refer simply to some aspect of the action of a mythical being, or perhaps the scent of the vegetation of the place, or the prevailing weather at the time of the event, but without tying any of these explicitly to both particular beings and sites all at once. The latter is usually done, if at all, by the participants using everyday language in a narrative or comment. (1987: 87)

Some authors have suggested that the nonexplicit nature of song texts is crucial for their maintenance. Marett has observed that "such a lack of explicitness is typical of Aboriginal discourse and forms part of a framework for the generation of further meanings which in themselves may give rise to, or emphasise a sense of community for those 'in the know'" (1994: 70). Clunies Ross also proposes that this "grammatically built-in ambiguity has been deliberately cultivated" in song language (1982: 15). Oblique and mysterious glosses are often provided by singers for song words, giving singers and knowledgeable elders control over how songs are shared and allowing space for shifts in song forms.

As song texts are largely unintelligible to an outsider, it is important to obtain exegesis after recording a song. As Hale explains, "The way you get the meaning is not by looking at the words, you get it by the story that goes with it. And the words evoke a story" (in Green 2001: 39). Francesca Merlan has also discussed the cryptic nature of song texts and the need for interpretation in her article about two song cycles from the Roper River area (1987: 144). She has proposed that "the predominance of these interpretive modes indicates the greater importance of "theme" as the organizing basis for song meaning over discursive meaning" (1987: 144). Tamsin Donaldson also highlights the increased understanding that she gained from people's interpretations of Ngiyampaa songs from northern New South Wales, where language loss is significant. Of particular interest is her observation that people who no longer understand the words of songs rely completely on embellished interpretations often surrounding a theme (1984: 240). Thus, obtaining exegesis is crucial in understanding the meanings of Aboriginal songs.

MUSICAL FEATURES

Many of the musical features of Warlpiri song are typical of Central Australian music more generally. Ellis has demonstrated that music is used in Central Australian song to convey meaning. Her examples show that particular rhythmic patterns relate to broad semantic topics (Ellis 1997: 65–67; 1998: 436) and that different ancestral paths have particular melodic contours, making them identifiable. Outside of Central Australia, in the Daly region, Marett has similarly shown that, "in Australian Aboriginal music, the power of music to signify rests primarily on a widespread convention that associates particular melodic forms with Dreamings, and by extension with the peoples and countries associated with those Dreamings" (2005: 200). Peter Toner's work in northeast Arnhem Land, however, shows clear links between melodies and social groups rather than Dreamings (2003). Musical analyses of the songs from across Australia, in particular their rhythmic and melodic forms, add significantly to our understanding of these kinds of associations and meanings. Turpin has illustrated that there is a sharp correlation between text and rhythm in the Katyetye women's songs genres (2005: 115). This extends broadly to other areas of the desert, as also noted by Ellis with respect to the Pitjantjatjara songs that she analyzed (1968: 24).

This interdependence of rhythm and text contrasts to the independence of melody and rhythm (and subsequently text), as illustrated in the example in figures 3.2–3.4. Central Australian songs are entirely vocal with no accompanying tonal musical instruments. Rhythmic accompaniment is common, however, with the use of clapsticks, two boomerangs being clapped together, or the thud of cupped hands on women's thighs as they sing. The thud of dancers' feet on the ground also provides rhythmic accompaniment to some songs. Often this rhythmic accompaniment is improvised at the time with whatever happens to be available—for example, a stick tapped on a tobacco tin or box. Particular song genres, however, make use of specific rhythmic accompaniments as "keys" to that particular type of song. An example of this is the use of two boomerangs to accompany the songs men sing for various *Jardiwarnpa*.[5] Boomerangs clapped in this way are also essential for the performance of men's *purlapa*. These accompanying beats are continued throughout the sequence of song items, which are repeated over a 30–40 second period until they speed up to a less consistent beat to finish, regardless of whether the same song verse is to be repeated again. The tempo or speed of this beating remains regular throughout the rest of a song series in most cases.

As there are no tonal instruments accompanying Warlpiri songs, the pitch is not determined by any outside reference. Generally, each song is led by someone who commences the singing of each separate song item and sets the pitch for the rest of the group. Sometimes these song leaders differ throughout the song series depending on the particular verse being sung or people's ownership rights or levels of knowledge concerning the song series. In the musical transcription in figure 3.5, the song leader sang at a higher octave from the rest of the group to assert her ownerships rights in these songs and associated country, distinguishing herself from the rest of the group initially before joining them at a lower octave for the rest of the session.

Like other Central Australian songs, the Warlpiri songs that I heard and recorded were sung in unison. As mentioned, a song leader would normally start singing, and the rest of the group would follow the pattern that they initiated. This was not normally negotiated ahead of time but assumed in the moment. Even in instances when someone without the proper authority took on the mantle of song leader, no argument occurred during the performance.

As illustrated in figures 3.2–3.4, a single repeated "melodic contour" (see Ellis 1985: 90) determines the "essence" of a song. This renders the song identifiable without making it necessary to understand the words (see Curran et al. 2019 for further examples). The text of a song is not set to this melodic contour in the same pattern with each repetition of the song item.

Figure 3.5. Musical assertions of ownership. *Wapurtarli yawulyu*, led by Bessie Nakamarra Sims, recorded December 2006 by the author with Jeannie Nungarrayi Egan, musical transcriptions by Calista Yeoh.

Often the singing will start and stop at various points in the melodic contour depending on where a breath is needed. Parts of the melodic contour may be assumed when the singer needs to take a breath and picked up again at the point where it would be expected that the rhythm would continue. The melodic contour is based on a flexible descending passage starting on a high tonic and descending to a low tonic (Ellis 1963: 88; 1966: 5; 1998: 434; and R. Moyle 1986: 156). Rhythm and text are integrated, with each song item consisting of two of these rhythmic text lines repeated until the end of the melodic contour. Musicologists describe this as "isorhythmic," where a rhythmic pattern cyclically repeats, although the corresponding melody may change (see Ellis and Barwick 1987; Barwick 1989: 13).

DANCING

Dail-Jones (1984) has described the dance patterns associated with Warlpiri ceremonies as she saw them in Willowra in the early 1980s. In her thesis, she argues that Warlpiri dance styles are ritualized patterns of movement that depict activities of the everyday. As examples, she parallels the styles of dance used in *yawulyu* performances with the movements made when women are hunting, emphasizing that similar implements, such as digging sticks and coolamons, are used for both of these activities. In dancing, these implements do not necessarily need to be present; the hands may be held in a fashion that imitates holding the tool instead. These implements symbolize different things, such as places, activities and people, which are intimately linked. Everyday implements are transformed when they are painted with ritual designs.

Dail-Jones (1984) also notes that the Warlpiri verb *wirntimi* can be translated firstly as "to dance" and secondly as "to hover like a bird." She provides examples of Warlpiri use of this verb to describe the action of bouncing a baby, indicating that it refers to a particular quality of movement that happens to be typical of Warlpiri dance. Dail-Jones has noted that for Warlpiri songs, "each genre of formal performance has a distinctive dance form" (Dail-Jones 1982: 81). These dance styles are thus important "keys" to particular genres of Warlpiri song. Cynthia Shannon has also described the range of body movements that are incorporated into Warlpiri women's dance from her fieldwork observations in Lajamanu (1971). She describes all Warlpiri women's dance movements as variations of the "dance jump," which adheres to a regular rhythm, and demonstrates that distinctions occur mainly in the arm movements, perhaps because many of these "dances" are also performed while seated, with the "knee quiver" being a notable exception (1971: 91).

Turpin has explained that dance movements can provide clues as to how the interpretation of the song texts were made in accompanying exegesis (2005: 111). Many of the participants of the *Kurdiji* ceremony, particularly the female dancers, derive their understandings of this ceremony from the dances they perform to accompany particular songs. They are learning primarily through these actions, and further associations become understood as they repeatedly dance in these ways by listening to the songs, paying attention to the surrounding conversations, and learning the associated ceremonial functions.

PAINTING UP

Several genres of songs incorporate the painting of participants' chests, backs, and thighs, as well as objects that will be used in the performance of ceremonies. Red, white, black, and yellow ochres are used. Often the songs sung while painting up are also sung in other performance contexts as well. Painting up in Yuendumu is done prior to the dancing component of a large-scale ceremony, often occurring in the late afternoon before a sunset ceremonial event. It is however, an integral part of the performance of the ceremony and follows strict conventions, which highlight the relationships among the song, the associated movements, and the designs. Visual designs are an important element of the ritual regardless of whether they are actually seen in the performance. Particular small songs are associated with particular designs, and these are repeatedly sung while painting up until the design is complete. Prior to *Kurdiji*, women paint up with Dreaming designs identifying the ownership rights of the boys central to the ceremony and their associated family members. For the performance of the *Jardiwanpa* ceremony, a song series that incorporates the travels of a number of different Dreaming ancestors, the designs that women use for painting up reflect the patricouple affiliation of the person being painted and the ancestor with whom they are associated. Men paint one another for some ceremonies and decorate themselves with white plant down in others, though I was not able to ascertain how the designs and songs are determined, as my participation was restricted in this genre. In Munn's extensive research into the visual symbols used during ceremonies, she highlights that "a characteristic feature is that the graphs [designs] always have explicit semantic reference; they are not merely decorative forms" (Munn 1973: 32). These references reinforce important symbolism associated with the broader ceremony for which the designs are being painted.

GENRES OF WARLPIRI SONGS

Defining songs through descriptions of their social purpose is by far the most common way Warlpiri people categorize genres. Songs are spoken of as being "for making young men," "for falling in love," or "for curing illnesses," emphasizing a highly functionalist focus on the purpose of songs and the rituals in which they are sung. Warlpiri people also distinguish song genres by the gender of the singers and participants in the associated ceremonies. Dussart has outlined the types of Warlpiri ceremonies that are performed by men (*watikirlangu*) or women (*karntakurlangu*), as well as those that may also be restricted to men (*watimipa*) or women (*karntamipa*) (2000: 52–57). She emphasizes, however, that there are joint performances involving both men and women (*wirikirlangu* = for businesspeople), but which still have components that are restricted to men and women.

Briggs and Bauman (1992: 132) have shown that genre categories are renowned for their inadequacy as there are always certain components that either do not fit a category or fit into more than one. The fuzziness of the boundaries between genres is acknowledged by Warlpiri people, as some songs are described as being of two genres and others are distinguished by not belonging to any particular genre.[6] There is, however, general agreement among Warlpiri people that songs can be categorized according to the genres outlined in this chapter. Firstly, there are songs that men sing in larger ceremonies in which women are involved, usually as dancers. Secondly, there are songs that men sing in smaller ceremonies—sometimes these are for men only and sometimes women participate. Lastly, there are songs that women sing in their own private spaces, which are sometimes also gender restricted. I want to emphasize that the genre divisions that I make in this chapter are classifications of types of songs rather than of the ceremonies in which they are performed. I have used an emic classification of Warlpiri songs that emphasizes, in most cases, the function of the song, or more specifically the particular purpose for singing it. Many of these categories do not have Warlpiri names, yet they are clearly seen by Warlpiri people to be of one type.

Songs Sung by Men in Large Ceremonial Contexts

In large ceremonial gatherings, songs are sung only by men, differing from other smaller ceremonial gatherings such as *purlapa* that women can join. Older men are the singers, and they sit in a group facing east, north, or west depending on the ceremony and context. Women sit in a group behind the men, who face away from them and at relevant points rise to dance. Dussart writes that these "joint" events are identified by Warlpiri people as *wirikirlangu* or *wirirlangu*—meaning "belonging to businesspeople" (2000: 53). She emphasizes that there are portions of these often complex ritual events that are restricted to women.

Kurdiji

The word *Kurdiji* (shield) refers to ceremonies for the first phase of initiation held each summer. It also refers to *Marnakurrawarnu*, songs that are central to the *Kurdiji* initiation phase and that are sung in the all-night part of the ceremony. Different song series are sung in different settlements across Central Australia, although the ceremonies are almost identical. The events of a particular performance of this ceremony in Yuendumu are described in chapter 4. A second phase of initiation called *Kankarlu*, which is no longer held, incorporates different genres of song (primarily *parnpa*, which I will discuss shortly). *Marnakurrawarnu* starts early in the morning and continues through the afternoon, when *yawulyu* and *parnpa* associated with the initiand's affiliated Dreamings are performed in their respective women's and men's groups. After this, the *Marnakurrawarnu* ceremony continues until sunrise the next day. The *Kurdiji* genre of song is performed during the all-night phase of *Marnakurrawarnu*, where it is sung by senior men from around 10 P.M. until sunrise the next morning. A day or so later, a ceremony named *Warawata* is held in the afternoon, leading up to the circumcision of the initiands shortly after dusk. Some songs from the *Kurdiji* song series are also sung at *Warawata*, but only for about half an hour. In the past, this final stage took the form of an elaborate ceremony called *Kirrirdikirrawarnu* (as described by Meggitt 1984: 285–98, and Wild 1975: 107–12), but in recent years, it has been replaced by the much shorter *Warawata*, a ceremony borrowed from Pintupi- and Luritja-speaking groups to the south. While Warlpiri people from Yuendumu participate in *Kirrirdikirrawarnu* when they go to other settlements (as they did in Napperby in 2008 and Mount Allan in 2006), it was not held in Yuendumu during my period of fieldwork from late 2005 until early 2007. A different song series is sung for *Kirrirdikirrawarnu*, which older Warlpiri men know well and of which I have elicited recordings.[7]

The *Karntakarnta* song series performed in Yuendumu for *Kurdiji* ceremonies follows the journey of a group of ancestral women from near Kunajarrayi (Mount Nicker). They actually start their journey further west at Yapurnu (Lake Mackay), a salt lake on the border of the Northern Territory and Western Australia, and end it at Yuluwurru (Lake Lewis), another salt lake just south of Napperby (refer to map 4.1 on p. 96, which marks the itinerary for this journey). In different settlements, other song series, which are also referred to as *Kurdiji* songs as they are used for the same ceremony, are performed. In Lajamanu, a different song series that follows the journey of a group of women from Minamina is sung.[8] In *Kurdiji* ceremonies that I attended in Mount Allan, which are predominantly populated by Anmatyerr-speaking people, the same songs are sung but begin at Yuluwurru, where the songs sung for *Kurdiji* in Yuendumu finish. Most senior Warlpiri men in Yuendumu know the song series sung in Lajamanu, Yuendumu, and Mount Allan and participate in *Kurdiji* ceremonies in these settlements frequently as well as many others across the Central Desert region.

Another ceremony, the *Kajirri* [Meggitt's *Gadjari*], is connected to the Warlpiri *Kurdiji* ceremony and has been outlined by Meggitt (1966) and Shannon (1971). This "religious festival" presents a further stage in boys' religious education. I did not witness this ceremony or even hear about it during my fieldwork—it may no longer be held. Meggitt emphasizes the links that the *Kajirri* ceremony has to the *Kunapipi* ceremony, which is widely performed across northern Australia (see Berndt 1951 for details), showing that this ceremony has come to the Warlpiri from the eastern Warumungu and that they obtained if from groups to the north. Wild (1971) describes this particular ceremony a few years later, discussing it mainly in the context of how it relates to positions of leadership and authority in the settlement of Lajamanu. Wild believes that in the early days of the establishment of the settlement, police officers, station owners, and missionaries did much to undermine traditional modes of authority, leading to decay in Warlpiri systems of leadership. He gives an outline of the *Kajirri* ceremony, saying that initiation, circumcision, subincision, and the *Kajirri* ceremony were all separate affairs in the past. Nowadays these once-separate affairs are all clumped together and performed over the six-week school holiday.[9] Wild indicates that at the time of his fieldwork in the 1970s, a man was ineligible to marry prior to the *Kajirri* ceremony and that a young man would have been ostracized if he had eloped without this establishment of his right to marry.

Songs Sung for Conflict-Resolution Ceremonies

Peterson (1970) has glossed these ceremonies as "fire ceremonies," as they involve the burning of long leafy poles. Many people, who are often required to come from distant places, participate in these ceremonies. Because so many people participate in cooperation, these ceremonies are useful in resolving conflicts. The songs sung by men for these ceremonies are all linked to *Jukurrpa* stories, which involve a fight that is resolved through joint performances of ceremonies (Rice, personal communication, 2007). In 2006 an attempt to perform *Jardiwanpa* was made (this has been described in Curran 2019), but after several months of trying to gather all of the people required for the ceremony without success, it was put on hold. *Ngajakula*, a similar ceremony owned by the opposite patrimoiety, is still known by a few older men. Harry Nelson (personal communication, 2006) stated that the primary function of these ceremonies was to open up the restrictions on remarriage for widows of deceased people associated with one of the *Jukurrpa* ancestors. A large part of one of the all-night ceremonies involves all the widows dancing in lines with flaming firesticks. Laughren (personal communication, 2009) noted that some women choose to avoid participation in order to avoid pressure to remarry.

Four different ceremonies have been described by Dussart: *Ngajakula*, *Jardiwanpa*, *Puluwanti*, and *Kura-kurra*. Dussart has shown an obligatory reversal and exchange of performance roles from one associated series to the next (Dussart 2000: 79). Peterson enhances this description, demonstrating that there are complex interrelationships among these ceremonies and emphasizing that *Ngajakula* and *Jardiwanpa* relate to different patrimoieties. The two patricouples within each of these moieties relate more directly to certain Dreamings along these lines. *Jardiwanpa* belongs to Jakamarra/Jupurrurla/Jangala and Jampijinpa patrimoiety. The Dreaming ancestor *yarripiri* (inland taipan) begins his travels at Wirnparrku; this place and the associated Dreaming belongs to the Jakamarra/Jupurrurla patricouple. Farther along this journey, the *yankirri* (emu) Dreaming joins in with the travels belonging to Jangala/Jampijinpa patricouple. Other Dreamings such as *wampana* and *ngurlu* (Nakamarra/Napurrurla) also join in at various points. *Ngajakula* revolves around the journey of *mala* (rat kangaroo) from *Mawurrungu*, which is associated with the Japaljarri/Jungarrayi patricouple. Intimately linked is the journey of the *puluwanti* (owl), which is associated with the country surrounding Willowra. This belongs to the Japangardi/Japanangka patricouple. Laughren (personal communication, 2009) and Peterson (personal communication, 2009) have both independently reflected that when they lived in Yuendumu in the 1970s, *Ngajakula* was performed more often than *Jardiwanpa*, as the eastern Warlpiri from Willowra were dominant in ceremonial activity. Nowadays, *Jardiwanpa* is the more popular of the two ceremonies. Many Warlpiri people use *Jardiwanpa* as a general gloss for these conflict-resolution ceremonies, which are performed almost identically despite their links to different Dreamings and country. *Jardiwanpa* has been performed several times over the last few decades, whereas *Ngajakula* has not been performed at Yuendumu since the 1970s.

A conflict-resolution ceremony generally takes about two weeks to complete, culminating in its spectacular final two nights. Before this, there is a period of waiting for everyone to arrive, which can be lengthy. During this period, people move their camps to the business area and gather together each night to rehearse songs and dances. The initial part of the event consists of men singing from the central song series associated with that particular ceremony in the early afternoon, while women dance with their hands raised beside their shoulders, hopping forward and singing "uh, uh, uh, uuuuuh" before switching to a "knee-quiver" style dance incorporating a hand movement similar to winnowing seeds in a coolamon. The dance style changes when the men are singing songs associated with the *yankirri Jukurrpa* (Emu Dreaming). This continues until all the people needed to perform the ceremony have gathered. The performance of these ceremonies entails ritualized assault and support. This is reflected in the layout in which people dance. On the final night, there is an elaborate ceremony that involves burning long poles wrapped with eucalyptus leaves. The owners of the ceremony are locked in a rounded shelter made of branches, and certain managers of the ceremony shake the poles over the owners, showering them in sparks in a kind of ritualized assault. The other group of managers is responsible for protecting them from getting too burnt.

There are also *yawulyu* incorporated into this ritual, sung by women in the afternoon preceding the nighttime ceremony. These are associated with the same Dreaming itineraries as the men's conflict-resolution songs. *Yawulyu* involve the painting of particular women's chests with associated designs determined by the woman's patricouple affiliation. The women's *yawulyu* and associated dances are also performed before the *Jardiwanpa* ceremonies begin, to "finish up" for someone associated with a *Jardiwanpa* site who has passed away a few years before.

Men's Songs

Some songs sung by men, such as *parnpa*, are restricted to a male-only audience. Others songs, such as *purlapa*, are sung in public situations and often incorporate women in various roles. *Yilpinji* are sometimes restricted and sometimes public. Being a female researcher, I could only record the public *yilpinji* and *purlapa*. Recordings of some of the restricted genres have been made by other male researchers and are housed in the Australian Institute for Aboriginal and Torres Strait Islander Studies (AIATSIS), although there are restrictions on who can access and listen to them.

Parnpa

Parnpa are often labeled "increase songs" in the literature, as one of their functions is to make food resources plentiful. These songs, however, have other functions too, such as to cure illnesses or alter weather conditions. The primary function of these songs, however, appears to be to educate men about Warlpiri religion and country. Dussart makes a parallel between this and women's *yawulyu* but notes, "*Parnpa* ceremonies tend to be directed at specific circumstances (*ngarrmirni* ['increase']), whereas the *yawulyu* are invoked for the more general maintenance of Warlpiri well-being" (Dussart 2000: 76).[10] These songs are sung during the first day of *Kurdiji* ceremonies, and they relate to those Dreamings and places to which an initiand has affiliations. Although *parnpa* are often discussed as being "secret" or "restricted" songs in this context, they are performed on the opposite side of the business ground to where the women sit. Far from pretending not to see these performances, women actively plan to be there when they are happening. Dussart pointed out in her observations from the 1980s that although these ceremonies "are performed less often now than when Munn undertook her fieldwork in Yuendumu [in the 1950s], their relevance in ritual life has in no way diminished" (Dussart 2000: 76). Similarly during my fieldwork, while there were only a few old men who actually knew how to sing the songs, the songs themselves were still a crucial element of ritual life, particularly in their performance as part of the *Kurdiji* ceremony.

In past decades, another stage of initiation called *Kankarlu* existed, in which young men were subincized. Peterson refers to these as "religious festivals" (Peterson 2000: 207) where men's songs associated with several different *Jukurrpa* were performed in a centralized area. People came from far away to camp nearby, and once everyone had gathered, the songs and dances associated with particular men would be performed. The ritual events surrounding *Kankarlu* no longer occur in Yuendumu today. However, the older generations frequently reminisce about *Kankarlu*, with older men recounting the songs, designs, dances, and stories they learned during this period of their lives. Older people in Yuendumu describe *Kankarlu* as similar to "high school" in that it was a period of instruction about Warlpiri religious life. The decline in Warlpiri people's knowledge of *Jukurrpa* stories, songs, dances, and designs in recent decades is often attributed to the fact that *Kankarlu* is no longer practiced and no other forum to learn about these elements of religious life has replaced it.

Purlapa

Purlapa is a genre of men's song associated with specific places. Meggitt has described these songs as "public entertainments" (1962: 244). Dussart has criticized this definition, saying that it suggests the function of *purlapa* is to serve as a "relatively inconsequential diversion," when instead *purlapa* allow people to "manifest ... their control over stories, sites, and the resources associated with them" (2000: 76). Wild has also noted that *purlapa* related to the management of particular sites serve a functionalist purpose (1975). He describes these songs, which were performed regularly during his fieldwork, as always being accompanied by a beat, created by clapping together two boomerangs or sticks or hitting a bottle on the ground. He also notes that women would join in, sometimes even with the singing, cupping their hands and hitting the insides of their thighs (*purrpu-pakarni*). He explains that these songs can also be performed without any dancing, where instead the men sit in a compact circle and the women and children surround them.

While I recorded versions of several *purlapa* song series with ritually senior men, the only *purlapa* that I have personally witnessed during my fieldwork was one associated with the Christian stories surrounding Easter. This is the only song series I encountered during my fieldwork that did not

Illustration 3.1. Warlpiri men perform the Easter *purlapa* with boomerang clapsticks. Photograph by the author.

center on ancestral beings and their journeys. A large group of people from Yuendumu traveled to Alekarenge in 2006 for the performance of this ceremony on Easter Friday and again at dawn on Easter Sunday. Neville Poulson (personal communication, 2006) explained that in the 1970s, this *purlapa* was composed by a group of older men and women to make sense of and pass on Christian stories. Men, women and children from many different places participated in the performance of this Easter *purlapa*. On Easter Friday, a session is held in the afternoon without dancing, the songs performed by seated men facing east and clapping together boomerangs, with seated women behind them also facing east.[11] The nighttime events consist of the same songs, accompanied by a march-like style of dancing by men and male children in which they are decorated with white fluff while they reenact the Easter story. The members of the Baptist church in Yuendumu are extremely proud of the Easter *purlapa* and showcase it to Christian visitors to the settlement as a kind of example of how Indigenous culture has incorporated Christianity.[12]

Juyurdu

These songs are known only by senior men, and they are rarely sung in contemporary Yuendumu as their intentions and consequences are so dire.

Older Warlpiri men informed me that as these songs are sung, a bone is pointed at a victim who becomes ill or in some cases dies as a result. As part of the mortuary rituals performed directly after someone dies, accusations are often made as to why the deceased has passed away. As most Warlpiri people are unwilling to believe that someone could have passed away from natural causes, senior men are often accused of singing *juyurdu*, and are cast out as sorcerers for a period surrounding these big "Sorry meetings."

Rice (2007) reported to me one day that he had gone to see two old men who had both gone quite senile in their old age, and he found them sitting innocently and singing *juyurdu*. He rushed to stop them, even though their senility meant they had not understood the impact of what they were singing and were merely just remembering something from the past. Rice explained that these songs are dangerous, as they can make people act strangely or dance like fools. He recounted that men would often sing these songs if their wife had a lover, causing the lover to act strangely and make the wife lose interest in him. When I asked Rice if I should record any of these songs, he said I should not, as he was too afraid of what might happen to me if I heard them.

Men's *Yilpinji* (Love Songs)

Yilpinji, often called "love songs" or "love magic" in the literature, have been the subject of much fascination in many studies of Aboriginal societies (Bell 1983: 145–46; Berndt 1950: 28; Kaberry 1939: 268; Meggitt 1962: 209; and Munn 1973: 45–47). Their purpose is to make people attractive to the opposite sex. These songs are targeted at a particular person, and the singing is directed to an item of their clothing. As the song is sung, this item of clothing is said to become "shiny"—shininess being a sexually attractive quality to Warlpiri people. The men's *yilpinji* that I recorded were all sung by small groups of men. The songs relate to particular sites and appear to be important in nurturing the *Jukurrpa* and associated country. Some men's *yilpinji* are performed in restricted men's groups, while others (such as those I recorded) are more open and can be performed in front of women.[13]

Women's Songs

Women's songs are generally sung in private female-only situations. Only certain *yawulyu* are restricted as such, but normally men do not attend their performance. Men, however, do come to the business ground while the songs are being performed if they need to see their female family members, suggesting that any restrictions are not terribly strong. When this occurs, though, women normally stop singing until the men have left. The songs associated with initiation and women's *yilpinji* are more restricted and women cease to sing them whenever a man is in close proximity. Some performances of *yawulyu*, particularly those that are danced while naked, are strongly restricted. This may have more to do with modern taboos on being naked in front of men. These *yawulyu* are still performed on the business ground visible from the settlement area, but a standing line of women always obscures any view of the dancers.

Women's Songs Surrounding *Jilkaja*

Women sing throughout the course of events that surround *jilkaja* journeys in which boys are picked up from their home settlements by a traveling party. Generally, women sing in the evenings or other quieter times while sitting around the camp, and the songs are particularly associated with the travels of the men. Women sing when the boys leave to go into the bush for men's business, then again to draw them back to the camp safely. During *jilkaja* journeys, women travel with the party of senior men, initiands, and their guardians to collect further candidates for initiation ceremonies. They sing to ensure the safety of the party. Older women explained to me that they had to do this so that the boys would not get homesick. During a *jilkaja* that came through Yuendumu in March 2006, a particular group of older women who were related to an initiand sang softly all night while the group of candidates and their guardians slept in the bush nearby. During the daytime part of *Kurdiji*, the men perform *parnpa* and the women perform *yawulyu* on opposing sides of a business ground. Women also perform other songs and dances that the men watch. Due to restrictions on recording these songs, I have not engaged in analysis of their features, but their content relates directly to the actions of the men at the time of singing. These songs were described to me several times as "not *yawulyu*," defining them as what they are not rather than giving them a distinct genre category of their own but indicating nonetheless that they are of a particular category of women's song. In the daytime part of the *Marnakurrawarnu* ceremony held in Yuendumu in January 2007, all able-bodied women were required to dance in a long line into the ceremony ground while a small group of senior women sang these songs. The men gathered on the opposite side of the business ground to watch this performance. When I began fieldwork in Yuendumu in 2005, no one had wanted to record these songs, as they were restricted from general public audiences. A younger woman explained to me then that

I should not record these songs, as "they were not like *yawulyu*." Nowadays attitudes have shifted, and I have been asked on a number of occasions to record these *jilkaja* songs but to keep the recordings restricted from public hearing.

Yawulyu (Women's Songs)

Yawulyu refers to the songs, designs, and dances that are performed by small groups of women and that represent the identity of a Warlpiri woman. These songs follow the Dreaming itineraries of ancestral beings across the country. Women associate themselves with particular *yawulyu* according to their connections with country along these Dreaming itineraries. The content of these songs may have a narrative component, but the emphasis is more on evoking places and the activities of Dreaming ancestors in a symbolic manner. *Yawulyu* may be performed in a song series or as individual verses, often in the broader context of a wider ritual. Dussart has described *yawulyu* as "an umbrella term for the most pervasive of women's rituals at Yuendumu," noting that it "defies easy translation because of its plural functions" (Dussart 2000: 75). Some *yawulyu* are labeled as *nyurnu-kurlangu* (healing songs) and are powerful in healing particular illnesses. In order to unlock their potency, animal fat or cooking oil is "sung" with these *yawulyu* and then massaged into the body of the sick person. Some *yawulyu* are also labeled as being *yilpinji*, as when they are sung for a particular person (or item of their clothing) that makes them more sexually attractive. Other *yawulyu* evoke places, encourage desired weather conditions, increase food resources, or recount Dreaming events. *Yawulyu* are performed in a long series of songs that follows the travels of Dreaming ancestors across the country, or individually, relating to their particular purpose. Individual verses are often sung while painting up.

Certain *yawulyu* are restricted to senior women while others are performed more openly. Those held when I was in Yuendumu tended to be female-only situations, although they were not restricted. Some performances of *yawulyu* involve elaborate dancing that is often hidden from the view of men by a group of women gathering in a cluster.[14] It is the performance of *yawulyu* that is private, but the songs are open for anyone to listen to.[15] During the time I have spent in Yuendumu, I have seen *yawulyu* performed in many different contexts. As I was working predominantly with women due to the gendered segregation in Aboriginal settlements, this is the genre of Warlpiri song of which I have made the most recordings.

Before *Kurdiji* ceremonies, *yawulyu* associated with the candidates for initiation are sung by a small group of women who paint their chests with designs. The Central Land Council organizes annual gatherings at which women congregate from many areas of Central Australia and perform *yawulyu* for a whole week. Many community groups use this as an opportunity to demonstrate and show off their styles of song and dance. Warlpiri women, who tend to dominate these events, use this opportunity to do important business such as "finishing up" for women who have recently passed away. These "finishing up" ceremonies are also held in Yuendumu beforehand, with senior women singing and dancing *yawulyu* associated with the deceased for several weeks, from just after sunset and into the night. These "finishing up" *yawulyu* involve all senior women shifting their camp to the business ground to sing. The final night consists of an all-night performance of the same *yawulyu*.

Yawulyu are also performed for settlement events, such as the annual Sports Weekend or the opening of new buildings. Dussart has noted that in the 1990s, *yawulyu* came to replace the men's public performances of *purlapa*, for example, in courts and at art exhibition openings (2004).

Women's *Yilpinji* (Love Songs)

Dussart recounts that "according to senior Warlpiri residents, *yilpinji* were the exclusive province of men prior to sedentarization. However, the performance of *yilpinji* was opened up to women in the wake of enforced settlement. A new population density and the accompanying social disruption stimulated a dramatic increase in the 'love songs' used to find lovers" (2000: 77). This indicates that *yilpinji* have in recent history been borrowed from nearby regions. I only recorded two *yilpinji* song series sung by women during my fieldwork, both of which were sung for my benefit.[16] One of them was from the Anmatyerr-speaking region to the northeast of Yuendumu, and the other was from the Lurtija-speaking region to the south. These *yilpinji* were identified as belonging to these other groups, supporting Dussart's comment that they were only the realm of the Warlpiri men before sedentarization. Unlike men's *yilpinji*, the women's versions seem not to be as intimately linked with places and *Jukurrpa*. While places and *Jukurrpa* may be referred to in some instances, evoking their characteristics does not seem to be one of their powerful functions (as it is with *yawulyu*); the primary function of *yilpinji* is to attract lovers.

Some individual *yawulyu* are said to be good *yilpinji*, and *yawulyu* relating to the same places are also performed in the middle of *yilpinji* song series (perhaps *yawulyu* are a way of grounding them in places and therefore making them meaningful for Warlpiri women).[17] This reinforces the multifunctional role of the genre of *yawulyu*. Laughren (personal communication, 2010), in comparing particular *yawulyu* and *yilpinji*, has noted that these two genres of women's song share some similarities, especially in their formal linguistic and musical properties, but they are clearly distinct in that *yilpinji* do not have the same structure to their performance, are performed by individuals rather than groups, and have clear narratives with overtly sexual themes, whereas the focus of *yawulyu* is on evoking country and Dreamings.

Warlpiri songs and the ceremonies for which they are sung are an aspect of "high culture," meaning that they have distinct features that set them apart from other aspects of Warlpiri life. Performances of songs and ceremonies nurture Warlpiri people's religious associations with Dreaming, country, and kin. In the next chapter, I present an example of a *Kurdiji* ceremony that was held in Yuendumu in 2007. This ceremony incorporated several of the genres of song described above, and its vibrancy in the contemporary Warlpiri world illustrates how these traditional song genres and associated inherited rights to country and *Jukurrpa* play out in a ceremonial performance context.

NOTES

1. Warlpiri people specifically use the word *kurdaitcha* to refer to male revenge killers who regularly haunt and attempt to seduce. This usage distinguishes *kurdaitcha* from the feather-footed beings that are believed to haunt wider Aboriginal Australia.
2. The conflict-resolution ceremonies also have central song series for which ownership changes along the itinerary followed. However, this is only within the same patrimoiety, i.e., the two patricouples of a patrimoiety may have ownership over different places along this journey.
3. In Lajamanu, however, the Minamina song series is used to initiate all boys, yet it still has distinct *kirda* and *kurdungurlu* who identify with this *Jukurrpa*.
4. The gloss "red bird" is used here, as there is some contention as to what species this bird is. The *Warlpiri-English Encyclopeadic Dictionary* (Laughren et al. 2007) glosses it as a "mythological bird." Ornithologist Robert Gosford (personal communication, 2008) has suggested that it is a red-capped robin (*Petroica goodenovii*).
5. Some of the song texts of the *Jardiwanpa* series describe the action of beating these two boomerangs together, as the older men stand behind the younger boys to teach them how to do it.

6. This situation most often came up when I asked someone what type of song was being sung. Normally I received a more specific response (e.g., the Dreaming, dance style, or place) associated with the song. Often if I asked if it was a specific genre—for example "Is that *yawulyu*?"—the response would be, "No, that's not *yawulyu*," with no further information given about a possible genre classification.
7. See Hansen 1954 for an account of this ceremony as witnessed in Yuendumu in January 1953.
8. These women also commence their journey at Yapurnu (Lake Mackay), crossing paths several times with the group of women traveling to the south of them.
9. Shannon observed in Lajamanu over the 1970–71 summer period that "the initiation rites lasted for two weeks. These were immediately followed by Kajirri which continued over the next five weeks" (Shannon 1971: 10).
10. *Ngarrmirni* is a verb used for the act of performing *parnpa*. *Ngarrmirninji* means "made plentiful or rendered abundant" (Laughren et al. 2007). *Ngarrmirni* also means "beget" as a father does to a child (Laughren 2010).
11. This seating pattern is similar to those for other ceremonies like *Kurdiji*. It is different from Wild's descriptions of how people sat when singing *purlapa* without dancing. In the *purlapa* that Peterson (2010) saw in the 1970s, the women and some men would sit in the east, and the men would dance toward them from the west.
12. In 2006, several months after this ceremony had been performed in Alekarenge at Eastertime, a group of schoolchildren and teachers from Mount Evelyn Christian School in Victoria came to Yuendumu as part of an exchange program. The songs associated with this ceremony were performed for them to demonstrate Warlpiri understandings of Christianity.
13. Egan also helped to record these *yilpinji*, indicating that they are open for Warlpiri women to hear and that an exception was not just being made for the purposes of recording the songs.
14. The more restricted *yawulyu* today are performed naked; more open yawulyu are performed with skirts but no shirts so that the chest designs can be seen.
15. The only restriction on playing *yawulyu* on the Warlpiri Media radio station was if one of the singers was someone who had recently passed away.
16. On both occasions, I was going to be seeing my boyfriend in the following days, and the women were singing these songs with this in mind.
17. Myfany Turpin (personal communication, 2009), in discussing similar songs in the Arandic area to the east, has noted that these terms are fluid, with cognate terms seeming to cover different types of rituals. Within Warlpiri songs, for example in the Minamina *yawulyu*, a song that evoked the movement of women's hips as they carried a baby in a coolamon attached to their body with snake vine, was said to be a "good *yilpinji*." Women were said to have obtained lovers through singing this song.

Chapter 4

Kurdiji, a Ceremony for "Making Young Men"

The summer of January 2007 was the first time in five or six years that *Kurdiji* ceremonies had been held in Yuendumu. Over the previous years, a bitter feud between two large families had reached a point where they could no longer cooperate to hold joint ceremonies. Many people had sent their boys to other settlements to participate in the ceremonies. The ceremonies in Mount Allan that I had attended the previous year had incorporated many boys from Yuendumu for this reason. While the feud had by no means been resolved, the emotions had not flared for some time. A further dispute with a family from another settlement had absorbed significant attention and the implicated family had been forced to side with their previous rivals. As such at that point in time the two families were on relatively harmonious terms.

As the people of Yuendumu prepared to hold *Kurdiji* there once more, there was a feeling of excitement: older people were overcome with nostalgia, the young with curiosity, and there was a feeling that the tradition would be continued in the proper way. Excitement filled the air, and Yuendumu became a different kind of place. The summer days were now much longer and hotter, meaning Yuendumu residents tended to rest for a long period in the middle of the day before exiting their houses and moving around the settlement in the evening. School was closed for the holiday, and most of the settlement organizations were closed as well. The structures that these institutions impose on Warlpiri lives had relaxed and were now unimportant, if only for a short time.

In mid-January, I attended a large-scale *Kurdiji* ceremony in nearby Wariyiwariyi in which twenty-one boys, including a significant proportion from Yuendumu, "went through business." The ethnographic descriptions of *Kurdiji* by Meggitt (1966) and Wild (1979) testify that in past decades, no more than two or three boys were made into young men in a single ceremony. The increase in the number of initiands significantly impacted how the ceremony was held, particularly in the numbers of people who would attend. Peterson (2008) has argued that a change in the demographic structure of the population in Yuendumu, with its rise in the number of youth, has also resulted in many more boys needing to be initiated each year with fewer older men with knowledge of the song series required for this ceremony. The result of these changes is that many more boys are being made young men at once, which relieves the older men slightly from the demand of singing all night on too many occasions.

It is not unusual to travel broadly for these ceremonies as part of *jilkaja* journeys, during which boys from distant settlements are brought to Yuendumu, with their families following closely behind. *Jilkaja* is increasingly encouraged as a way of establishing alliances among people from geographically separate places (Peterson 2000). The ceremonies held in Mount Allan were, however, quite different in many ways due to the influences of the large Anmatyerr population in this settlement. The excitement of holding *Kurdiji* the Warlpiri way, in Yuendumu, added to the buzz in the air.

On 27 January 2007, after a lot of build-up and discussion about when it would start, the first lot of boys went through business in Yuendumu. This was a large ceremony with eighteen boys and all the necessary family members gathered in the east of Yuendumu. I was enthusiastically asked to record the singing throughout the all-night period, and I had now begun to recognize a loosely organized but clear pattern to the sequence of events surrounding a *Kurdiji* ceremony (see figure 4.1).

The population of Yuendumu was on a high that night and for days following this ceremony. The mother of one boy, however, had not been able to travel to Yuendumu, as she lived in Alice Springs and required medical services that were not locally available. For this reason her son had not been "caught," though he was certainly of age.

§

A few days later, I was having a late night cup of tea outside with Napurrurla before we headed off to bed. In the distance to the north, we heard a few shrill, high-pitched cries. Napurrurla whispered to me that they must have caught more boys, and that meant that *Kurdiji* would be on again in the next few days. These cries were loud enough for everyone in the settlement to hear, serving as a warning for the women to stay inside their houses or camps. The boys that had been "caught" were now being taken out into an area immediately north of the settlement that is restricted to adult men and

"Getting caught"	Anytime during the day, often over several days
Marnakurrawarnu	Afternoon
	Women's *yawulyu* (painting up)
	Men's *parnpa* (dancing)
	Sunset
	Men's *parnpa* while women "sleep"
	All night until sunrise the next morning
	Men singing and women dancing
Warawata	Late afternoon until just after sunset
Coming back from the bush	Later afternoon until just after sunset (several weeks later)
	*in the past this part was done in the morning just before sunrise

Figure 4.1. Temporal overview of the *Kurdiji* ceremony. Created by the author.

hidden from view by bush. Women were not meant to see them as they were escorted out of the settlement.

A short while later, an eleven-year-old boy who lived next door to us came over to tell us excitedly that he had been at the disco when one of the boys was "caught." His *juka* (brother-in-law) and *rdiliwarnu* (elder brother) had disrupted the disco by coming in and solemnly leading him out of the room. The sparkle in our neighbor's eye indicated that while the process was reputed to be a tough and arduous one for young boys, as their social and behavioral expectations significantly changed as a result of it, the life event is also anticipated with excitement by young boys of this age group.

When I woke up the following morning, I found out that three boys had in fact been caught the day before. The older men had wanted to catch Japangardi for the ceremony a few nights earlier, as they did not want to have to hold another *Kurdiji* ceremony. Despite difficulty traveling, his mother was able come up to Yuendumu for a three-day period, so they had decided to catch him now rather than wait until the following year. As it would have been strange to hold *Kurdiji* for a single boy, the other two boys were caught so that all of them could go through the ceremony together. These boys were twelve to fourteen years old, showing signs of physical maturity but still appearing and acting as children. The older men had been carefully watching all the boys around this age group until they decided who would go through that year. The boys that were caught were of two subsection groups: Jampijinpa and Japangardi, and one boy had two skin names, Jampijinpa/Japangardi, as his parents had not been first choice marriage partners (as set out on in figure 2.2 on p. 35). In initiating the boy with two subsections at the same time as the other boys, the ceremony would be easier to hold as all relations to this boy would have roles at all times. The boys that had been caught to go through together were thus classificatory brothers-in-law (sisters' husbands). This also meant that the mothers of these boys who were classificatory "cousins" (mother's brother's daughter, father's sister's daughter) for each other could thus potentially also act as "mothers-in-law" for each other's sons—important for marriage exchange. Japangardi and Jampijinpa/Japangardi shared a common great-great-grandfather (i.e., one man was both Jampijinpa's father's mother's mother's father, and Jampijinpa/Japangardi's mother's father's father's father; refer to figure 4.2), whereas Japangardi's family was more distantly related still (see figure 4.3).

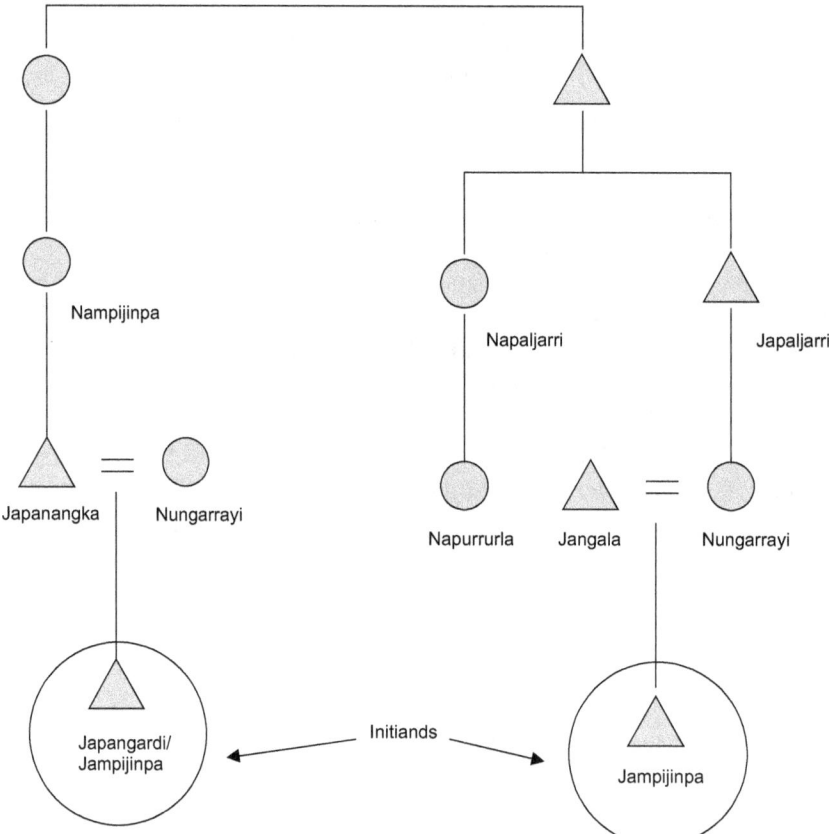

Figure 4.2. Genealogy of the families of Jampijinpa and Japangardi/Jampijinpa. Created by the author.

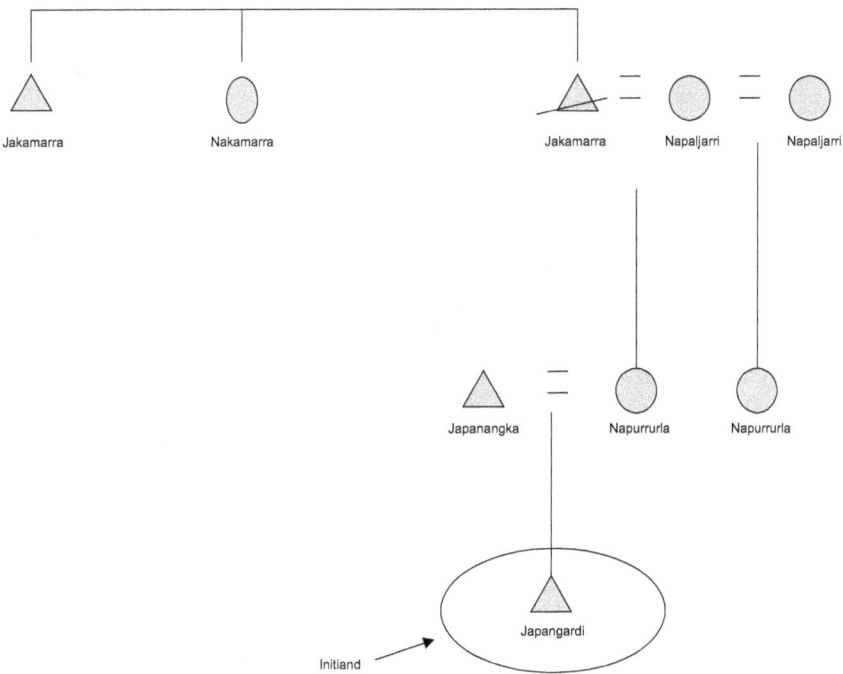

Figure 4.3. Genealogy of the family of Japangardi. Created by the author.

This ceremony would forge closer kinship ties among all these families. In the past, a key collective motivation for holding *Kurdiji* was to form alliances between families whose children would one day marry each other. In contemporary Yuendumu, promised marriages rarely eventuate, as younger people now choose to marry outside of these systems; however, the bonds between families are still significant.

A few days after Japangardi was caught, his mother from Alice Springs arrived on the bush bus, a public transport system operating several times a week so that people living in settlements can travel around independently. She was staying with her mother and sister at a house very close to the business ground at east camp in Yuendumu. As it was widely known that she could not stay long, her arrival signaled to other people that *Kurdiji* would be held within the next day or so.

ROLES OF KIN

I do not go into detail here about the roles of specific kin during this ceremony, as they are apparent in the description that follows. I do introduce, however, a few terms for the groups of people, emphasizing their normative roles rather than those for the particular ceremony described in this chapter. These terms are used throughout my description, clarifying that alternate generation moieties are the basis for the organizational structure of *Kurdiji* ceremonies. One's own generation moiety is referred to as *ngarnarntarrka* (also sometimes *yarlpurru-kurlangu*), whereas the opposite moiety is called *jarnamil-jarnpa* (also sometimes *ngawu-kurlangu*). In discussing these terms, Laughren (1982: 77) notes that "the social significance of this division is great," emphasizing that marriage contracts must be made between two people who belong to the same generation moiety. First-, second-, and third-choice marriage partners are therefore all found in one's own generation moiety, and taboos on marriage occur with those in the opposing generation moiety.

Young men who go through *Kurdiji* and other maturity rights in the same ceremony form an important bond that lasts throughout their lives. They refer to each other as *yarlpurru* when they belong to the same subsection. There is also a special set of terms that is formed by adding the suffix *-lyka* to the morpheme that designates the relations between co-initiates (refer to Laughren 1982: 78). These terms are summarized in figure 4.4.

Juka (sister's husbands, either actual or classificatory) are responsible for caring for the boys over the period of their initiation. Initially, they must inform the father of a boy when they think that he has matured enough to be ready to go through initiatory business. The *juka* must also prepare a camp for the boys in an area used by men for ritual and help the boys' elder brothers escort him there. In the camp, *juka* act as guardians, preparing boys by rubbing them with red ochre and fat and tying their hair in a *pukurdi*–a knot behind the head that reveals the forehead and peak of the head (Meggitt 1962: 283).[1] Glowczewski also explains that the *juka* prepare hair strings that are put on the young men when they are brought out of seclusion and re-

yarlpurru	in the same subsection (brother)
lampanilyka	in the mother's brother's/ sister's son's subsection
pirlpirlilyka	in a mother's mother's brother or daughter's son's subsection
wapirralyka	in father's subsection
marrkarilyka	in wife's brother's subsection
wajamirnilyka	in wife's mother's brother's, mother's mother's father's or sister's daughter's daughter's son's subsection
ngarrmaralyka	in mother's father's subsection

Figure 4.4. Co-initiate kin reference terms. Created by the author, adapted from Laughren 1982: 77.

introduced to their families (1983: 234). The hair string is then passed over as a gift from boy to mother-in-law—this action strengthens the ties between the initiand's family and that of his future wife. The *juka* play a crucial role in this ceremony, as they represent the family into which the boy will potentially one day marry. Glowsczewski (1983) has illustrated that hair among the Warlpiri is a powerful sexual symbol, promoting virility in men and fertility in women, and therefore it symbolically represents the marriage liaison that results from this ceremony.

The *rdiliwarnu* (elder brothers), also known as *jarrawarnu*, are involved in deciding whether or not the boys are ready to be initiated. Once the boy is caught, the *rdiliwarnu* helps to reassure him by explaining to him what will happen (Meggitt 1962: 282). *Jarrawarnu* is also the word used for the siblings of a dead person. Warlpiri mortuary rituals also emphasize the role of siblings in a similar way. Northern Warlpiri speakers use the word *jarrardili*, which translates as "flame." The *jarrawarnu* are involved in catching the boys and taking them to the camp where they are initially secluded. During the rituals, the *rdiliwarnu* are responsible for explaining the significance of ceremonies, supervising the painting of the shields with *Jukurrpa* designs associated with the initiand's patrilineal identities, and lighting fires during the nighttime phase of *Marnakurrawarnu*. The initiand's *warringiyi* (father's father), who is of the same generation moiety and subsection as the initiand, also performs a similar role, but less actively. As these older men have acquired ritual knowledge over their lifetimes, they are there to supervise that the *rdiliwarnu* are actively learning about the *Jukurrpa* songs, designs, and dances in the *parnpa* (men's dancing) phase while also taking on the ritual responsibilities in looking after the younger brothers throughout the entire series of ritual events. The *warringiyi* plays a particularly important role today, as the fathers of the boys nowadays are a lot younger than they were in the past and have not developed their ritual knowledge to the point where they could perform their duties on their own. The female *rdiliwarnu* (sisters, mother's brother's daughters, and father's sister's daughters) are also active participants in this ceremony, particularly the younger generation. Dussart (2000: 70) explains that they introduce the initiand's sisters into ritual life. They often get *yawulyu* designs painted on their chests in the late afternoon and dance in the all-night ceremony.

A shield is painted for each boy and used throughout the *Marnakurrawarnu* ceremony (see illustration 4.3 on p. 92). During the all-night ceremony, the *rdiliwarnu* dance on the northern and southern ends of the line of women, making the sound "puh, puh, puh, puuuuuh." The mothers' mothers and fathers' mothers are also considered *rdiliwarnu*, as they are of the same generation moiety, but, in a similar way to the male *rdiliwarnu*, they do not take an active role as the younger women and girls do. Nowadays, these older women lead and guide the *yawulyu*, as younger generations do not know the songs and their associated designs with as much detail. This will be illustrated shortly in the description of women's painting up in the late afternoon.

The *yulpurru* (fathers and mothers' brothers) are responsible for singing both the *Karntakarnta* song series during the night and the *parnpa* during the day, painting the shields and generally making sure the ceremony goes as it should. Today, not many men of this age group know these songs, although they actively participate by sitting with the older men while they are singing. As young men no longer go through the secondary phase of initiation called *Kankarlu* that was described in chapter 3, they are having children at a much younger age than in the past. It used to be that young men would not finish their full initiatory rites until they were around the age of thirty, meaning that they would be around forty-five when their sons were ready to go through business. Today most men become fathers in their late teenage years, only a few years after their initial circumcision ceremonies, and as such may only be as young as thirty when their sons are initiated. As a consequence, there is now an extra generation of *yulpurru* present. There is usually one senior man from this group called a *wati-rirri-rirri* who takes on the role of boss for the entire sequence of ritual events. The women of the opposite generation moiety to the initiand are called *jinpurrmanu* (mothers, fathers' sisters, and mothers-in-law). They dance in the middle of the line of women during *Marnakurrawarnu* and make high-pitched sounds for the length of each phase of their dancing. The differing ways in which these women dance and the accompanying props that they use (such as firesticks, digging sticks, coolamons, and dancing boards) bring about certain transformations in relationships among the participants of the ceremony. The roles of men and women of all generations are vital for this all-community ceremony, and Warlpiri people take them very seriously.

MARNAKURRAWARNU–DAYTIME

The day after the extra boys has been caught, I went out in the bush to collect honey ants. It was a perfect day for this, as a lot of rain had fallen that summer and the honey ants were close to the surface. The day had the crisp, clean air following rain in the desert. Napurrurla was renowned for her hunting skills—her extraordinary strength mixed with a delicate touch meant that she rarely squashed the fragile honey-filled backs of the ants, causing them to spill open. Our neighbor, Napanangka also came along in a separate car with her large extended family. Napanangka's daughter had been living in Queensland for the last few years with her four children after she had separated from her partner who still lived in Yuendumu. She had been heavily pregnant with her fifth child when the family arrived back in Yuendumu. She had recently come to me, upset that they had caught her eldest son only a week after they had arrived back to the desert after many years of east coast living. She cried that she didn't know what to do or what was expected of her during *Kurdiji* as she had lived away from Yuendumu for so long. Despite her worries, I watched as she and her younger sister, who was also heavily pregnant, danced all night as their son went through business at the big ceremony in Mount Allan earlier in the month.

Her son had come hunting with us that day, recently having returned to Yuendumu from spending several weeks in the bush under the guidance of the senior men. It was clear that he still enjoyed hanging out with his mothers and younger siblings. Perhaps because he had recently come back to live in Yuendumu, he did not feel as close to his age peers. Unlike other men who have just been through business who take on a sudden mature swagger, he still appeared childlike, although at the age of sixteen he was actually one of the older boys. This didn't last long. Within months, he was absorbed into the world of male teenagers and youth, a world in which I as an adult woman rarely engaged.

Women's *Yawulyu* in the Late Afternoon

When we came back from hunting honey ants, crowds of people had begun to gather at the business ground to the northeast of Yuendumu. Napaljarri waved me down from the side of the road—she wanted me to drive her elderly and quite senile sister back to their house. *Kurdiji* would be on all night, and she didn't want her to stay there as she might get lost or become confused during the night. Napaljarri was sitting with a small group of six women who had gathered to sing *yawulyu* and paint up for the nighttime ceremony. I knew Nakamarra and Nampijinpa from Yuendumu. Nampijinpa's grandson (son's son) was going through that night. Three Nampijinpa sisters from Willowra had also come down for this *Kurdiji*, as their grandson was also going through that night. Napaljarri told me to come back after I had taken her sister home, as they were going to start painting up and singing *yawulyu*. Some younger women in their thirties, forties and fifties, including the mothers of the boys, were sitting nearby, but they did not come over to participate in the painting up or even acknowledge that it was happening.

The first *yawulyu* they sang was from the *Watiyawarnu* "Acacia tenuissima" *Jukurrpa* song series, mainly associated with places around Willowra, a settlement about 150 kilometers to the northeast of Yuendumu. Three Nampijinpa women from Willowra took part in the singing. One of the Nampijinpas from Willowra was painting Nampijinpa from Yuendumu with red and white ochre as the women sang. This *yawulyu* is sung in sections by women from both Willowra and Yuendumu, providing an important link between different Warlpiri groups (see Curran et al. 2019).

Ngurlu-lirri-nyinanya x 2	There it is at Ngurlulirrinyinanya [place name]
Watiyawarnu panjapanja kujurnu x 2	The Acacia seeds spread all over the ground.[2]

The grandson Jampijinpa/Japangardi of the Nampijinpa who was being painted was to "go through" that night, and she was excited. Nonetheless, she planned to go home before the all-night ceremony because of her asthma, which would be worsened by the night air. Nampijinpa was being painted with a *Watiyawarnu Jukurrpa* design associated with her father's country and therefore one for which she held a *kirda* role (see illustration 4.1). Each

Illustration 4.1. Peggy Nampijinpa Brown painted with *Watiyawarnu yawulyu* designs during *Kurdiji*, 2007. Photograph by the author.

yawulyu was associated with the patriline of each of the boys who wo~ through business later that night though the range of relationships and ~ terconnections was complex.

The second *yawulyu* to be performed that afternoon was associated with Pawu (Mount Barkly), a hill in the country just to the south of Willowra, belonging to Jampijinpa/Jangala. This hill is also the starting place for the *Watiyawarnu yawulyu* sung by the women from Willowra and an important central location for many of the Willowra-based *yawulyu*. Nakamarra showed me a bump on her back and explained that she needed the other women to sing *nyurnu-kurlangu*, as she was in a lot of pain. Two of the Nampijinpas from Willowra sat on either side of her to hold her while the third Nampijinpa painted her stomach. They sang a verse from the *Pawu yawulyu* song series as they held and painted her, as this is a good *nyurnukurlangu* for this type of pain. The design they painted was a filled-in oval over her belly button with four semicircles arching away from this central circle. The song sung is private and for women only due to its powerful healing qualities, and I have therefore not written the words in this book. This *yawulyu* appeared to be sung solely for the purposes of healing Nakamarra—a powerful *nyurnukurlangu yawulyu*. It is also a *yawulyu* owned by the three Nampijinpa women from Willowra, connecting them closely to the country at Pawu, and in singing it they emphasized in this important social moment that their grandson, through them, also had links to this country.

The final *yawulyu* sung that afternoon was *Warlukurlangu yawulyu* ("Belonging to the fire" Dreaming), a favorite of women from Yuendumu. This song had only recently been "opened up" again after a period in which it had not been sung following of death of a much-loved woman who was an owner (*kirda*) for this *Jukurrpa*. This *Jukurrpa* is associated with country to the south of Yuendumu. Nampijinpa is an owner (*kirda*) for this *yawulyu*, and Napaljarri is a manager (*kurdungurlu*). After Nakamarra had sung *nyurnukurlangu* for Napaljarri's stomach, Napaljarri also complained that she had very sore knees and needed the women to sing them to make them better. The women from Willowra first massaged her knees with red ochre and then painted the *Warlukurlangu Jukurrpa* designs on her chest (see illustration 4.2).

Jangalajarra layampirra x 2	Two Jangalas, [the smoke came up] right where they are standing
Lirranji layampirra x 2	The smoke clouds forming, right where they are standing.[3]

Napaljarri told me that this verse from the *Warlukurlangu* song series is particularly good for pain such as that caused by arthritis. *Warlukurlangu* is

Illustration 4.2. Ruth Napaljarri Oldfield painted with *Warlukurlangu yawulyu* designs. Photograph by the author.

the country for Napaljarri's mothers and their brothers. Napaljarri's niece (brother's daughter) Nungarrayi's son, Jampijinpa, was going through business that evening. This *Jukurrpa* related to him, as both Napaljarri and his mother's father were managers (*kurdungurlu*) for the *Warlukurlangu Jukurrpa*.

It was getting quite dark by the time they finished singing. We all quickly rubbed more red ochre on our legs so they would be strong and we could dance that night, after which Napaljarri and Nampijinpa went home. It was clearly not essential that they attend the all-night ceremony, as it was more about the younger generation taking an active role than about the knowledge of the older people.

Parnpa

During the afternoon, while the women had gathered for *yawulyu*, the men sang and danced *parnpa* on the opposite (eastern) side of the same cleared area. The women sat on the western side, with the men in clear view (see figure 4.5). The group of women occasionally laughed or chattered about

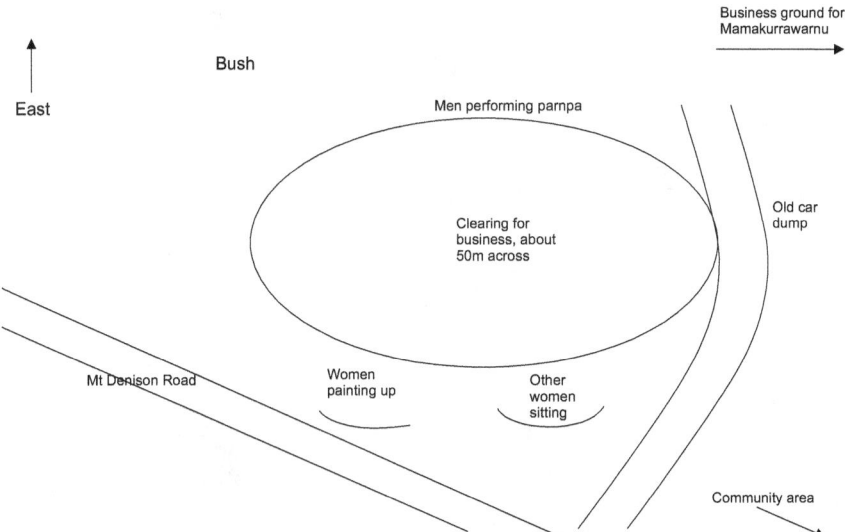

Figure 4.5. Ground plan for afternoon *yawulyu* and *parnpa*. Created by the author.

which men were dancing. *Parnpa* is a genre of men's song that is well known to be restricted from women, but the nature of these restrictions becomes more evident in context—these songs and dances can be seen and heard faintly from a distance.

Several days after the ceremony, I asked some of the older men who had been present at the *parnpa* performance what they had done during the daytime part of *Marnakurrawarnu*. While it was clear that they did not want me to document details of the songs and dances, they did explain that earlier in the day, the fathers of the initiands had painted shields with the *Jukurrpa* designs belonging to their patrilineal line. The fathers did not know how to paint these designs, so they required instruction. The older men were pleased that one of the fathers in particular had made an effort to learn this skill. After painting, they rested during the hot part of the day. In the afternoon, while the women had been singing and painting up with *yawulyu*, the men performed the *parnpa* associated with the designs they had painted on the shields. The boys who were going through this business were not present for the painting of the shields or the *parnpa*. They were out in the bush in their secluded camp with their *juka*, presumably resting up for the big night ahead of them. The day had been predominantly used to educate the fathers of the initiands on their *Jukurrpa* designs, dances, and songs, for which they were gaining increasing responsibility. After these afternoon gatherings had dispersed, there was a flurry of activity as many men and

Illustration 4.3. The *kurdiji* "shields" painted for ceremonies in 2007. Photograph by the author.

women went home, where they would stay or collect their swags and return for the nighttime ceremony.

Parnpa after Sunset

The majority of women dragged their swags, cooking implements, and food a few hundred meters up to the cleared ground, to the south of where we had been performing *yawulyu* and *parnpa* during the day, on which the all-night phase of the *Marnakurrawarnu* ceremony was to take place. Once our group of women had collected all our swags and lined them up north to south, we lay down with our heads covered and pretended to sleep. By this point the sun had set, and it was almost completely dark. After a few minutes, the *wati-rirri-rirri* came over to tell us to move further east because the men were sitting too far away. He wanted us to be about ten meters away from where the men were (see figure 4.6). Once we had repositioned, our group again lay down on our swags and recovered our heads.

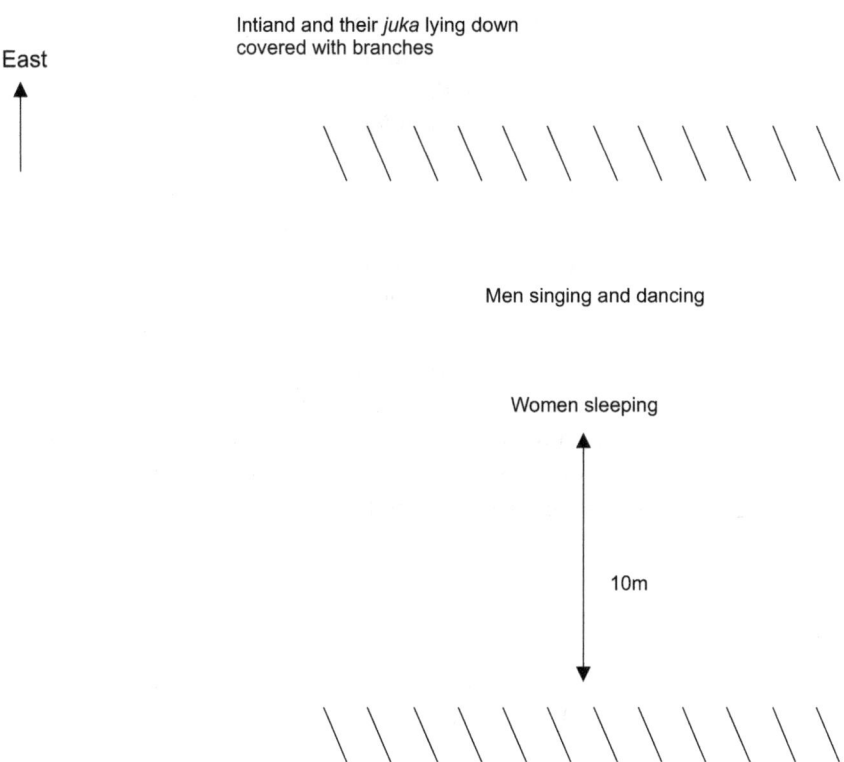

Figure 4.6. Ground plan for *parnpa* just after sunset. Created by the author.

While the women rested, the men performed the same *parnpa* songs they had danced earlier in the afternoon (belonging to the initiand's *Jukurrpa* through his father's father). They sang softly as they sat in a group just to the east of the women's heads. Though the women were not allowed to *see* the men, the singing was clearly audible. At the end, the men got up and danced close to our heads. I could hear the thud of their feet on the ground. After about an hour, the *wati-rirri-rirri* told the women to get up, as the men had finished. All the actual mothers (i.e., mother or mother's sisters) of the young boys walked to the eastern side of the windbreak, just to the east of the old men (see figure 4.6).[4] As Japangardi's mother was in a wheelchair, she was pushed closer before standing and hobbling over with her walking stick. The three boys, Japangardi, Jampijinpa, and Jampijinpa/Japangardi, were lying on top of their *juka*, facing upward, and covered with large leafy branches. The *wati-rirri-rirri* pointed each one out to his mother when the women got there. They hit their own sons on the chest lightly with their dancing boards before rejoining the group of the women. The boys were then led by their *juka* around the northern end of the windbreak, past the singers and through the middle of the group of female dancers, who had at this point separated into two groups to form a path for them to be guided through. From there the boys walked up to the far western end of the business ground where another windbreak had been set up. This was about fifty meters behind the large group of women in the middle. The *juka* and *rdiliwarnu* for the initiands sat at this end of the ceremony ground too. All the male *yulpurru* and some older *rdiliwarnu* remained sitting in the group at the eastern end, facing east, where they remained all night (see figure 4.7). The only senior men who got up and moved around (for reasons other than stretching or toilet breaks) were the *wati-rirri-rirri* and his brother, who were responsible for making sure everything was happening the right way. They would occasionally check on the boys and make sure the other *juka* and *rdiliwarnu* knew what they were supposed to be doing.

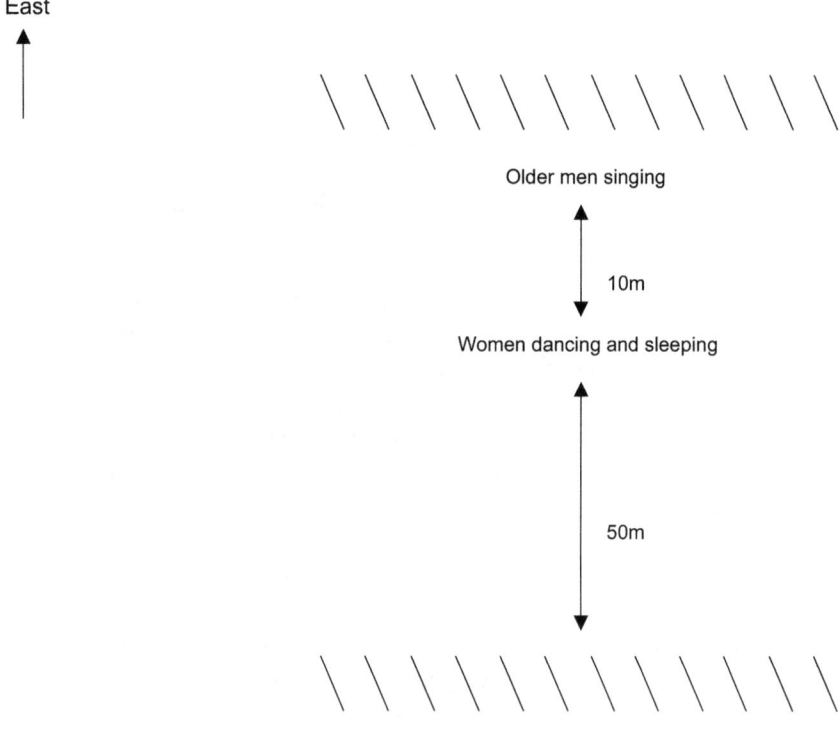

Figure 4.7. Ground plan for all-night phase of *Marnakurrawarnu*. Created by the author.

MARNAKURRAWARNU–SUNSET TO SUNRISE

Around 10 P.M., the older men gathered in a small group at the eastern end of the business ground. They sat in a semicircle facing east. I was informed that this was "so they could see the sun rising in the morning." The women all sat upright on their swags, which were positioned in a line from north to south. The women had haphazardly placed their swags behind the area in which they would dance to make it easy to sit down and rest at various points. *Yulpurru* would dance in the middle of this line, with *rdiliwarnu* on the northern and southern ends. Most of the women, however, sat in their tight-knit family groups with their own mothers and children and walked over to the appropriate places to dance. The *wati-rirri-rirri* yelled for me to start recording–I had received his permission prior to the ceremony to make a sound recording of this event. While the *parnpa* sung earlier in the evening were not to be recorded and documented, the men sang public songs for the rest of the night, which are open for all to see and hear and which guide the women's dancing for the all-night period. The group of men sang songs relating to the journey of ancestral women who traveled from a salt lake called Yapurnu near the Western Australian border on an eastwards journey (refer to map 4.1). The series of songs follows the women's journey along a series of named places across Warlpiri country. As these ancestral women travel, they sing about the places and associated *Jukurrpa* events. These places, particularly those close to Yuendumu, are well known to Warlpiri people, and the actions of the *Jukurrpa* ancestors are intimately linked to these places in the minds of the singers. In the *Jukurrpa*, these ancestral women sing and dance as they travel along this journey. The same songs and dances are performed in the *Kurdiji* ceremony. However, in this instance, the men are the singers and the women are the dancers. As these two realms are symbolically interlinked in ceremonial space, in this book I alternate my focus on the *Jukurrpa* story, as sung by the ancestral women, with the actual performance of the *Kurdiji* ceremony in which the senior men are the singers. Some of these songs relate to places or to how these ancestral women danced, and some are directly concerned with the events of the ceremony. *Jukurrpa* and ritual act merge in ceremonial space, and for this reason I do not wish to separate these two realms in the analysis presented in this book.

The women's dances are associated with these songs, and they use firesticks, digging sticks, dancing boards, and *yinirnti* necklaces depending on the song. These dances are often performed without props; the particular style of dancing is the important factor. Songs have different functions: some describe specific places, some the environment that the ancestral women traveled through, and some the different dances and other events of the cer-

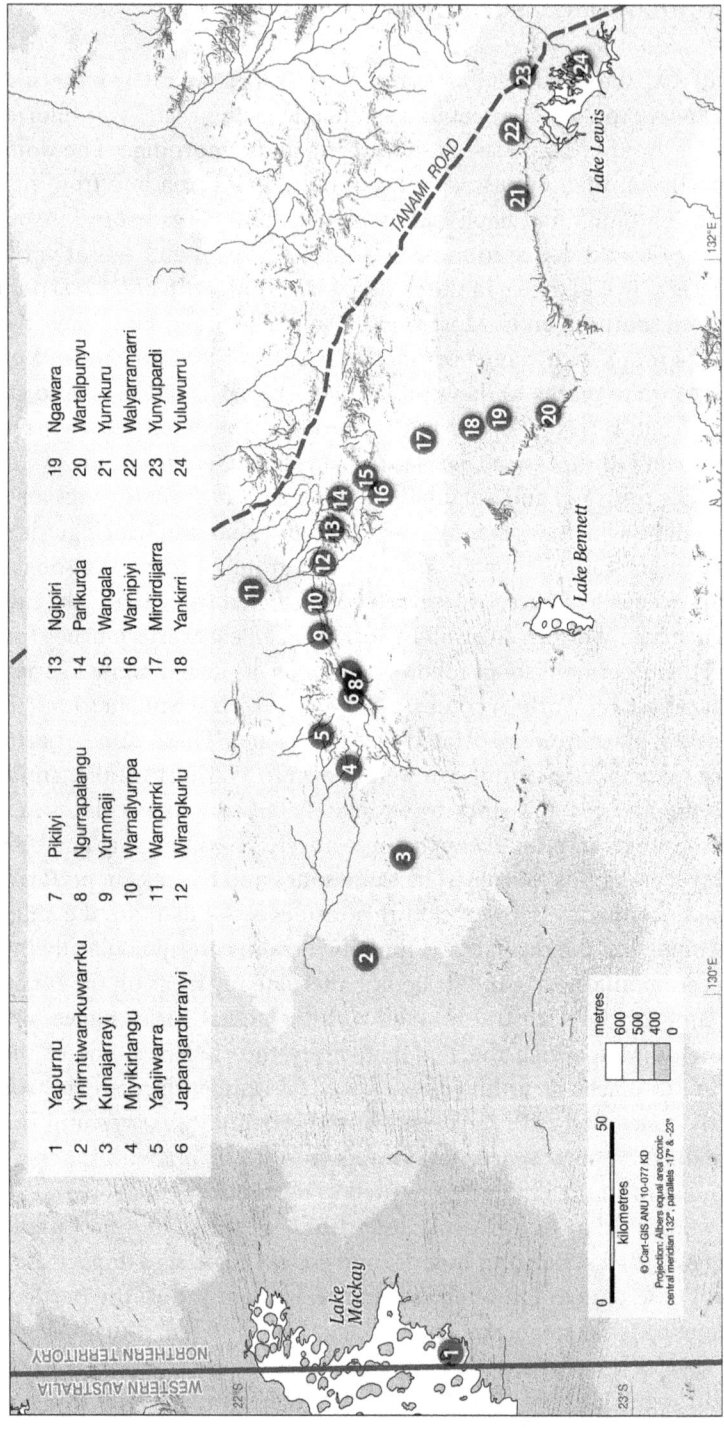

Map 4.1. Places along the *Karntakarnta* "traveling ancestral women" *Jukurrpa*. Created by CartoGIS Services, CAP, Australian National University.

emony. According to Rice's analysis, there are three different types of songs: those associated with the particular places and associated *Jukurrpa* events that can be plotted along an itinerary and follow the journey of the ancestral women (see map 4.1); those designated as "traveling songs," which are associated with repeated events and landscapes and repeated often throughout the night; and those designated as "business songs," which are sung solely for functional purposes in the performance context (Curran 2013). I identified only one of these "business songs," but it served such a different purpose and took such a different form to the others that I have classified it on its own. In the ceremony described, forty-nine different verses were sung over the course of the night, which were sung several times each and repeated at certain stages (refer to the appendix for a full summary of the order of these song verses in the *Kurdiji* ceremony held on 4 February 2007, as well as additional exegesis). Some of these song verses, in particular certain "traveling songs," are repeated much more often than others are, as the type of landscape that forms their content is abundant in the country through which this *Jukurrpa* travels. Dail-Jones, in her analysis of movement patterns associated with the *Kurdiji* ceremony as it was performed when she was in Willowra in the early 1980s, notes that

> after the men begin to sing, the women start to dance. The women "follow" the song. They know which movements to perform from the song content, and from what has preceded. For example, the women must dance facing north when a certain song verse begins, for the next successive song item, though it may be the same verse, they must dance facing south. The women finish dancing prior to the end of each song item—when the men begin the descending melodic contour. Within the limits of the song item, a woman has a certain amount of freedom to choose when she will start and stop dancing. (Dail-Jones 1984: 138)

I draw on Dail-Jones's description of nine different types of dance movements performed by women throughout this ceremony, all of them having slight variations. She terms these "dance verses," as they match up with particular verses. Many of these "dance verses" are danced, however, to multiple song verses. Therefore, I refer to them more generally as "dance movements" (from here DM) in my discussion to differentiate them from any neat correlation with particular song verses. The songs specifically relating to particular places are all accompanied by a version of DM 1. The traveling songs incorporate the rest of the dance movements, which are often described in the song texts as the ways in which the ancestral women danced. Particular ways of dancing appear to be associated with the types of landscape in particular places.

Over the first two hours of the ceremony, the men performed a sequence of song verses that follow a straight path from Yapurnu to Yurrkuru (near

DM	Description of movement and its variations (based on Dail-Jones's description)
1	Version 1 Arms hang down at sides, performed by everyone, performed en masse in an arc. Version 2 Also performed by mother and father's sisters with a firestick in two hands and pointed towards the center of the group, performed while facing east either as individuals or couples (one behind the other), also performed when the partitioned arc of women faces the initiate's center path. These two versions of this dance movement are performed for two-thirds of the night and commonly occur between the other dance movements.
2	Version 1 Hands on the back of head, performed by everyone, the ancestral women were "carrying things" like children, performed as individuals in a line facing east or when the partitioned arc of women faces the initiate's center path Version 2 Holding coolamon on back of the neck, performed by the real mothers (or their representatives) and fathers' sisters of the initiands, performed as Version 1 but these women do it individually rather than in a group.
3	Version 1 Hands on waist, performed by everyone, performed in an arc facing east.
4	Version 1 Hands together behind back at or below waist, performed by everyone, older sisters dance in a single file line travelling either toward the north or the south.
5	Version 1 Hands under or holding breasts, swinging arms in and out and clicking fingers toward the east, performed by everyone, performed in an arc facing east.
6	Version 1 Preceded by picking up handfuls of dirt, letting dirt drift through fingers while arms move forward and back, performed by everyone, performed in an arc facing east.
7	Version 1 Alternately moving hands forward and up and backward and down, oppositionally tossing "nothing" over each shoulder, performed by everyone, performed in an arc facing east.
8	Version 1 Sliding the hands, palms facing each other, forward and backward oppositionally, performed by everyone, "kana" digging stick, performed in an arc facing east. This initial movement is sometimes followed by picking up a digging stick that lies in an east-west direction between the dancers' feet, moving the stick slightly up and down almost in a passive reaction to the leg movement, at the end of the verse the stick is replaced on the ground between the dancers' feet, performed by mothers and fathers' sisters, performed by facing east travelling first forward and then backward.
9	Version 1 Preceded by throwing dirt to the west toward the initiates, moving both arms forward and backward, performed by everyone, performed in an arc facing east or west, takes place only on the second night of *Kirrirdikirrawarnu*.

Figure 4.8. Dance movements (DM) for *Kurdiji*. Created by the author, altered from Dail-Jones 1984: 144–48. Dail-Jones notes that DM9 is only used for *Kirrirdikirrawarnu*.

Mount Denison station). At this point, they "backtrack to Warnipiyi" (Rice, personal communication, 2008), with the singers going back to sing verse 27, and the sequence of the following thirty-nine verses is in exactly the same order until they reach the area around Yurrkuru again (see appendix, which shows the order of verses). Singing the verses associated with these same places continues for another hour. From here, and for the rest of the night (i.e., another seven hours), they "circle around from Yunyupardi to Yuluwurru" (Rice 2006). It is the repetitive circling of the ancestral women as they keep dancing this path that creates the large salt lake named Yuluwurru, "Lake Lewis." The verses are centered on places and often describe significant physical features, and the "traveling songs" depict the landscape that exists between these places. The repetition of the verses may also contribute to the ways in which they are remembered by the singers and hence the ways in which they guide the performance of the *Kurdiji* ceremony.

While the men were singing, the women were dancing just in front of their swags, shuffling toward the east with their arms hanging limply at their sides. At the end of each phrase of the song verse, the *jinpurrmarnu* called out a trilled cry, and the *rdiliwarnu* sang "Puh, puh, puh, puh, puuuuuuh" throughout. At various stages throughout the night, different dances were performed that related to the particular verse that the men were singing. Most of the time the women danced in "traveling style," shuffling from west to east, representing the journey of the ancestral women. This could vary, as they would hop sideways from north to south and back again on occasion. Also, on occasion, the women danced with their hands behind their head, and the mothers-in-law danced with the firesticks belonging to the initiands. One senior woman, Nakamarra, danced with a digging stick pointing forward into the ground at particular stages. Other women did not dance. Many went to sleep when it got late—particularly the younger girls. Some women, like Napurrurla (Japangardi's mother) and Nungarrayi (Jampijinpa's mother), hardly sat down all night. Another older woman, Napaljarri, whose daughter's son was an initiand that night, spent most of her time cooking and making tea for the men, sitting toward the back of the group of women. These unspoken roles were clearly known by the women due to their connections to the initiands and their families.

The places along the journey of the traveling women have been plotted on map 4.1, and they are sung in the same order as the ancestral travels. They are not repeated frequently over the course of the night, as the traveling songs or business songs are. They relate specifically to particular places, and therefore the ancestral women do not return to these places once they have journeyed past them until the singers decide to backtrack on this sung journey (as described above). These songs depict the events of the *Jukurrpa* ancestors at these places, often in esoteric ways. The actions of these women as they journey from east to west can be seen as symbolic depictions of the journey of the initiands and their families as they go through the initiatory process, as the events of the ceremony have many parallels with the journey of these ancestral women. The dance movements accompanying these verses do not seem to vary much; they are all accompanied by a loose-kneed shuffle eastward with the arms hanging limply by the sides (see DM 1 in figure 4.8) or a north-to-south shuffle with hands on hips or the waist before turning around to repeat this south-to-north (see DM 4). The choice between these two dance styles may depend on whether a particular verse is associated with the symbolism of east/west, which depicts movement from the female to the male world (this will be discussed further in chapter 5), or north/south (the Japaljarri/Jungarrayi/Japangardi/Japanangka patrimoiety being represented by the north and the Jangala/Jampijinpa/Jakamarra/Jupurrurla patrimoiety by the south).

The song series that structures the performance of this ritual from sunset until sunrise is concerned specifically with the journey of a group of women of the Napaljarri/Nungarrayi patricouple who come from Kunajarrayi. As they travel along into country belonging to different patricouples of Warlpiri women, they incorporate women from these places in their journey eastward. They sing and dance the appropriate verses for particular places, and they acknowledge the features and landscape of the country they are traveling through, as well as the activities of other *Jukurrpa* ancestors that are occurring around them. All these places have Warlpiri names, which help to bring them and their features to the mind's eye. Toner has emphasized that

> for the Dhalwangu . . . a deeply-felt sense of place is built up through naming: naming is a central poetic feature of songs, and the singing of names articulates both the knowledge of geographical places and a profound nostalgia for those places as imaginative constructions which anchor personal and group spirituality. (2007: 166)

The names of the places in the *Karntakarnta* song series are sometimes included in the song texts, but they are often evoked in more esoteric ways through descriptions of landscape or significant *Jukurrpa* events that occur at these particular places. Further exegesis from someone with a good knowledge of these places and associated songs is required to make the links. Often a significant feature of the landscape is evoked in a verse such that people who know a place can bring it to their mind.

The journey of the ancestral women begins at Yapurnu (Lake Mackay). Accompanying stories like this are frequently, though certainly not always, told in conjunction with the singing of a song series as a way of explaining some of the more esoteric ideas present in the verses. These ideas and their inherent associations pervade the ceremonial space in cognitive ways for the singers, but they also appear in embodied, unconscious ways for the other participants. For these reasons, I now turn the discussion to a more textual analysis, which is intended to follow the thought path of the singers as they guide the ceremony. These stories may differ in detail depending on the occasion, and the interpretations below (and explicated upon further in the appendix) were given by key senior men who participated in this particular ceremonial event, most of all Rice, whom I worked with extensively on this account following the ceremony.

The ancestral women who undertake this journey are of the Napaljarri/Nungarrayi patricouple and are owners for Kunajarrayi (Mount Nicker); they begin their journey at Yapurnu. Verses 1 and 2 are sung to begin the all-night phase of *Marnakurrawarnu*. In these verses, the song texts mark this starting location at Yapurnu through the use of this place name and an accompanying locative suffix.

Yapurnurla kaninjarra	Deep down at Yapurnu.
Jirrpijirrpi parnkayarra	Fingernails dancing from side to side.
Walyangka juturu nyina	Sitting still on the ground
Yapurnurla juturu nyina	Sitting still at Yapurnu

Verse 1 reveals that the women are coming out of the ground here, as do all *Jukurrpa* when they begin their journeys. Glowczewski (1991: 98) has summarized the associations of coming from deep in the earth rather than from above. The verse commencing the night's singing is not always associated with Yapurnu; for example, the *Kurdiji* ceremony held on 27 January 2007 started with verse associated with Yanjiwarra. Rice (2006) sited Yinintiwarrkuwarrku, a place near Kunajarrayi, as the real home of these ancestral women. Meggitt writes that the "'immortal initiated man' arises at Miliwanu Hill near Yenindiwaguwagu [Yinintiwarrkuwarrku], the place of the bean trees (*Erythrina vespertilio*) which in turn is far to the west of Bigilyi (Vaughan Springs) [*Pikilyi*]" (1966: 131). The starting location for the all-night singing is clearly flexible and decided upon according to the particular senior men who are present.

The idea of coming from *kaninjarra*, "deep down" in the earth, is associated with strong links to ancestral beings. Coming from the surface of the earth or higher, such as from the sky, *kankarlu* is associated more with the everyday living world, a public domain. While not expressed in the song text, exegesis provided by Rice for verses 1 and 2 reveals that a man named Wirdangurla of the Jungarrayi subsection, and therefore a potential brother or father for these women, is also dancing beside them, imitating their movements. Wirdangurla is from Western Australia, and he came to the salt lake for a drink; however, when he sees the women's fast, animated dancing, he becomes sexually aroused. He copies their movements in an effort to seduce them. He has long toenails that he uses to scratch marks on the surface of the salt lake as he dances. When the women see Wirdangurla following them, they think he is mad because he is dancing like a woman and interested in an incestuous relationship with them. To make him stop following them, they sit quietly on the side of the lake, their stillness unattractive to Wirdangurla. This is represented in verse 2 by the verb *juturunyina* (sitting around doing nothing).

Wirdangurla has not let the women out of his sight, though, and he continues to follow them to their home at Kunajarrayi. This place is not stated explicitly in verse 10, but it is alluded to by a reference to the type of grass that grows there.

| *Kalpalpirla rarra wapa* | Swarming in the soft grass |
| *Yatingkarna rarra wapa* | I am swarming in the tree roots |

This "soft grass" is glossed as "native lemongrass" and "lemon scented grass" in the Warlpiri English Encyclopaedic Dictionary (Laughren et al. 2007), and it is soft enough that emus lay their eggs on it and witchetty grubs rest on it as they swarm out of trees and roots, as is depicted in verse 10. The yellow excrement that comes from the witchetty grubs can be seen everywhere. In the story associated with this verse, one witchetty grub ate another, and then they all turned into little snakes, and then finally into one big snake with wings. This snake flew to the Granites.

Wirdangurla sings about his actions as he copies the way the women dance with wild, animated movements. He is on the side of a creek a few hundred meters away from the women, and he becomes more aroused as he watches their bottoms and legs move as they dance. The women think he is crazy and ignore him, continuing to dance eastward along their journey.

As the ancestral women sing about passing through Miyikirlangu it is raining and there is water running all over the claypan, as alluded to in verse 14.

| *Yalkiri rapawala pawala* | The sky is all in the cracks in the ground |
| *Yalkiri jawirri jawala* | Only sky in the cracks in the ground |

This place is evoked by describing how the water flows across the claypan into the cracks in the ground. The sky in the description is being reflected in the large expanse of water. Other Warlpiri songs also use optical illusions to refer to places appearing differently from how they actually are. Exegesis has revealed that Miyikirlangu gets its name from all the vegetable food, particularly *mukaki* (bush plum), that grows here in abundance. Miyikirlangu literally translates as "vegetable food-belonging."

Next on the ancestral women's itinerary is Yanjiwarra, a flat rock with a hole in it, as depicted in verse 15. Here they cross paths with two kangaroos.

| *Yanjiwarrarra rdaku* | There is a hole in the flat rock |
| *Yanjata patarrpala* | The kangaroos are stretching their limbs |

At this rockhole, two kangaroos are drinking. They are from another Dreaming itinerary, and they have traveled from the north near Gurindji country. They are on their way south when they encounter the traveling women. When they see the women, they too get aroused and stretch out their legs, showing off so that the women will notice them. They keep looking at the women sideways as they continue to drink. In verse 16, the kangaroos sing about the big holes in their noses, in which they can put nose pegs.

| *Mulyurna wilypiri* | I am a nose with a big hole |
| *Yajanpurrukarri yajanpurrukarri* | Enticing further and further |

The kangaroos are trying to entice the women to come with them. When the women are not impressed by their nose pegs, despite the indication of their ritual importance, the two kangaroos decide to continue their journey south, again singing about themselves as they stand up to leave.

| *Wawirrirna parnkaparnka* | I am a kangaroo, running |
| *Yilimirntirrirna karri* | I am two legs going farther and farther |

In verse 18, as the women travel through Japangardirranyi, the next place on their itinerary, they sing about a large group of baby *kakalyalyas* (Major Mitchell's cockatoos) that are sitting in a tree and crying out for food.

| *Wujuju wangkaja* | Called out in complaint |
| *Wujuju wangkaja yatingangakarrarra* | Called out in complaint, calling out from the nest in the tree. |

This *Kakalyalya Jukurrpa* starts on the eastern side of the Mount Davenport range, from which they fly north to Yumurrpa and to a place near the Tanami. The ancestral women travel past this *Jukurrpa*. The women reach the range, and after climbing a hill, they stop to have a rest. In verse 21, they sing about preparing *minyi*, a type of small, strong-smelling black seed that is found in this place.

Minyi ngapangaparla parrakurra kujurnu	Threw the black Acacia seeds in the water toward the sun
Warlu yintiyintirla parrakurra kujurnu	Threw into the heat toward the sun

The verse describes how they lay them out in the heat first to dry before putting them in water to make flour for damper. They go to Ngurrapalangu, a cave above the Pikilyi waterhole. In verse 22, they sit inside the cave, and their voices echo around inside.

Ngurrapalangurlu kaninju rdatirla	Quietly from the cave at Ngurrapala
Yangungu kurrangka yangungu kurrangka	Echoing around, echoing around

They sit inside the opening to the cave, and the noise echoes around them as they talk and eat their seedcakes. Ngurrapalangu gets its name from two grooves in the rock where the two kangaroos were sleeping. They sing about this in verse 23.

Ngurrangurra punju	Two camps at the rockhole
Kujarrala	Two kangaroos

They travel on to Wirangkurlu. The older women are left here, as they have no energy to continue on with their journey. In verse 31, they sing about how the "old women" dance with their bodies slumped over because they are so tired.

Wirangkurlurla rdanjiwirnparanya	Hanging off their bodies at Wirangkurlu
Yanangkurlurlu rdanjiwirnparanya	The old women are hanging down

At Ngipiri, all the mother snakes leave their eggs while they go off hunting. In verse 33 a python from Yarliyumpu comes and eats them all.

Ngipiri ngarnungarnu	Desiring the eggs
Warapija	Moving around

Today there are little rockholes on the flat rock at Ngipiri where these eggs were lying. The python continues on to Palkurda. When the mother snakes come back and find their eggs gone, they start fighting with each other.

Wirdangurla has been following the women the whole time, keeping his distance. He leaves them at Warnalyurrpa and continues north to Wijilpa, Warnpirrki, and then Wakurlpa. At Warnpirrki, a big rockhole, he dances with a firestick, still imitating the way the women are dancing. From here, he sends his penis under the ground to where the women are dancing at the swamp at Ngarnawilypiri and tries to penetrate them as they urinate—his penis being referred to as a firestick in the verse. The women sing about this in verse 34.

> *Ngurra jangiyi pirlirli* At home, the rock has a firestick
> *Wari jangiyi manta* Get on it, without the firestick

They get out their digging sticks and cut off his penis as he tries to push it up through the earth beneath them. Wirdangurla reconstitutes himself several times as he repeatedly tries to rape these women, but he eventually dies in the country close to Ngarlikirlangu.[147]

They travel on to Yipilanji and sing about retrieving pink and white witchetty grubs from the sides of the red river gum trees (*Ngapiri*) in verse 34.

> *Ngapiyataka yataparrkara* Standing with crossed legs at the red river gums
> *Waraparrpa karrinya* Farther and farther into the bump

They stand with two legs crossed over, protectively guarding the *yipilanji* as they remove them from the sides of the tree with small hooked twigs called *narnngu*. They also stand this way so that they do not arouse the men, who become so when the women dance with their legs spread apart.

The women then travel to Jarlji. They use their digging sticks to penetrate into the sandhills for big, fat, edible frogs. In verse 36, they sing about burrowing for these frogs.

> *Yanakirri jantarra* Searching for frogs
> *Nyarla panturru* Escaping downward

At Jarlji these frogs are everywhere, burrowing into the sandhill, sometimes a meter deep, to avoid being caught. (Rice said that this verse was particularly tricky to sing, as the words are hard to get around one's tongue.)

At Wangala, a crow of the Japanangka subsection is sitting on top of the hill watching the women dance for a *Kurdiji* ceremony. Japangardi, the goanna from Mount Theo, also goes past, but he does not stop as he is keen on finding his mother-in-law Nungarrayi, with whom he had fallen in love. Japanangka, the crow, is the owner of this country, so all the women bring him lots of food as payment for having the ceremony there. He sits on top of the hill watching one of the Napaljarris, a mother-in-law for him. He stretches around like crows do, trying to attract her attention. In verse 41 the women sing about this.

> *Wangalarlanjirringirli nyina jarlarra pata* Coming from the place of the crow, sitting down
> *Yanurrupungurlu nyina jarlarra pata* Getting things, sitting down

Napaljarri is embarrassed because the crow keeps looking at her. He comes down and joins the ceremony, but instead of facing eastward like everyone else, he faces westward, toward the women who are dancing (like Anmatyerre and Luritja people do), so he can watch Napaljarri. He has one hand over his eye so that no one can tell that he is watching her. When the ceremony is finished, everybody leaves, but Japanangka holds on to Napaljarri's dog. When Napaljarri comes to get it, he grabs her and has sexual intercourse with her.

Though Rice later explained that verses 40 and 41 are sung in the wrong order in the ceremony, it does not affect the performance in any way. This order originated when one man started singing the verse out of its place, and instead of correcting him, the other older men joined in with him.

A Jampijinpa and a Jangala from Warnipiyi who had joined the traveling women blindfold Japanangka. In verse 40 they sing about how he struggled as they took him to a nearby creek where they lit a fire.

Wipiya wipiya rdijipiya	Stretching out as set alight
Ngarnkirrinya kutakuta rduluya	Struggling toward the hole near the creek's edge.

They throw him into the creek and into the fire as punishment for his unacceptable behavior. A swarm of black crows comes out of the fire as he burns, which is where they all come from today.

As the women travel past Mirdirdijarra, they see a group of emus standing at Rdukirri. These emus have come from Wawurrwawurrpa in the west on their way to Yarliyumu. They sing about these emus in verse 42 and how they sit with crossed legs, ready to get up if they need to run.

Larnkatipi kanpirriya	Two crossed legs with emu fat
Larnkajarra pajurrima	Two legs, two knees

The emus all sit in a semicircle, watching the passing women as well as the fire from the *Warlukurlangu Jukurrpa*. In verse 43, the women sing about the rough skin and sharp claws of the emus.

Mirdijirijirirla	At Mirdirdijarra
Malantakurra lantirni japa	Sharp nails scratch as they move along

At Yankirri, the emus sing about the way they bob their heads as they search for food. This movement is depicted in verse 44 by indicating that the emus are searching for food.

Mirdijintilyiyirna	I am two knees
Parrarna yangkurrngurla	I am the daylight in the green vegetation

At Ngawara, water covers everything from the *Ngapa Jukurrpa* from Wartarlpunyu. The women sing about the water in verse 46.

Ngapakurla jurarri jurarri ngunanya	There in the water, streams lying around
Ngapakurla parlawamu ngunanya	There in the water, leafy branches lying around

This *Ngapa Jukurrpa* travels alongside them for a while, as they are going to Yurnkuru too. Just before Yurnkuru, the women dance with firesticks at Walyaramarri. They sing about this in verse 47.

Walyaramarrirla marrirla	At Walyaramarri
Walyara jangijirna ngurla	I am belonging to the ground

In a variant of the above verse, they sing about the hard ground at Walyaramarri and how it makes their feet sore.

Walyarna tapatakijirla	I am the ground
Walyarna jangijirna ngurla	I am the ground, I am away from the firestick

The women are now in Anmatyerr country. They pass through the gap in the hills to Yunyupardi. They create a hole in the rock as they travel through. Here they have a large *Kirrardikirrawarnu* ceremony. This is an Anmatyerr *Kirrardikirrawarnu*. On the ground in the rocks, the ceremonial ground can be seen: a windbreak for the men with an anthill on the west side and two fires. There is a long section leading up to the mother's windbreak on the far western end.

At Yuluwurru they are still dancing but getting tired—they slump over and have headaches. They sing about this in verse 48 as they continue to dance and create the salt lake.

Yuluwurru rdajiwarnpungu	Getting tired at Yuluwurru
Rdajiwarnpungu	Tiredness

Unlike the verses about particular places described above, there are numerous verses in the *Karntakarnta* song series that recount the women's travels between these places. The content of these verses revolves around descriptions of the particular landscape, the ways in which the women dance, or other events that are often repeated when they set out from one place to go to another. As similar landscape recurs along their travels, certain verses are sung and repeated whenever the ancestral women encounter a certain type of tree or scrub. This further adds to the mental map that can be made of the country. These verses differ from those described above in that they are not linked directly to one particular place. They are used to "travel" between one named place and the next—the verses, however, are linked specifically to particular landscapes and are therefore associated with the country of certain places. These verses also often depict the dancing of the ancestral women at particular places as they move along their journey. These verses and the landscape they describe are important to the overall story and sequence of the ancestral women's travels.

"TRAVELING SONGS"

The traveling songs take several forms: they may give descriptions of landscape, such as particular trees, grasses, or other physical features; they may describe dance styles used by the ancestral women as they travel; and they may depict repeated events along the women's journey, such as climbing hills, resting, or anticipating the sunrise. There is often a complex intermingling of these themes. For example, certain landscapes can evoke particular dance styles, and the associations are commonly known among participants of this ceremony. In the ceremony, women know to dance in a certain way upon hearing particular verses —the younger women pick this up quickly through their active participation. However, there is not always a parallel between the dance styles being sung about and those being performed in the actual ceremony. This will be pointed out in the examples presented below.

For someone who has never visited the country along the journey of the ancestral women, the verses sung between these two places along the song series provide a kind of mental topographical map that features the types of trees, scrub, and other environmental elements that exist there. Verse 3 is the first traveling song that was sung during the February 2007 ceremony. This verse is associated with *pakarli* (inland ti-trees) and sung numerous times at two points along the ancestral women's journey. The first time is when the ancestral women leave Yapurnu and travel in the country to the west of Kunajarrayi. It is repeated later as they travel through the country around Warnpirrki.

Pakarli yanjawarra　　The special place of the inland ti-trees
Yarlipilykipilyki　　They are shaking

In this verse there are raindrops dripping through the *pakarli* trees. Many associations can be made from this image. *Pakarli* branches are commonly used in other ceremonies (including the *Kirrardikirrawarnu* ceremony) and are always shaken around vigorously. *Pakarli* trees also evoke the knee quiver of the women's legs as they dance.

Mulga trees are also common in the landscape through which the ancestral women travel, and therefore verse 4 is also sung frequently over the course of the night.

> *Lardiji lanja kuruku kurrku*   A thick group of mulga trees all together
> *Rdalyaranga larranya*   There it is, broken off firewood

The women sing about all the dry firewood lying around as they travel through this country. There are three other verses relating to mulga country (verses 5, 13, and 26) that are often, but not always, sung in sequence with verse 4. From the points along this journey where this verse is sung, it is evident that mulga trees are common across Warlpiri country, in particular in the area to the west of Kunajarrayi, between Kunajarrayi and Miyikirlangu, on the eastern side of Mount Davenport, on the eastern side of Wangala, and surrounding Ngawara.

Verse 5 is also associated with mulga country, and it is sung each time the women encounter country with the associated prickles in the ground.

> *Jilkangka larrujarru jaru*   At the prickled country, they dance on the prickles.
> *Walkangka larrujarrujaru*   On the ground, they dance on the prickles.
> *Jilkangka rdilyilpi nyiwi*   At the prickled country, the prickles break in their feet.

They sing about the prickles breaking in their feet and the pain as they try to get them out. The particular prickles they sing about are called *yarnajakarlarla*, and they cover the ground in the country where mulga trees grow.

In verse 13, the women sing about the sweet sugar that is found on the mulga trees.

> *Ngapirlirli marraya*   The sweet sugar is swaying
> *Ngatulampa kurraya*   Dripping down

Ngapirli is a type of sugar that forms on the leaves of the mulga trees. When it gets hot, this sugar turns to a liquid and drips to the ground. The women sing about this liquid falling to the ground as it sways in the wind. As this verse is also associated with mulga country, it is often performed alongside verses 4 and 5.

Verse 26 is also associated with mulga country, in which the women sing about *ngaru* growing everywhere.

Watijiyimarurla (ya)   Ripe bush tomatoes growing everywhere
Ngaru wilyiwilyi (ya)   The dense foliage is blocking the view.

Ngaru grow in the mulga country. The women are singing about foliage that is so dense they cannot see through the trees. Rice said that this verse can be sung with a slight variation (below), if the scrub they are singing about is not as thick.

Watijarntakurlka (ya)   Lighter foliage, seeing through
Ngaru wilyiwilyi (ya)   Ripe bush tomatoes everywhere

These songs vary according to how thick the mulga country is.

For someone who knows the song series and the associated country as intimately as Rice, it is possible to point out exactly where in the women's journey particular traveling songs should be sung. Verse 45 is associated with particular places.

Yarrajipirli   At Yarranjipirli
Yarrajipirli ngipipurla ngara   A dense forest of mulga trees

Rice explained that this verse is about traveling through the country where there are lots of *yalpiyaru* trees. He also said that this verse could be sung at Yuwalinji by varying it slightly. The similarity between these two versions is based on the thickness of the scrub rather than the presence of a particular type of tree.

Yuwalinjirli place   At Yuwalinji
Yuwalinjirli ngipipurla ngara   A dense forest of mulga trees

While some other traveling songs have variants, this was the only one that had a direct link in the variant song texts to particular places.

Some of these traveling songs are concerned with the type of food that grows in the places the women travel through. In verse 12, the women sing about *kurarra* (dead finish) seeds that hang down from the trees.

Nyarla kurarra rdangka   The seeds are hanging down from the dead finish tree.
Nyarla jurrparna janji   Collecting them as they hang down.

The women collect these seeds in their coolamons. This verse is performed often throughout the night, as the trees on which these seeds grow being common landscape during the journey of the ancestral women. They sing this verse when they leave Kunajarrayi on its eastern side and when they leave Wirangkurlu on their way to Ngipiri, indicating that the seeds grow on the trees in these areas.

Many of the traveling songs depict how the ancestral women danced as they journeyed across the country, with particular dances being associated with certain types of country as well as having distinct ceremonial functions. Months after the *Kurdiji* ceremonies, Napurrurla and I were driving through the country to the north of Yuendumu near Wakurlpa, and she motioned for me to look out the window. "See that hill there, that's Ngarningirri, the one like this [motioning with her two hands clasped behind her head] where they dance with a *parraja* [coolamon]." She reminded me of the *Kurdiji* the previous summer where the women had been dancing in this way, and emphasized again that the hill we had just passed was the place for which they had been dancing. This indicates an intimate connection in Warlpiri minds between particular places, certain features of the landscape, and the songs and associated dance styles that are performed in ceremonies.

Jurnpurla rulawama	Dancing and throwing up soil into a mound
Parlanji wirriwirri	Dancing with flattened feet so the tracks are forming a channel

A big mound is building up on the sides of where Wirdangurla is dancing and a deep groove is being worn in the sand where his feet are shuffling along. He dances along, throwing the soil up with his feet to create these tracks. *Parlanji* (also translating as a termite mound) is used to describe the deep groove formed by dancers' feet in the ground with mounds of soil built up on the sides. He dances this way at several points along the women's journey: between Yapurnu and Kunajarrayi, between Yanjiwarra and Japangardirranyi, and between Warnpirrki and Yipilanji.

Wirdangurla is still dancing in verse 8 as he watches the women at Kunajarrayi.

Yinjirinpunganya palarrararrara	Dragging feet along through the swamp grass
Parlanji yatampurrukarri	Flattening feet and standing still

Here, Wirdangurla dances through the ground, dragging his legs. He makes a track through the grass, which is represented by the word *parlanji* as in the previous verse. In the ceremony, the women dance with their legs wide apart, first northward and then back to the south again. He dances in this way at the same places where he dances in song 7.

In verse 9, the women sing about the way they are dancing with wide legs. They dance from north to south stopping at each end.

Yamanarna japara wapa   I am dancing with wide legs, eating as I move
Yamanarna japiri nguna   I am dancing with wide legs, eating as I stay still

They dance in this way at two points along their journey: just to the west of Kunajarrayi and to the west of Wirangkurlu.

Throwing soil as the women dance is also a theme in verse 24.

Walyarna pinaru wapa   I am throwing up the soil as I move
Jurrmarlinjirna   I am dancing with knees quivering

This verse is sung at two points along the journey: as they leave Ngurrapalangu and come down from Pikilyi and as they approach Wangala. The significance of "throwing soil" in ceremony will be discussed further in chapter 5.

In verse 27, the women sing about dancing in a line with firesticks.

Ngiji juturrungkarni   Dancing with a firestick, pushing up the soil
Juturrungkarni   Dancing pushing up the soil

The women are dressed up with *ngamirdingamirdi* (a type of circular prickle found in mulga country, several of which are put together on a stick to make a comb) in their hair, *yinirnti* necklaces and headbands, and *jinjirla* (tails) hanging from around their heads. They sing this verse when they travel through Yurnmaji.

Everyone had firesticks in the Dreaming, but nowadays only the mothers-in-law, fathers' sisters, and mothers dance with them. They dance in lines while the others hold their waists from behind. For a mother-in-law to dance with a firestick is for her to promise her daughter, who may be a small child or still unborn, to the boy whose firestick she is holding.

In song 28, the women sing about combing their hair and making themselves look pretty.

Wakurlunjarri wilyarri wulya (ya)   They have long hair.
Wakurlunjarri linjalja (ya)   They have short hair.

Rice (personal communication, 2008) also noted that in the old days, they would put on *wanya*, a headband made of emu feathers placed at the hairline. For this verse the women dance by throwing each hand alternately behind the head (DM 7 in figure 4.8). Rice said that this verse can be sung at both Yurnmaji and Yinirntiwarrkuwarrku, farther back to the west of Kunajarrayi.

In verse 29, they sing about the events of *Kirrardikirrawarnu*.

Karntawurrurlparna parlintirri	I am a woman dancing low in defense
Yati nganjalalyanganja	A long spear with hairstring

At *Kirrardikirrawarnu*, the boys give a long spear with hairstring wrapped around it to their mothers-in-law. The mothers also line up to give food to the boys to take into the bush. Afterward, the brothers-in-law who are acting as ritual guardians bring out their spears and put them in the middle of the ceremony ground until the morning. Then the mothers-in-law give it to the fathers. Today *Kirrardikirrawarnu* is no longer performed, so the boys give the spear directly to their fathers. The men still sing this verse, though, as a part of *Kurdiji*, and the mothers and the fathers' sisters dance in a line with a digging stick held out in front of them (see DM 8 in figure 4.8 on p. 98). They sing this as they leave Yurnmaji.

At Wirangkurlu, the ancestral women sing about dancing in this way in verse 32.

Wirangkurlu nampunampu	The thud of Wirangkurlu
Wirangkurlu wintijarna	I danced at Wirangkurlu

At Wirangkurlu, the ancestral women leave the older women, as the latter are too tired to continue traveling. Nakamarra danced while leaning on her digging stick, as this style of dancing is associated with the older women.

In verse 37, they sing about dancing in a line.

Waparlaku karrimarnkarra	Dancing in a line, holding on to each other from behind
Karrimarnkarrimarnkarra	Holding on to each other from behind

The older women dance at the front, and the younger girls dance behind them while holding onto their waists or shoulders (DM 3 in figure 4.8). This was often performed in the larger ceremonies I saw in Mount Allan, where there were many dancers and not enough room to dance in a single line across the front.

In verse 38, they sing about dancing with *yinirnti* necklaces cupped in their hands.

Yinirnti jilpirri jilpi (ya)	Cupped hands full of *yinirnti*
Yinirnti nanparri nanparrirna (ya)	The *yinirnti* seeds are making a noise.

Rice's exegesis for this verse described how the ancestral women danced: shuffling up and down, the necklaces making a distinctive sound as they shook in their cupped hands. Dail-Jones (1984) describes the way the women dance in ceremonies at Willowra with their hands cupped underneath their breasts (DM 5 in figure 4.8). This style of dancing is perhaps used when there are no *yinirnti* necklaces available. These necklaces were not used in the ceremony described in this book. The ancestral women sing this verse as they leave Jarlji on their way to Warnipi.

In verse 49, the ancestral women sing about how they are dancing with their hands behind their heads (DM 2, version 1 in figure 4.8) and their bodies bent over as far as possible ("low down").

Walarakuraku walarakuraku wirnpirla	Dancing low down in the soft sand
Wakumintirrirla wakumintirrirla wirnpirla	Dancing low down, arms joined

This was described as an Anmatyerr style of dancing, with no order—they dance anywhere. In many *yawulyu* performances that I have seen over the last few years, dancing low to the ground in this way was highly desired, with the *kurdungurlu* often yelling throughout the performance for the dancers to dance "lower." They sing this verse at Yarrukunulu when they meet up with Anmatyerr women.

There are a few other repeated events along the travels of the ancestral women that have accompanying verses. Verse 19 is sung each time the women have to climb a hill, which occurs a number of times along their journey. In particular, they sing about the fat women trying to get up.

Yarlkinjirrpa	Up high
Yurrupa yurrku	The fat people

This verse is sung as the ancestral women climb Mount Davenport and Warnipi, the two major hills they cross in their journey.

Another event that occurs a number of times stopping to rest—normally after climbing a hill. In verse 20 the women sing about how tired they are.

Yimirta nyarrurrangka nyarrurrangka	Tired with aching legs
Yapata nyarrurrangka nyarrurrangka	Groaning with weakness

This verse is initially sung when they reach the top of Pikilyi and sit down for a break. It is sung again as they travel from Pangkunaparnta toward Warnipi. This time they stop for a rest before they climb the hill.

Lastly, two verses (slight variants of each other) are sung when the night is getting long to make the sun rise more quickly, to bring the light over the horizon. These functional ceremonies can also be classified under business songs as well. I have included them in my discussion of traveling songs, however, as the ancestral women sing them in the *Jukurrpa* at particular places.

Verse 30 is sung several times throughout the night to make the sun rise.

Wurrumpu parntirninya	There it is hidden
Ngarnampu parntirninya	Desired to come up

For this verse, the women dance while they click their fingers toward the eastern sky, which they hope to fill with light (DM 5 in figure 4.8). They sing this verse just before they reach Wirangkurlu.

The verses continue to be sung from this point circling around the places near Yuluwurru, this movement forming the salt lake that is there today.

§

The initiands slept for the first few hours of the ceremony while the voices of the senior male singers and the female dancers brought the symbolic associations in to the ceremonial space. At around 2 A.M. they woke up and their *juka* decorated them with white fluff. After this, they sat in a crouched position for the remainder of the night. Their *juka* looked after them and sat with them throughout. Their elder brothers also sat up with them. A few times during the night the men sang a particular verse with a slower rhythm that allowed the boys to stand up and stretch their legs (verse 6). The *wati-rirri-rirri* stood up and told the women to form two lines facing each other on the northern and southern sides to provide a passage through which the singing men could see the initiands as they stood up. The women danced, shuffling on one spot with their hands behind their head while they were doing this. The initiands, decorated with white fluff, looked spectacular standing in the firelight. Their *juka* helped them to stand and warmed their hands on the fire to massage their legs. The actions of the *juka* mirrored the content of the songs the older men were singing. Verse 6 stands out in the song series in that it serves a ceremonial function only and significantly differs in form from the other verses sung during the course of the night. It was sung at three different intervals a number of times during the ceremony, and it served the functional purpose of allowing the initiands, sitting in a crouched position, to stand up, stretch their legs, and go to the toilet. While the language used in this song text is not straightforward and almost impossible to translate, exegesis provided for this song text literally described the actions of the initiands and their guardians. Some vulgar and simplified Warlpiri words were easily translated.

Jaka yangawa	The guardians are holding the initiand's buttocks to help lift them up.
Kaka yarrarnta	They are rubbing them with warm hands from the fire.
Jaki yarringki	They are fixing up the fluff on their heads.
Rima yarrarnta	They are holding under their arms to support them while they stand.

While the men sang this verse, the ritual guardians of the initiands helped them to stand and led them off to the side. They were weak and needed help to walk, as their legs were stiff from crouching all night. The guardians fix up the adornments of white fluff and other ritual paraphernalia with which the initiands are decorated. The old men keep singing this verse until everything has been done. When the women heard this verse they divided into two groups, with two lines of women facing each other (one facing north, one facing south) and danced with their hands behind their heads (DM 2, version 1 in figure 4.8). This formed a clear passage down the center through which the singing older men could see the initiates. In an elicited version of the *Karntakarnta* song series that I recorded, where Rice sang the songs along the itinerary for no ceremonial purpose, he did not sing this verse, indicating that it is not part of the song series as such but nonetheless has a solely functional purpose in the performance. Other than these few moments when they stood up, the initiands did not move from their crouched position until the morning.

In the morning, as the sun was rising, the *juka* led the initiands eastward through the middle of the women who had once again parted into two groups to let them through. The initiands were clearly weak from crouching for many hours and needed help from their *juka*. Napurrurla, Nungarrayi, and Napurrurla, all mothers of the initiands, were holding the firesticks as they came through facing towards the initiands. They stopped at the section where the women had been dancing all night, and the *yulpurru* rushed up to them, wailing and picked off the bits of white fluff that clung to them. The female *rdiliwarnu* spoke to the initiands, telling them to be careful in the bush. All of the women then gathered their swags as quickly as possible and ran away to their individual houses within the settlement. The men stayed to do men's business. This did not last very long, though, as I saw many of them around the settlement within the next half hour.

WARAWARTA

After a long, sleepy day, the cool of the afternoon finally set in, and a large group of women began to gather underneath a shade in the west of Yuendumu. The west camp in Yuendumu is slightly removed from the rest of the settlement, with a football-shaped oval marking in between the camp and the settlement separating it spatially. A group of men also gathered nearby, just to the north. Nampijinpa came over and told me to face south, as the men were doing something on the northern side that we were not meant to see. All I could hear was chanting and the sounds of thudding feet on the ground as they ran along in a slow jog—having seen this ritualized movement many times before, I was able to identify it by its sound. When the men had finished, Napaljarri and her daughter Napurrurla asked me to help them take their cooking implements home in my Toyota. They had come to this shade to make lunch for the boys earlier in the day, as it was Napaljarri's duty as the mother's mother of the young man, Japangardi. Some of the older men had come to get the food and take it to the young men in the bush. Napaljarri had hurt her leg earlier in the year and did not want to attend the next part of the ceremony where she would have to move quickly. Napurrurla and I dropped Napaljarri at home with all the cooking implements and then came back to the business area. When we got there the *wati-rirri-rirri* came over to the group of women and told us to go over to a cleared space farther west, but still within the public space of the settlement. Many men were there, including the *juka*, but not the young men themselves. The *wati-rirri-rirri* stood up and spoke to the group who was sitting down in a squared-off area according to generation moiety group (see figure 4.9). The same generation moiety of the young men who had just "been

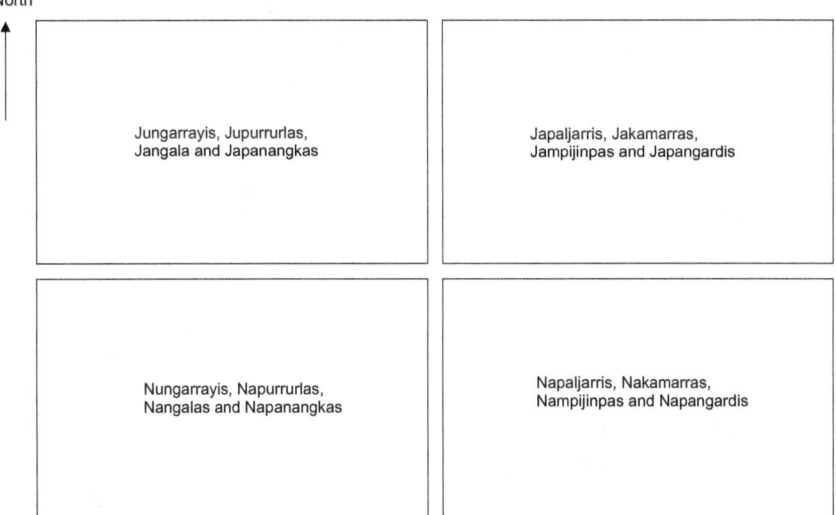

Figure 4.9. Seating arrangements prior to *Warawata*. Created by the author.

through business" (*ngarnarntarrka*) were sitting on the eastern side and the opposite moiety (*jarnamiljarnpa*) were sitting on the western side.[5]

The *wati-rirri-rirri* stood up in front of everyone and lectured us about how important it was to perform business properly and to take it seriously. He then referred specifically to two individuals who were going to circumcise the young men later that day. He introduced one man as Jangala, who was to circumcise Japangardi, as he was the father of the woman who had been promised as a future wife for Japangardi's in the ceremony the night before. Then the *wati-rirri-rirri* introduced another man as Jampijinpa, who got up and made a joke that he was the husband for Nungarrayi now after the ceremony the previous night. Normally as a man of Jampijinpa subsection would be a classificatory son for Nungarrayi, but as she had danced as a mother-in-law for Japangardi in the ceremony, it now made her his classificatory wife. Normally a Jangala man would be required to circumcise a Japangardi (as his father-in-law), but due to a non-ideal marriage of the initiand's parents, the relationship roles were skewed. These shifts in the normalized expectations of kin were met with laughter.

The *wati-rirri-rirri* then instructed everyone to move farther west into the bush behind the houses on the periphery of the settlement. All the men sat down facing west, and some older men sat in a half-circle and sang (see figure 4.10). The Jangala and the Jampijinpa that the *wati-rirri-rirri* had introduced before stood on the eastern side behind these men holding sticks at both ends behind their necks. The women danced in their two separate generation moieties toward the west in the same shuffling style as they had done the night before. Everyone was having a lot of fun, especially the children. The men on one side sang while the women of the same generation moiety danced, and then those on the other side sang and danced in the same way. Some of the verses had been sung the night before, but they now were sung in rapid succession. Because the verses were sung quickly, some women had to sit out certain verses because they were too exhausted. At the end of all this, the gathered group declared that the Nungarrayis, Napurrurlas, Nangalas, and Napanangkas were "winners," because this group of women had danced the fastest and had the most women still dancing at the end.

When we had finished dancing, all the young male children went to the fire on the east side behind where the women had been dancing. The *juka* were adorned with red ochre, and they stood on the southern side. The young boys threw firesticks at them, though they clearly missed intentionally, and the *juka* ran through the middle of the group picking up the young boys and ran with them on their shoulders back to the southwest side. They threw them up in the air a few times, and then the young boys ran quickly toward the east, back to the main settlement area in Yuendumu, laughing delight-

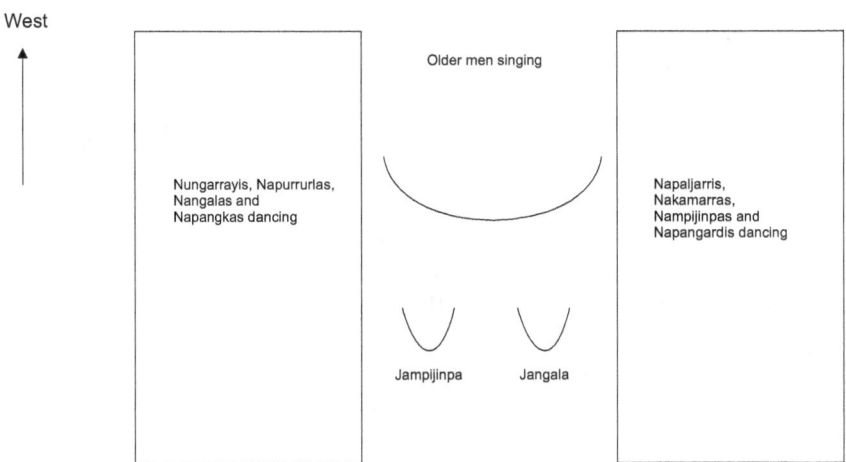

Figure 4.10. Ground plan for *Warawata*. Created by the author.

edly as they did so. The children's mothers followed them excitedly as these boys were now candidates for these initiatory rights in the coming years.

The initiands appeared from the bush to the west and came to where the men were sitting. Once they were in front of the men, all the women stood up, wailing and reaching out to touch the young men. This was the last time they would see them before their circumcision. All women then turned around and ran back to their camps in Yuendumu. Several men followed, yelling out from behind to go faster. These young men were once again going to their secluded bush camp with their *juka* and *rdiliwarnu*. From this point until when they returned a few weeks later, they were referred to as *purunyungu*, and no one from the settlement could see them except for their *juka*, male *rdiliwarnu*, and some of the senior men.

COMING BACK FROM THE BUSH

All the women moved back to their regular camps within Yuendumu directly after the *Marnakurrawarnu* and *Warawata* ceremonies. The boys, their *rdiliwarnu*, and their *juka* stayed in a secluded camp in the bush under the guidance of a group of senior men. The mothers of the boys continued to cook for them in their camps and send food out at regular intervals. After about a month, the boys were brought back in to Yuendumu, and the news rapidly spread of their arrival. Due to the constraints of the start of the school year, this period in the bush must necessarily be cut short, allowing enough time for their circumcision wounds to heal but little else.[6]

In the afternoon, all the women gathered together near the business ground in the east of the Yuendumu settlement area and hurriedly massaged red ochre into their hair and skin—the shiny quality that this gives to skin makes them attractive. As I rubbed ochre into my own skin, Napaljarri told me that, in the past, this ritualized event in which the boys are reintroduced back into settlement life would have happened early in the morning; nowadays, it always occurs in the late afternoon, as it did in this particular instance. I walked with the group of women a bit farther, to the northwest of the cleared areas. The male *yulpurru* (fathers and mothers' brothers) were sitting in a small group facing eastward. We waited until the men called out in a loud, high-pitched "brrrrr" sound. Traditionally a wake-up call, it signaled to these young men, their *rdiliwarnu*, and their *juka* in this contemporary context that it was time to come back in to the settlement. A group of the senior men who were sitting in a group began to sing a series of songs. The singers did not want me to record these songs—they described the content as open in this context but the function restricted. The content, they later explained, was descriptive. One verse, which was to make the sun rise, described the orange-colored sky—transmitted from a past period when this ritual event would have been held early in the morning just prior to sunrise. These same songs were still sung, although the time of day in which this ritualized event occurred had changed. The sun rising in this context was a powerful metaphor that functioned to draw the boys and their guardians out from their seclusion in the bush. Another verse was about the sun being fully up in the sky—again representing the boys as being out of their period of seclusion and back in the public world of the settlement.

Following this, the senior men continued to sing songs that described the actions of the *juka* as they led the young men, covering them by walking in front of them and on the sides so no one could see them, toward their mothers and the other women. They also sung about the young men having long whiskers and long hair—again, a verse from a past era in which these men would have long hair and beards, as they would not have cut them during their time in the bush camp. Nowadays, as they only spend around a month in the bush, their facial hair does not grow very much, but this verse remains powerful in this performative context. These young men, however, were adorned with hair strings that crossed their chests and with white fluff in their hair. The songs the men sang also made mention of these bodily adornments. The mothers of these young men sat on the ground at the front of the group of women facing their sons. As the young men walked toward the group, we waved white feathers from side to side and rhythmically called out "brrr, brrr, brrrr" while the men sang. The other women stood in a group behind the mothers. Once the young men had taken their place just in front of the group of men, everyone stood and the mothers placed tea and damper, which they had prepared beforehand, on the ground in front of them. Then they rose to greet their sons, picked the fluff from their hair, took off the hairstrings, and massaged their limbs. Now young men, they could return to their daily lives and commitments in Yuendumu, yet had still to navigate the reformed kind of sociality expected of them as men, rather than children.

NOTES

1. This makes the initiands look like budgerigars, a metaphor that has also been noted by Elias (1997). Elias discusses the travels of initiands as similar to the travels of flocks of these birds in *Jukurrpa* stories, where they stop at various places before continuing on their journeys.
2. This verse has been published in Warlpiri women from Yuendumu (2017a), but in this context it is sung by women from the settlement of Willowra. The interconnections between these two groups of women who share this song have been set out in Curran et al. (2019).
3. This song has been published with the other songs in the *Warlukurlangu yawulyu* series (Warlpiri women from Yuendumu 2017a). This book incorporates further stories that contextualize and give additional meaning to the song.
4. Senior Warlpiri men told me after this event that the windbreak should have been separated in the middle and the boys should have been escorted through this, but in the moment this had proved too difficult and the *wati-rirri-rirri* had decided it would be smoother for them to walk around the windbreak instead.
5. Myers (1986: 231–32) describes a very similar ceremony among the Pintupi. Warlpiri people also attest that this ceremony has been borrowed from the group living to their south. Myers notes that the first day of initiatory rights for Pintupi groups consists of the *Kurdiji* ceremony borrowed from the Warlpiri. This indicates that the trading of ceremonies between these two groups may be quite common.
6. In the "old days," the initiands would spend a long period of time in the bush, from which they were eventually taken to the secondary phase of initiation called *Kankarlu*.

Chapter 5

Holding Warlpiri Songs
Addressing Musical Endangerment

In the previous chapter, *Kurdiji* has been used as a case study of a vibrant contemporary ceremony held in Yuendumu. It has social import to Warlpiri lives and the establishment of relationships among groups of people across Central Australia. In this chapter, I also draw out that ceremonies like *Kurdiji* are vital in passing on cultural values across generations, doing so through their incorporative performance practices. It is through these shifts in ceremonial practices in recent decades that songs and associated content remain powerful in contemporary Warlpiri lives. As I have emphasized, however, tension exists because few senior men who know how to sing the songs that hold these ceremonies together are still alive. This is the fragile situation of the musical practices facing many Indigenous groups around the world. As has been pointed out by Catherine Grant, this "intangible cultural heritage," as recognized by the United Nations Education, Scientific and Cultural Organisation (UNESCO), "includes, among other things, the theatre, dance, music, language, and the rituals of a people, as well as the spiritual and philosophical systems that inform them" (2014: 1). *Kurdiji* and other Warlpiri ceremonies still performed today hold on to the unique and valuable cosmologies and worldview of Warlpiri people.

Although many younger participants in *Kurdiji* may not understand the words of the songs, there are nonetheless some core themes that surround the ceremonial practices and accompanying ritual events. Tambiah has emphasized that "a marriage of form and content is essential to ritual action's performative character and efficacy" (1985: 129). The symbolic content of the song series that the senior men sing as part of the all-night phase of

Marnakurrawarnu is a crucial aspect of the performance of this ritual as it guides the actions of the other participants. A theoretical trend in recent analyses of ritual toward emphasis on aspects of performance and the formal sequence of actions that make up a meaningful whole has made it such that some songs and other instances of ritual language are often ignored. The language used in rituals is often seen as being passed on in such a way that it is recited verbatim with little actually being understood, the words simply memorized for the purposes of performing the ritual. I argue that with respect to the performance of the *Kurdiji* ceremony, the song content and language is highly important in guiding what happens and how this is understood, making the meanings, however esoteric and subject to interpretation they may be, crucial for these ceremonies. For these reasons, song text analysis has formed a central place in the previous chapter's ethnographic description of this ceremony. For Warlpiri people, songs are a perfect medium to inexplicitly transmit the values, themes, and ideas surrounding social maturity. However, the esoteric references of the songs make it such that many of the participants of this ritual do not understand in much detail the specific content. This creates a dilemma, as despite this ceremony's importance to younger generations, it is dependent on the capacity of older men who understand and can sing the songs.

Based on his fieldwork in the Warlpiri settlement of Lajamanu in the 1960s, Mervyn Meggitt wrote that,

> should [a Warlpiri boy] fail to pass through these rites, he may not enter into his father's lodge, he may not participate in religious ceremonies, he cannot acquire a marriage line, he cannot legitimately obtain a wife; in short, he cannot become a social person. (1984: 241)

While the priorities of young men today are in many ways very different from those of young men at the time Meggitt made this statement, it still holds that without going through this ritual at this point in his life cycle, a young Warlpiri man cannot fully participate in social life as an adult person in this Aboriginal settlement.

Kurdiji ceremonies have remained an essential part of Warlpiri life while many other ceremonial forms have disappeared. Warlpiri people would argue that this is because these ceremonies are essential for "making young men": it is the only way for boys around the age of thirteen or fourteen, as well as their male and female family members (particularly their mothers and sisters), to be socialized into new roles, in which they have different responsibilities and are expected to behave in different ways. And although other traditional ceremonial forms would also seem essential for other important elements of people's lives—such as ceremonies for curing sickness, for falling in love, or for increasing food resources—the frequency with which they are held, however, has declined in recent decades, such that today they are only known by a small group of older people.

Peterson has suggested that the expansion of the number of people involved and the distances that people travel to attend these Warlpiri initiation rites is due to the ceremonial emphasis on the participation of the younger generations rather than the specific knowledge of songs, designs, and dances, which are predominantly known by older people (2000: 213). In the 1980s, Erich Kolig noted a profound change in the role religion played compared to previous decades, arguing that religion, once something used to divide and differentiate people,

> is now rapidly becoming a powerful force binding the Aboriginal people together and fostering mutual recognition and solidarity. Religious practices have now created a modern network of communication and interaction that serves as a paradigm to instill a sense of belonging together. (1981: 1)

While it is true that more emphasis is placed on the roles of younger generations in the *Kurdiji* ceremony, making it more inclusive, the crucial song series is only sung by a small group of older men. Therefore, despite the importance of this ceremony in creating widespread social networks in contemporary Warlpiri lives, it maintains a precarious position, as the ceremony will have to change form significantly when there are no longer any singers left.

Despite participation by the majority of the population of Yuendumu in *Kurdiji* ceremonies, the full song series central to it is only known by a small group of older men. It is clear, though, that the other participants derive meaning from this ceremony in other ways. In the previous chapter, I have shown how the participants of this ceremony engage with the songs sung by the older men, such that these men direct the performance and hence the understanding of the ceremony. In this chapter, I explore how Warlpiri people come to understand shared cultural values and broader themes relating to initiation through their participation. Additionally, I show that it is through their participation that the symbolism and associated cultural values of the *Jukurrpa* is brought into people's experienced lives. In line with performance theorists (see, e.g., Ortner 1978 and Shieffelin 1985) who argue that meaning is derived from ritual symbols through their enactment rather than by mentally processing their often abstract meanings, I demonstrate that the symbolism of the songs and associated stories is not understood by the participants through a rational, intellectual analysis but rather through the experience of singing, dancing, and holding the ritual in a meaningful social context. I show that symbolic meanings are effective not because the participants understand their underlying logic (Kapferer 1979) but because they are enacting them in less conscious ways, predominantly through their collective bodily experience of this ritual (Jackson 1983). Jennifer Biddle has also noted the power of Warlpiri bodies moving together en masse with respect to the biannual Milpirri festival held in Lajamanu since 2005 (2018) (see illustrations 5.1 and 5.2). I demonstrate how the central themes surrounding liminality, distinct male and female realms, and the forging of widespread relationship networks come to be understood through the actions of the participants. *Kurdiji* ceremonies today are not so much about learning the complexities of religious knowledge (though this does still happen to some degree) but more about gaining an understanding of these broader themes, which are central to Warlpiri ways of being through performative means.

Illustration 5.1. Warlpiri men sing *kurdiji* songs at Milpirri, 2016. Lajamanu/Tracks Dance Company Milpirri 2016 (*left to right*): Leslie Jampijinpa Robertson, Henry Jakamarra Cooke, Jerry Jangala Patrick, and Norbert Jampijinpa Patrick. Photo: Peter Eve.

Illustration 5.2. Warlpiri women dance *yawulyu* for Milpirri, 2016. Lajamanu/Tracks Dance Company Milpirri 2016 (*left to right*): Remeika Napangardi Simon, Denise Napangardi Tasman, Ursula Napangardi Marks, Merinda (Napangardi) Johnson, Valerie Napanangka James, and Agnes Napanangka Donnelly. Photo: Peter Eve.

LIMINAL SOCIAL SPACES

Van Gennep (1960) identified three core moments in a rite of passage: separation, marginalization, and aggregation. He argues that these moments inform the symbolism of the rites at many stages of the ceremony. Victor Turner (1967) picked up on the intermediate stage of "the margin," emphasizing that the liminal period is particularly well marked in initiation rites. He stresses that in this stage, the participants are "in between" their old and new roles in society and therefore do not adhere to its rules. Turner points out that during a transitional period, symbols typically surround "the biology of death, decomposition, catabolism, and other physical processes that have a negative tinge, such as menstruation (frequently regarded as the absence or loss of a foetus)" (Turner 1967: 96). Marett has noted themes of "liminality" in the *wangga* genre of song performed in the Daly region of Northern Australia, which highlight the marginal state between being alive and being dead. He comments that

> the association of *wangga* with liminal states of being—dream states, and the states of being in the twilight zone between life and death, or between child-

hood and adulthood—is enacted in ceremony and reflected in its poetics. Animals who can exist in both salt- and freshwater environments, the mixing of fresh and salt water at the Marri-ammu *wudi-pumininy* spring, the ebb and flow of the tide: all these allude to the intermingling of the living and the dead within the liminal context of ceremony. (Marett 2005: 5)

In the *Kurdiji* ceremony, the emphasis is on being reborn into the world in a new role with a new social function, albeit after the symbolic death. It is held at night, a time associated with sleep and death, and thus the morning equates to reawakening and rebirth when the sun rises. The social status of the participants of the ceremony also ceases to be as it once was, as during the ceremony they neither hold the relationships they had prior to its start nor do they yet attain those that they will have at its conclusion.

The majority of this ceremony is directed toward the east where the sun will rise in the morning. The journey of the ancestral women who are the subjects of the central song series also has an eastern directional focus, as they come out of the ground in the far west of Warlpiri country and dance toward their eastern goal. The association of the west with women and the female world and the east with men and the male world will be discussed later in this chapter. The journey of the ancestral women from west to east is symbolic of the transition of the initiand from the female world (in which he spent most of his time as a child) to the world of the men. The ceremony, which takes place from sunset one night to sunrise the next morning, is itself a liminal state. There are several songs in the *Karntakarnta* song series that involve "making the sun rise," alluding to this symbolism.

Verse 51, shown again below, reveals that the rising of the sun is a desired outcome and that the participants of the ceremony consider the sun to be "hidden" at nighttime. The sun becomes unhidden in the morning as it rises out of this liminal state, which is the same time the initiands are reborn into the world of adult men.

Wurrumpu pantirninya
Ngarnampu pantirninya
"There it is hidden, coming up from the ground."

This similar notion is expressed through imagery in a variant sung during the night, shown below.

Mangakijakiji-rla larnpirripirri
Mangapantipantirla
"The kingfisher is digging a burrow."

This song verse was described to me as being an Anmatyerr version of verse 51 and is accompanied by the same dancing style where fingers are clicked toward the eastern sky (DM 5, see figure 4.8). The action of the kingfisher burrowing through and coming out the other side is symbolic of the movement of the sun as it sets in the west in the evening and comes out on the eastern side in the morning. The bright yellow glint of the kingfisher's feathers, similar to that of the sun appearing over the horizon, further reinforces this imagery. The liminal state in this song is represented by the bird within the burrow. Like the participants of the ceremony, it is "in between" one state and the next.

Peterson has shown clear symbolism of rebirth in the performance of the *Kurdiji* ceremony (2006). As described in chapter 4, the initiands crouch down behind a windbreak at the back of the ceremony ground for the majority of the night. At various points, the actual (i.e., not classificatory) mothers of the boys move around to the back of this windbreak and circle around the boys a few times. Then they rejoin the other women. The boys are decorated with white fluff, and as dawn breaks, the fluff is removed from the top of their heads and replaced with red ochre. Once the sun has fully risen, they are covered from head to toe with red ochre. Peterson argues that this can "be understood by the anthropologist as gestating in a womb and one identified with women, rather than appropriated by men" (2006: 6).

Throughout the night, certain actions are performed that result in complex changes in relationships. Certain women establish themselves as mothers-in-law by dancing with firesticks, which has the effect of promising their daughters as wives to the initiands. Their husbands establish themselves as fathers-in-law the next day when they circumcise the young men. Strong, lifelong bonds are created between the young initiands and their *juka*, who look after them throughout this process. The initiands' sisters begin their ritual careers dancing in this ceremony, as they also transition into adulthood but in a less formalized way. The mothers lose a child but gain an adult man as a son, thereby increasing their social status. All the participants of this ceremony are "reborn" as new social beings with new sets of relationships, a process established and symbolized through the song texts, dances, ritualized actions, and other aspects of the ceremony. Here I illustrate two important themes that are central to *Kurdji*, which come through in the analyses of song texts and are evident in the ceremonial practice.

REESTABLISHING MALE AND FEMALE REALMS

Jeannie Nungarrayi Egan (personal communication, 2006) explained to me when we began working on the texts of the *Karntakarnta* song series that "these songs were sung by women in the *Jukurrpa* but now only men can sing them." This reflects the complex interplay between gendered roles when considering the actions of *Jukurrpa* ancestors and present-day Warlpiri people. Glowczewski (1991: 98) has counterpoised the world underneath the ground with that above, noting that underground is associated with female ancestors of the *Jukurrpa* yet is the secret domain of men, whereas aboveground is associated with male ancestors yet is the more public domain of women. In Verse 28 discussed in the previous chapter, the ancestral women sing about their long hair and making it look beautiful with red ochre and other decorative features. Ernest Giles has written of the Pitjantjatjara in 1875 that "some wear their hair in long thick curls, reaching down to their shoulders, and beautifully cultivated with iguana's fat and red ochre. This applies only to men; the women wear their hair cut short" (1875: 61). As the ancestral women sing about their long hair, it identifies them with men (in a traditional style). However, men sing this song in the ceremony, associating them with the ancestral women. These kinds of inversions again reflect the men's role in ceremony as similar to that of the women's in the *Jukurrpa*, with the ancestral women being symbolic of a male world. In *parnpa* ceremonies, men throw a handful of earth to one side at the start of the dance to mark their emergence from the underground spirit world. In the *Kurdiji* ceremony, women throw soil at the boys in the morning after they walk through a central path on the business ground symbolically entering the the world of adult men. This action can be seen as a symbolic move of the initiands from their place with the women, associated with the everyday, to the realm of the men, associated with the *Jukurrpa*. Complex transitions between male and female realms occur in both the *Jukurrpa* story and the ceremonial enactment that reinforce the distinct separation between male and female realms in Warlpiri life. These kinds of inversions are common, reveled in by Warlpiri people as they express fundamental values and ideas in such an inexplicit way.

Wild too has noted that "two principal themes mark the circumcision rituals: transition from the ranks of women and children to the ranks of men, and transition from family of orientation to family of procreation" (Wild 1975: 92). The west-to-east symbolism discussed above can further be analyzed as a symbolic journey from the world of women, associated with the west, into the world of men, associated with the east. This ceremony is thus a journey from being a boy who predominantly socializes with women and other children to being a man. After the *Kurdiji* and associated rites are finished, men spend the majority of their time with other men of the same age and older. The association of the west with women and east with men is reflected in many other parts of Warlpiri life, including in other ceremonial contexts such as mortuary rituals (see Musharbash 2008b) and *Kurdiji* seating arrangements: men sit at the far east of the ceremony ground, while women sit further to the west; boys who are "going through business" sit at the far west of the ground. At the end of the night, the boys move from this far western position through the women eastward until they are with the men, thus symbolizing their transition from the world of women to the world of men. Men refer to and address women as *Karlarningintipatu*, literally "west side ones."

After the rituals are finished and the boys return to camp with their families, they are encouraged to affiliate more with men of similar age or older and less with their mothers and other groups of women and children with whom they socialized as boys. It would be simple to assume that this ceremony is about dividing male and female realms as distinct from one another and repositioning a man of adult age within the male realm. Much of this symbolism would suggest a harsh division between the worlds of men and women. This, however, is not the case. Dussart highlights the problems with trying to categorize such things as "men's," "women's," "secret," and "open," pointing out that "women know about what is not proprietarily (in a ritual sense) 'theirs,' and that while much of this knowledge cannot be performed by women formally, they nevertheless exert influence in performative domains technically off-limits to them" (Dussart 2000: 59). She also explains that "the Warlpiri at Yuendumu seemed to transfer their ceremonial material via networks of kinship that accommodated, indeed revelled in, discrete expressions of cross-gender exchange" (Dussart 2000: 59). In singing *parnpa* so close to women just after sunset, men reemphasize that women can hear but not see these ceremonies—a contrast to the relaxed daytime performance in which women can see the men dancing from afar. While not commonly discussed openly, these performances of supposedly "restricted" men's songs are clearly intended to be seen by women or more effort would be made to place them out of sight and hearing.

Dussart asks the question, "How do the men and women of Yuendumu exchange material that might appear, to the outside, to be restricted to one group or another?" (Dussart 2003: 4). The restrictions surrounding male- and female-specific information are reinforced through distinct gendered roles in the performance of events associated with initiation. However, there are many areas where these distinctions between male and female knowledge are blurred. After being initiated, young men are encouraged to learn the songs, designs, and dances associated with their fathers and fathers' fathers. Before this, they would have gone along to women's *yawulyu* ceremonies with their mothers, but now they will participate in the men's ceremonies. Throughout my fieldwork, Rice was keen to help me understand women's *yawulyu*. I had not expected him to know much about these women's songs because the men always sit somewhere else during their performance. However, he said that while he could not sing the songs, he knew about them and could help transcribe them and provide exegesis, particularly those to which his mother was affiliated and which he had thus listened to as an uninitiated man hanging around predominantly with his mother and other women. Men learn about aspects of women's business in their childhood years that they remember throughout their lives.

As recounted in the previous chapter, the ancestral women who are the subjects of the song texts are pursued by a man named Wirdangula at various points along their journey. At the beginning of the song series at Yapurnu, Wirdangula sees the women and starts dancing like them in an effort to seduce them. Dancing in an animated way with lots of emphatic movements is a sexually attractive action among Warlpiri people (Egan, personal communication, 2006). However, Warlpiri exegesis for these song texts revealed that this was only a dance that women did, and Wirdangula's attempts to act in that way made the ancestral women think he was mad. Although the women do not react to Wirdangula's advances, he continues to follow them, dancing along like a woman just beside them. Eventually he takes his leave. However, as the women are urinating some time later, they see something emerging from the ground underneath them. They poke at the ground with their digging sticks and find out Wirdangula has sent his long penis underneath the earth and is trying to rape them. They cut off his penis with their digging sticks, resulting in his death.

Wild addresses a similar point when he looks at the Warlpiri men's dance styles and their relation to sex roles within Warlpiri society (Wild 1977/78). He argues that "men dance in women's style in part as a symbolic celebration of the complementarity of sex roles, and partly as a symbolic appropriation of women's procreative and nurturing role" (1977/78: 14). After providing a description of the underlying factors of Warlpiri ritual life, Wild discusses female symbolism in men's rituals, particularly the *Katjiri* (*Kajirri*) ceremony. The underlying theme of the *Katjiri* is fertility and the regeneration of Warlpiri society, which can be seen in the men's dance movements as they adapt women's styles. Thus men's rituals are collectively and metaphorically conceptualized as female (Wild 1977/78: 20). In a similar way, Wirdangurla dances like a woman in the *Karntakarnta* song series as a way of playing with these associations and therefore further emphasizing them. I have elsewhere argued that women too, in female-only private contexts, dance like men for similar reasons.

During ceremonial gatherings that I attended in Yuendumu, a practice called *jiliwirri* was also performed in an exclusively female realm. *Jiliwirri* involves raucous joking to the point where everyone is laughing hysterically by the time it is finished. Certain women were renowned for "making *jiliwirri*" and could often found at the center of these events. This type of behavior occurred even more often in highly restricted women's groups, but it also happened in situations where men had gone away for the day to attend their business and women were required to stay in the one place until they returned. At one event at Mount Allan in 2006, the women mocked the *parnpa* style of dancing while wearing red headbands similar to those men wear for business. When the men returned, the women scrambled to get rid of the headbands so that the men would not see what they were doing. Often women would pretend to have penises and strut around with a masculine stagger, teasing the other women by pretending to make sexual advances at them. Like the *jiliwirri* language described by Hale, this behavior was also about "turning up-side-down" the normal roles of women in Warlpiri society (1984). These examples from the performance, song texts, and surrounding activities of the *Kurdiji* ceremony demonstrate clearly Dussart's point that male and female realms are not exclusive and that there is a large degree of knowledge sharing between these groups. The ways in which this knowledge is shared, however, clearly mark the differentiation between male and female realms. In playing with these gender divisions, Warlpiri people reinforce their distinction.

FORMATION OF WIDESPREAD SOCIAL INTERCONNECTEDNESS

Myers summarizes the overarching purpose of initiation ceremonies in the Central Desert in saying that "the production of the social person involves an elaboration of the ties of relatedness to others" (1986: 228). As the ancestral women travel along from west to east, they continually meet up with women from the country they are traveling through who join with them to hold ceremonies, so that by the end of the journey, the group of women is composed of people from all the countries they have crossed. At the end of this journey, these Warlpiri women meet up with Anmatyerr women. They perform a large *Kirrirdikirrawanu* ceremony together, which consolidates bonds of relatedness between the two groups.

Many Warlpiri songs follow routes across the country that meet up with other *Jukurrpa* ancestors—marked in the more incorporative, large-scale ceremonies popular in the contemporary world, thus emphasizing the importance of the performance of ceremony in bringing people together to form relationships as well as the role of ceremony in creating a wider polity. The encounters that the ancestral women have with the two kangaroos and the *Kakalyalya Jukurrpa* (Major Mitchell's Cockatoo Dreaming) at Pikilyi and with the *Ngapa Jukurrpa* (Rain Dreaming) going to Warturlpunyu that travels along with them represent new relationships formed through these travels—they parallel the new relationships formed during *Kurdiji* ceremonies. It is the wider polity and the new relationships formed that must be continually renewed, because once people disperse from a ceremonial gathering, bonds start to weaken or fall apart. These encounters with other *Jukurrpa* characters also play on the temporal dimensions of the *Jukurrpa*, as all these *Jukurrpa* events are presented as happening simultaneously despite the sequential order in which the individual stories are presented. This indicates that a chronological and logical order of events in time is not the focus of notions of the *Jukurrpa* but rather an emphasis on the country visited by the ancestral beings.

As a boy makes the progression from child to young adult during the course of the *Jukurrpa* ceremony, he strengthens and gives meaning to relationships with people whom he may have only known distantly before this. Boys initiated together form a strong bond that lasts for the course of their lives, and they become known as *yarlpurru*. These boys may be from the same settlement, but they may also be from geographically remote places. Such people come together through *jilkaja* journeys, in which a candidate for *Kurdiji* travels with his *juka*, often over great distances, to bring other initiands back to his settlement (Peterson 2000). This party of travelers includes senior men as well as women who help to look after the boys by cooking and singing songs. Myers describes Pintupi initiation ceremonies, which have a similar practice:

> Like many ceremonial forms, it addresses the problem of differentiation among people who live in geographically separated areas. The symbolic action of the initiatory process, prescriptively including people from "far away," converts difference into relatedness. (1986: 229)

The families of the boys who go through *Kurdiji* ceremonies together also form new relationships through the establishment of marriage ties, through the connection between the mothers of the initiands, and of course through the strong bond between the boys initiated together and their brothers-in-law who are the boys' guardians through the ceremony. Peterson (2000: 209) notes that after Aboriginal people in the Central Desert area gained independent access to cars in the late 1960s, *jilkaja* expanded significantly. He highlights one journey from Tjuntujuntjara to Lajamanu and back again, a distance of approximately forty-five hundred kilometers, which involved twelve hundred people at its peak. Peterson shows that the reproduction of this wider regional sociality is now taking place primarily through initiation ceremonies. It is these ceremonies, which are still vital to the production of social persons, that are also reproducing the conditions of widespread relatedness. (2000: 212)

The new relationships formed in the process of organizing and performing this ceremony prepare young men for the next phase of their lives, a time when they commonly travel widely around the Central Desert visiting different settlements—often ones they have come to know from traveling with *jilkaja* parties. Nowadays young men frequently enter and exit relationships during this period; nonetheless, they typically do not "settle down" with a wife until they are well into their thirties (see Musharbash 2003: 68).

In a similar way, "relatedness" is also transformed between the initiand's family and the members of the boy's future wife's family, who may have previously only been known as distant kin. This relationship is initially established with the boy's sister's husband acting as guardian to the boy throughout the ritual. During the *Marnakurrawarnu* ceremony, the initiands' future mothers-in-law dance with a firestick, which is provided by the initiand's father's sister when the initiand initially goes into seclusion. This action confirms her approval for her very young or perhaps even unborn daughter to marry the boy being initiated. As well as making this promise, the mother-in-law also forms a bond between her and the boy's mother. Once she has danced with the firestick and promised her daughter as a future wife for the other woman's son, these two women can no longer call each other by their names, using the term *yinjakurrku* (firestick) instead. The bonds between these two families are further established when the future father-in-law acts as the young man's circumciser. The actions performed during the *Kurdiji* ceremony thus firmly intertwine the family of the initiand with the family of his future wife. These relationships are also seen when someone dies, with the principal female mourners being the mother, wife, and wife's mother. In contemporary Yuendumu, the marriage contracts arising from the initiation ceremonies no longer commonly eventuate, as women prefer to marry men of their own choice and age. However, as Musharbash noted in the late 1990s, "Even if promised marriages do not eventuate, the respective "promised" spouses are linked to each other in everybody's minds" (Musharbash 2003: 68). The relationships established between these families during *Kurdiji* ceremonies are still important even if the union they have anticipated does not work out in actuality. The avoidance relationships that have been established in this ceremony between an initiated man and his mother-in-law remain regardless of whether or not the marriage eventuates.

The song texts set out in the previous chapter also emphasize these "correct" marriage relationships. Men lusting after their mothers-in-law is a recurring theme throughout Warlpiri *Jukurrpa* stories, because it is typical of these stories to outline the inverse of everyday situations, or the way things should be. The women central to this song series are being pursued by men of the wrong subsection throughout their journey, which again emphasizes an inverted situation. While still adhered to in some ways today, these avoidance relationships were important in the past, as wives were typically fifteen years younger than their husbands at the time of their first marriage (Meggitt 1962). As such, a man and his mother-in-law were often of a similar age and therefore were potential sexual partners. Nowadays the avoidance relationships established in past *Kurdiji* ceremonies are still strictly maintained. The story of Wangala the crow, who is burned for pursuing a potential mother-in-law, emphasizes the consequences of pursuing women of the wrong relationship category. The ancestral women also cross paths with a Japangardi from Mount Theo who has fallen in love with his mother-in-law, Nungarrayi, and chases her many hundreds of kilometers; the result is that he is ostracized from social life. Other taboo relationships are also highlighted, such as Wirdangurla's affection for the traveling women (he too is a son-in-law to these Napaljarri/Nungarrayi women). In the ceremony, the future mothers-in-law of the initiands promise their daughters to them, and the future fathers-in-law are responsible for circumcising the young men to further reinforce this promise. The establishment of these marriage relationships is central to initiation in Yuendumu, and the participants form strict avoidance relationships especially between the initiand and his future mother-in-law as well as the women who call each other *yinjakurrku*. These relationships continue for life and are respected within the wide polity that is created through forming networks of relationships.

Warlpiri people gain an understanding of some core themes in Warlpiri life as a result of holding and participating in *Kurdiji* ceremonies. This understanding comes from the symbolic content and meanings of the central series of songs and the *Jukurrpa* story sung by the older men. I argue that, instead of the process being consciously thought out, experience dictates an understanding of these ideas, as people often participate in these ceremonies many times. Therefore, these thematic emphases become known by Warlpiri people as "techniques of the body," which they carry forward throughout their lives (Mauss 1973). The central song series used to structure this ceremony alludes to core symbolism surrounding maturity rites that are enacted in other parts of the ceremony and associated events. In this way, Warlpiri people come to share an understanding of the symbolism surrounding this ceremony. While there is a small group of older men who sing and can give detailed exegesis surrounding the song texts, the majority of the participants in this ceremony cannot. However, they do appear to understand the symbolic associations in an unarticulated way. The central themes of liminality, the distinguishing of male and female realms, and the forming of widespread relationships have been highlighted in this chapter and are central to the journey of all participants in this ceremony and in other areas of Warlpiri life as well. The emphasis on the themes in this ceremony perhaps contributes to its popularity, as these themes are recognized as integral to the lives of younger generations of Warlpiri people.

MUSICAL SHIFT OR ENDANGERMENT?

This book has illustrated, as expected, that Warlpiri musical practices and their ceremonial contexts have shifted in response to the dramatic social changes of recent Central Australian history. Nowadays, Warlpiri ceremonies tend to center on large-scale affairs incorporating many people, who often come from a wide region of Central Australia. In the past, site-specific ceremonies that nurtured individuals' connections to country held far more importance, but these smaller-scale practices have declined significantly in the last few decades. As has been observed across the world, many musical genres successfully adapt to changing circumstances, and in some instances they experience a revitalization. Warlpiri people are acutely aware of the highly endangered status of their songs and ceremonial life, and many make efforts to engage in projects that involve creative shifts to traditional performance contexts. These efforts often involve development or arts organizations, which support these contexts with logistical management and funding (see, for example, illustration 5.3).

Ceremonies like *Kurdiji*–perhaps the only Warlpiri ceremony held today without significant external support–are crucial for sharing fundamental cultural values among Warlpiri people, many of which become known via performative means and ceremonial contexts. In the *Kurdiji* ceremony, many participants gain knowledge of ritual symbols through dancing and participating in the context in which ritual symbols pervade. Rituals such as *Kurdiji* are important because they maintain traditions that give meaning to people's lives in a rapidly changing world where traditional values are often hidden. The effectiveness of rituals in doing this derives precisely from their emergent nature, which gives the participants a great degree of control.

Warlpiri people go to immense effort to hold ceremonies like *Kurdiji*, indicating the events' continuing importance to Warlpiri lives. People travel extraordinarily long distances to attend them, often a number of times, re-

Illustration 5.3. Warlpiri women dance *Ngapa yawulyu* as part of Unbroken Land in September 2018. Led by Pamela Nangala Sampson (*left*) and Maisy Napurrurla Wayne (*front right*). Video still: Anna Cadden, © Incite Arts Inc.

turning to collect other family members who also need to attend. Large sums of money are spent on food, fuel, and blankets—many people contribute the majority of their already small income so that these ceremonies can take place. Over the weeks surrounding the ceremony, people often camp in rough conditions and in extreme heat. Often there is no running water and little shade, and the shops selling food maintain irregular hours over the summer holiday period. As recounted in the introduction, the older women need to obtain *yurlpa* by digging into hard rock. The older men are required to stay up all night to sing, and certain women must also dance until morning. Despite the extreme effort and the hardships that must be endured, Warlpiri people often consider these times as some of their happiest. Of course, if it were easier to hold ceremonies such as *Kurdiji*, they would certainly prefer it, but the ritual is so important to their lives that they will endure the hard conditions in order for it to take place, a fact that illustrates the vital role of ceremony in contemporary Warlpiri lives.

Conclusion

I began this book by describing my experience attending a *Kurdiji* ceremony in Wariyiwariyi (Mount Allan) shortly after I first arrived to live in Yuendumu. This experience was one of overwhelming spectacle, intense sensation, many unknowns, patience, hard work, and, most of all, communality. These feelings were no doubt enhanced in my case, not only because it was the first *Kurdiji* ceremony I had been to but also because I was new to life in this Central Australian Aboriginal settlement and was still absorbing at great speed the new faces and experiences of everyday life.

The *Kurdiji* ceremony that I attended a year later was different. I had spent the preceding year in Yuendumu, immersing myself in Warlpiri culture and intensively researching songs and ceremonies every day. By the time the *Kurdiji* season came around in 2007, I had a good knowledge of who the people in Yuendumu were and how they related to each other, as well as the many contingencies of their lives at that point in time. I knew enough that I was able to anticipate the sequence of events that was likely to occur that evening—enough at least that I did not oversleep and miss important parts. I had also spent a great deal of time recording elicited versions of *Kurdiji* ceremonial songs, transcribing and translating them as well as obtaining exegesis concerning the meanings of their content. I could recognize songs and understand the associated abstract symbolism at particular points of the ceremony. These experiences over my year in Yuendumu impacted and enhanced my understanding of the *Kurdiji* ceremony, which I have described in this book. Nonetheless, it was made clear to me the first time I attended *Kurdiji* at Mount Allan that its true significance in Warlpiri lives comes from the experience of participating and the intense emotive responses that go along with sustaining a tradition in this way.

This book provides an ethnographic account of the place of songs and ceremonies in contemporary Warlpiri life. My description of *Kurdiji* serves to show the vitality of this particular ceremony in Yuendumu today. This understanding is pinned against the significant historical factors and specific modes of life of the people who today live in the settlement of Yuendumu. Contemporary notions of the *Jukurrpa* and the inherited connections that Warlpiri people have to country are also fundamental and serve to guide the performance of ceremony and the ways in which individuals engage with its various parts. Regarding these songs and ceremonies as Warlpiri "high culture," this book has laid out the special features of Warlpiri songs, including their language, musical features, dances, and designs. Several different genres of Warlpiri songs are evident based on lines of gender and publicity, which have deep effects on their performance contexts. The *Kurdiji* ceremony is a particularly interesting case study for this book because it is held frequently in the contemporary world, while many other ceremonies are not. Its contemporary importance is evident in that it brings together many different family groups and has a vital social function in the modern world. The content of the songs—which follow the ancestral beings of the *Jukurrpa*—though only sung by a small group of older men, relates intimately to the performance of this ceremony, guiding the dancing and associated actions. This gives the older men a significant degree of control and power over the ritual, yet the tradition is left in a fragile state because of it.

As stated in the introduction, one of the most pressing motivations for Warlpiri people's involvement in this kind of research is the desire to record detailed religious knowledge that is today only known by a dwindling group of older people. It is important for the most senior generation, who understand the intricate details and power that Warlpiri songs and ceremonies have, to document this cultural phenomenon, and it is important for younger people to receive this knowledge as it adds significant meaning to their identity as Warlpiri people, detailing their connections to their kin, country, and related *Jukurrpa*. No Warpiri person questions the power of song to change the world, and the senior men and women with this knowledge are given significant respect. Despite the apparent threat, knowledge such as this and its associated practices do not die out in a clear-cut way. As I have illustrated in chapter 5, younger people, through active participation in *Kurdiji* ceremonies, are absorbing knowledge about *Jukurrpa*, country, and ceremony and the esoteric references that surround these. A decline in traditional learning contexts such as *Kankarlu* means that younger people do not learn about this knowledge in the same way or in as many contexts as they did in previous decades. It is true that they do not appear to be learning songs and their detailed associated knowledge, but their participation in ceremonies such as *Kurdiji* indicates that they are absorbing knowledge in another way. In turn, the important roles that younger people are given in ceremonies like *Kurdiji* empower them to take on greater responsibilities within Warlpiri ceremonial life.

The description of *Kurdiji* in this book illustrates the importance of context, of contingency, and of the capacity of these ritualized practices to encompass change and emerge in new forms, which both adhere to tradition and continue to respond to and shape the circumstances of people's lives at a particular point in time. Aboriginal people often describe the *Jukurrpa* as an unchanging structure that shapes the way the world is and the practices of human beings within it. The performance of ceremonies, which symbolically represent the events of the *Jukurrpa*, counter this view in many ways. Rather than prescribing ceremonial performance, the *Jukurrpa* provides a framework for the participants to decide, through complex negotiations, how ceremonies will be held. It is precisely in their ability to adapt that rituals remain meaningful to people over a long period of time, making them effective in maintaining traditions through times of change. If the ceremony were inflexible, it would not have any place in modern life or be able to achieve its functional goals, and it would not see a future. Kolig noted that

> traditional Aboriginal religion, though in one sense the reservoir of the autochthonous Aboriginal heritage, the symbol of unchanging continuity, has nowadays clandestinely become the vehicle of change. As the religion is being transformed, it alters and shapes Aboriginal consciousness accordingly. (1981: 1)

Nowadays this is still the case, with ceremonies like *Kurdiji* being particularly accommodating to Warlpiri lives; therefore, it is still performed several times annually in various settlements. Many other Warlpiri ceremonies have rarely been performed in the last few decades (see Curran 2019). Meggitt's and Wild's normative accounts of *Kurdiji* ceremonies in Warlpiri settlements in the 1950s and 1970s, respectively however, show that there are also some remarkable patterns of continuity given the dramatic changes that have occurred to Warlpiri life in the last few decades. *Kurdiji* continues to be a significant part of the coming-of-age process despite many significant social changes and additional pressures that come with modernity. Why this is so is particularly interesting when considering the place of ceremony more broadly in contemporary Warlpiri life.

In many ways, *Kurdiji* appears to have lost some key aspects of its significance. The marriage contracts that are established through this ceremony rarely eventuate, with initiands of the younger generation often choosing their own marriage partner. While alliances are still forged between the participating families in this ceremony, they by no means hold the same relevance and necessity within Warlpiri social life. However, it is apparent to anyone visiting Yuendumu over the summer that *Kurdiji* ceremonies are the focus of Warlpiri lives, particularly those of the younger generation, who take their duties quite seriously. Following Kolig's (1981) suggestion that Aboriginal religious life, which once was about exclusion and separation, has in recent decades become defined by its ability to unite and establish networks, Peterson (2000) has suggested that the emphasis on active roles, particularly those taken on by the younger participants, is what makes this ceremony so popular. In a world where *Kankarlu* is no longer held, Warlpiri men have no forum in which to learn religious knowledge. Therefore, younger people can no longer perform the ceremonies emphasizing this knowledge, particularly those associated with sites. The younger generation, particularly young men, are empowered by the roles entrusted to them in *Kurdiji*—through these roles they attain an important place in this religious realm.

The emphasis on younger generations has given rise to the large-scale ceremonies of today. As noted in chapter 2, an increase in birth rates over the past few decades has resulted in significantly more young people in Aboriginal settlements than people of their grandparents' generation. Thus, many more boys need to be initiated each year. In chapter 3, I discussed the general increase of large-scale ceremonies in Yuendumu, alongside a trend for inclusivity, in recent decades. I covered how sweeping ceremonies in Yuendumu in the 1980s incorporated large numbers of people in inclusive ways. The "Balgo business" describedbed in chapter 3 is an example of this trend. Today *Kurdiji* and *Malamala*, a mortuary ritual, are the most frequently performed rituals in Yuendumu, with both of them taking on an inclusive form and often featuring hundreds of participants. As both emphasise inclusivity, and as established relational networks increase across the Central Desert, the ceremonies grow in size.

Even though the emphasis is on younger generations, older men are still the only ones who know how to sing the songs that are so central to the performance of *Kurdiji*. Over several decades now, while middle-aged men join in and participate as part of the group of male singers, the lead singers remain the same elderly men, increasing the pressure on them. This creates somewhat of a dilemma, as younger generations view this ceremony as necessary for them to continue their relationships and transition into their roles as adult men, yet it is difficult to imagine how this ceremony will be held when the core group of older men passes on. The medium of song is important for this ceremony, as it is through singing that the older men control the sequence of events for the night. The songs are such a crucial element that if there are no longer any men who know them, the ceremony will have to dramatically change form. Song is a perfect medium to allude inexplicitly to the central themes of maturity rites. Merlan (1987) has noticed the importance of theme in song texts that make esoteric references. A broader theme is often more crucial to understanding a song text than the specific meanings of particular words. Donaldson has also emphasized the importance of themes in understanding song texts in languages that are no longer understood by the singers (1984). General themes also come to be understood in other ways. As I showed in chapter 5, the participants in *Kurdiji* and related events absorb themes surrounding liminality and transitions, male/female realms, and the establishment of relational networks—these are crucial components of what it means for a boy to become a man and for relationship to change accordingly surrounding this. Marett (2005) and Ellis (1985) have noted how themes (particularly with associated Dreamings) in other parts of Australia are expressed through the melody of particular songs, and that upon hearing particular melodies, the associations are brought to mind. On one occasion when Peterson was in Yuendumu during my fieldwork, Rice explained to him that many of the young men did not really know these songs, they were "just humming." This opens up some interesting questions about the nature of learning and the types of knowledge being transmitted. These younger men are clearly learning the tune of these songs and most likely the associated themes. They are also probably learning quite a few words even if they do not acknowledge this outright. Perhaps they lack the confidence to sing or feel that they must submit to authority. Whatever the case, it is such that senior men consider that they are not learning the songs. But what form will this important ceremony take, and how can it be sustained after the current generation of older men passes away? Perhaps faced with no other option, younger generations of men may just step up to the task of singing.

In many other places around the world and in other parts of Australia, the contexts needed and the knowledge required for initiation rituals that serve similar purposes to *Kurdiji* no longer exist, and subsequently they are no longer performed. Gabriele Sturzenhofecker has studied a similar situation in Papua New Guinea, where the *Palena* initiation rites have declined:

> The demise of the Palena cult may also be seen as having contributed to male anxiety. One thing the cult accomplished was the removal of boys from domestic life with their mothers and their institutionalized socialization into male personhood under the tutelage of ritually pure bachelors.... This time of separation no longer exists, and in a sense boys pass in an unrecognized and amorphous period of limbo from boyhood to manhood without a context in which they are unambiguously taught the proper ways to be men. Many later filled this void by seeking work outside of the local area as laborers on coastal plantations or, more recently, on mining sites (1998: 171).

As I have demonstrated, *Kurdiji* entails much more than the social transition of a boy into a man. Other relationships are also forged and change form: friendships (solidarity relationships) are created among boys who "go through" in the same ceremony, and alliances are made between distantly related families. The ceremony remains vital in contemporary Warlpiri lives, and the void will have to be filled in creative ways. One way in which this ceremony is sustained is by calling upon broader relational networks. Older men from different settlements in the Central Desert who know the songs required to hold *Kurdiji* are called on to travel to various settlements during the summer months. Laughren (personal communication, 2009) has pointed out that in the East Kimberley, one or two families have become the specialists whose presence is needed to perform ceremonies.

Ceremonies and their associated songs clearly have an important place in contemporary Warlpiri lives. Recent decades, however, have seen a shift of emphasis. In the recent past, songs were valued for the intrinsic religious knowledge they contained and for the power they had to change the world and maintain social order. While these aspects of songs still hold importance today, the ceremonies in which they are sung are no longer as relevant to Warlpiri lives as they used to be. Instead, ceremonies such as *Kurdiji*, which do encode important religious knowledge but also emphasize performative aspects, overarching themes, and wide-scale incorporation, are taking over as the dominant ceremonial forms. The significance of these ceremonies in Warlpiri life was apparent from the first *Kurdiji* I went to at Mount Allan a few weeks after I first moved to Yuendumu, and it remained apparent in the 2007 ceremony I describe in this book. The same emotions, the same dedication to hard work, the immense effort to stay up all night, the spectacular nature of the whole affair, the large numbers of people, and the great sense of sustaining tradition all combine to drive Warlpiri people to hold this ceremony year after year.

Appendix
Song Verses from the *Kurdiji* Ceremony

I refer to the song verses presented in this appendix throughout this book, but I list them here in the order in which they were sung during the all-night *Marnakurrawarnu* ceremony on 4 February 2007. The order would not necessarily be the same for other *Kurdiji* ceremonies, although some similarities would exist. Many of the words are special "song words" or skewed versions of regular Warlpiri words. Many are also in various other Aboriginal languages and further analysis is required to determine individual words. Morphemes that are from regular Warlpiri (or have roots clearly traced to regular Warlpiri) are referenced from the *Warlpiri- English Encyclopaedic Dictionary* (Laughren et al. 2007). All other morpheme glosses come from exegesis from Rice and Egan (Rice and Egan 2008), who assisted with these transcriptions and translations. Some of the words could not be glossed in any exact way. Related words or words possibly related are preceded by an asterisk. A basic translation is also given directly after the song text.

Verse 1 (place)

A *Yapurnurla kaninjarra*
B *Jirrpijirrpi parnkayarra*

A Deep down at Yapurnu
B Fingernails dancing from side to side.

Yapurnu *proper noun*. Lake Mackay, a salt lake near the Northern Territory and Western Australian border
*yapurnu *noun*. salt lake (Laughren et al. 2007)

-rla *noun suffix.* at, in, on, near (Laughren et al. 2007)
kaninjarra *noun.* inside, down, underneath, downward, way down in
   (Laughren et al. 2007); a depression in the ground (Rice and Egan 2008)
jirrpijirrpi *noun.* long fingernails and toenails (Rice and Egan 2008)
parnka- *verb.* run, fly, dart, speed, race (Laughren et al. 2007); dancing
   really quickly (Rice and Egan 2008)
-nya *verb suffix.* presentative, used commonly in songs
-rra *verb suffix.* away (Laughren et al. 2007)
-nyarra *verb suffix.* side to side, back and forth (Rice and Egan 2008)

Wirdangurla is dancing quickly from side to side at Yapurnu on the salt lake. He comes from Western Australia. He has come to the salt lake to drink and sees the women dancing there. He watches them and thinks they look pretty. Then he joins in their dance, trying to impress them by making a mark on the ground with his long fingernails. He thinks his fast dancing will allure them toward him.

Verse 2 (place)

A *Walyangka juturu nyina*
B *Yapurnurla juturu nyina*

A Sitting still on the ground
B Sitting still at Yapurnu

Yapurnu *noun.* Lake Mackay, a salt lake near the Northern Territory and
   Western Australian borderline
*yapurnu *noun.* salt lake (Laughren et al. 2007)
-rla *noun suffix.* at, in, on, near (Laughren et al. 2007)
juturu *preverb.* unmoving, quiet, still, unanimated (Rice & Egan 2008)
*jutu *preverb.* cease, leave, desist (Laughren et al. 2007)
*junyuku- *preverb.* lifeless, apathetic, listless, quiet, loner, reserved,
   uninterested (Laughren et al. 2007)
nyina *verb.* sit (Laughren et al. 2007)
walya *noun.* ground, earth, land (Laughren et al. 2007)
-ngka *noun suffix.* at, in, on, near (Laughren et al. 2007)

At Yapurnu, the women sit quietly on the ground. By sitting quietly, they are trying to lose the attention of Wirdangula so that he does not follow them any farther. Their animated dancing has attracted him to them. Dancing with a lot of movement makes women very sexy, whereas stillness and rigidness has the opposite effect.

Verse 3 (traveling)

A *Pakarli yanjawarra*
B *Yarlipilykipilyki*

A The special place of the inland ti-trees
B They are shaking

pakarli *noun.* inland ti-tree, paper-bark tree (Laughren et al. 2007)
yanjawarra *noun.* Dreaming site (Rice and Egan 2008)
*yanjarra *noun.* Dreaming site, Dreaming place, Dreaming, Dreamtime (Laughren et al. 2007)
yarlipilykipilyki *noun.* shaking, quivering, trembling, moving loosely [opposite: lalka *noun.* solid, hardened, stiff, firm, frozen stiff, congealed, rigid, dried up (Laughren et al. 2007)] (Rice and Egan 2008)

The raindrops are falling through the leaves of the *pakarli* trees, and the women are dancing shake-a-leg style. They dance like this in the cool of the afternoon, after the rain. The way the rain falls through the leaves of the *pakarli* and the movement of the women's legs as they dance are both evoked in the word *yarlipilykipilyki*.

Verse 4 (traveling)

A *Lardiji lanja kuruku kurrku*
B *Rdalyaranga larranya*

A A thick group of mulga trees all together
B There it is, broken-off firewood

lardiji *noun.* mulga (Rice and Egan 2008)
*wardiji *noun.* mulga (Laughren et al. 2007)
lanja *preverb.* thickly grouped (Rice and Egan 2008)
*laja *preverb.* amassing (Laughren et al. 2007)
kuru *preverb.* in one place (Laughren et al. 2007)
kurrku *noun.* heap, pile, mass, lot, large quantity (Laughren et al. 2007)
rdalyaranga *noun.* dry firewood (Rice and Egan 2008)
*rdaaly(pa) *noun.* broken (of solid entity) off, snapped, split in two, in pieces, apart (Laughren et al. 2007)
*laarr-rdangka *preverb.* broken off, split off from
*laarr(pa) *preverb.* out of (Laughren et al. 2007)
*rdangka *preverb.* apart from, away from, separate from (Laughren et al. 2007)
larra *noun.* cracked, split, slit, torn (Laughren et al. 2007)
-nya *noun suffix.* presentative suffix "there it is," "here it is" (Laughren et al. 2007)

The women stop in a dense forest of mulga trees, they cannot see through them. The branches have broken off, so there are piles of dry firewood lying everywhere. There is an Anmatyerr song just like this.

Verse 5 (traveling)

A1 *Jilkangka larrujarru jaru*
A2 *Walkangka larrujarrujaru*
B *Jilkangka rdilyilpi nyiwi*

A1 At the prickled country, they dance on the prickles.
A2 On the ground, they dance on the prickles.
B At the prickled country, the prickles break in their feet.

jilka *noun.* prickle
*jilkarla *noun.* prickle (Laughren et al. 2007)
-ngka *noun suffix.* at, on, near, with (Laughren et al. 2007)
larrujarru jaru *verb.* dancing fast on the prickles, getting them in their feet (Rice and Egan 2008)
*larrungka *noun.* mulga gall (Laughren et el. 2007)
*jarala *preverb.* all over (the place), everywhere, up and down (Laughren et al. 2007)
*jararr(pa) *noun, preverb.* ground, digging (of ground) (Laughren et al. 2007)
*jaru *preverb.* curved downward, sloping downward, bent over, on a slope, on its side (Laughren et al. 2007)
walka (=walya) *noun.* ground, earth, land (Laughren et al. 2007)
rdilyilpi *noun.* broken (Rice and Egan 2008)
*rdilyki *noun.* broken, rent, torn, fractured, smashed (Laughren et al. 2007)
nyiwi (-nyili) *noun.* thorn, prickle, sticker, spike, spine (Laughren et al. 2007)

They are dancing on the prickles around the mulga country. The prickles break in their feet and are really painful. They sit down remove the prickles. The prickles are called *yarnajakarlarla*—there are lots of them where mulga trees grow. Three sharp points extend from each. Pieces of them get stuck in the women's feet and throb with pain (wiyingkiwiyingki = stinging, irritating, hurting)

Verse 6 (business)

A *Jaka yangawa*
B *Kaka yarrarnta*
C *Jaki yarringki*
D *Rima yarrarnta*

A The guardians are holding the initiands' buttocks to help lift them up.
B They are rubbing them with warm hands from the fire.
C They are fixing the fluff on their heads.
D They are holding the initiands under their arms to support them while they stand.

jaka *noun.* buttocks, behind, rear, backside, bottom, rump, arse (vulgar) (Laughren et al. 2007)
yangawa *verb.* fixing their dress (headbands, fluff, etc.) (Rice and Egan 2008)
*nawaya *noun.* headband (Laughren et al. 2007)
kaka *noun.* defecates (for a small child) (Laughren et al. 2007)
yarrarnta *verb.* moving off to the side (Rice and Egan 2008)
Jaki (=jaka) *noun.* buttocks (Rice and Egan 2008)
yarringki *verb.* standing up (Rice and Egan 2008)
*yarriyarri *preverb.* rising, going up, high up (Laughren et al. 2007)
*yarrinki *noun.* new growth, fresh vegetation, green grass (Laughren et al. 2007)
rima
*riwariwa *noun.* toilet (Laughren et al. 2007)

This is a special song for business. The young men get stiff legs from crouching all night, so they sing this song to give them a break to stand and stretch. Their *rdiliwarnu* help them stand up. They hold the young men under their arms to support them. The women move apart from each other in two groups so the men can see the boys in the back. The women dance in two lines facing each other, while the men look at the young men through the middle. The woman at the front of each line of dancers holds a firestick and dancing board, and there are others behind her holding on to her waist. The cousins and sisters dance sideways and make a "puh, puh, puh" sound. The mothers, mothers-in-law, and fathers' sisters hold the firesticks. The singers make an undulating sound at the end of this song.

Verse 7 (traveling)

A *Jurnpurla rulawama*
B *Parlanji wirriwirri*

A Dancing and throwing up soil into a mound.
B Dancing with flattened feet so the tracks are forming a channel

jurnpu *preverb.* raised, humped (Laughren et al. 2007), the mound of sand made on the side of a dancer's tracks (Rice and Egan 2008)

-rla *noun suffix.* on, at, with, in (Laughren et al. 2007)
rulawama *verb.* moving feet that throw up soil while dancing (Rice and Egan 2008)
parlanji *verb.* flattening feet so they are wide apart (Rice and Egan 2008)
*parlaparla *noun.* flat ground (Laughren et al. 2007)
*parlanji *noun.* termite mound (Laughren et al. 2007)
wirriwirri *noun.* deep tracks (Rice and Egan 2008)
*wirri *noun.* watercourse, floodway, channel, floodplain, gutter, runoff areas, drainage channel, valley (Laughren et al. 2007)

Wirdangula is singing about himself and the way he is dancing and making tracks. He dances with the women, copying them and joining in as they dance first with their feet flat, making a deep track, and then throwing them out to the side to make a mound of soil beside their tracks. He's dancing like this because he wants the women to notice him and be attracted to him.

Verse 8 (traveling)

A *Yinjirinpunganya palarrararrara*
B *Parlanji yatampurrukarri*

A Dragging feet along through the swamp grass
B Flattening feet and standing still

yinjiri *noun.* swamp grass, spear grass (Laughren et al. 2007)
punganya *verb.* fight, present
pala *preverb.* tight, secure, fixed (Laughren et al. 2007)
rarra-rarra *preverb.* drag feet along the ground (Laughren et al. 2007)
parlanji *verb.* flattening feet so they are wide apart (Rice and Egan 2008)
*parlaparla *noun.* flat ground (Laughren et al. 2007)
*parlanji *noun.* flat termite bed (Laughren et al. 2007)
yatarnpa *noun.* calm, still (Laughren et al. 2007)
karri- *verb.* stand (Laughren et al. 2007)

Jungarrayi is dancing with wide legs because he is copying the women. He starts dancing in the grass and then moves out to where the women are dancing. He makes a clearing in the grass where he is dancing. This happens at a place called Wirdangula, not far from Kunajarrayi. This is where he lives. He sees the women harvesting witchetty grubs at Kunajarrayi and joins them there. The women are dancing with wide legs, sideways, from north to south and back again.

Verse 9 (traveling)

A *Yamanarna japara wapa*
B *Yamanarna japiri nguna*

A I am dancing with wide legs, eating as I move
B I am dancing with wide legs, eating as I stay still

Yamana *noun.* wide legs (Rice and Egan 2008)
*yamalanypa *noun.* numb and cramped (Laughren et al. 2007)
-rna *noun suffix.* first-person singular subject suffix (Laughren et al. 2007)
japara *preverb.* eating while on the move (Laughren et al. 2007)
wapa *verb.* moving along (Laughren et al. 2007)
nguna *verb.* lying (Laughren et al. 2007)

The women are dancing around the rock at Kunajarrayi. They move their feet from being up on the outside to being flat on the ground. They dance from side to side, making the dust come up and pushing the sand along. They eat witchetty grubs as they dance.

Verse 10 (place)

A *Kalpalpirla rarra wapa*
B *Yatingkarna rarra wapa*

A Swarming in the soft grass
B I am swarming in the tree roots

kalpalpi *noun.* lemon-scented grass, native lemon grass (Laughren et al. 2007); soft grass to put delicate items on (Rice and Egan 2008)
-rla *noun suffix.* at, on, near, with (Laughren et al. 2007)
rarra-wapa-mi *verb.* stream in and out, swarm, go in all directions (Laughren et al. 2007)
yatingka. *noun* tree roots (Rice and Egan 2008) [syn. *kuturlurla*]
-rna *noun suffix.* first-person singular subject suffix (Laughren et al. 2007)

The witchetty grubs are moving around on the back of the rock at Kunajarrayi. They come together to form into a single snake. This snake eats another witchetty grub, and then turns into many smaller snakes before turning into one big snake with little wings—*rimpirimpi*, who flew to the Granites.

Verse 11 (place)

A *Warnampa warna pirrirdi japa*
B *Warnampa warna jarridi japa*

A The snakes are going around in a circle
B The snakes are flying off

warna *noun.* poisonous snake
jarrirdi japa *verb.* fly off (Rice and Egan 2008)
pirrirdi japa *verb.* going around the rock in a circle (Rice and Egan 2008)
*japiya *noun.* big, much, many, large amount of, great quantity of, big number of, numerous (Laughren et al. 2007)
*jarri *noun.* singing (Laughren et al. 2007)
*pirdi *noun.* whole, cave, cavity, cavern (Laughren et al. 2007)

The witchetty grubs have come together to turn into snakes. The women are dancing around the rock in a circle, and they sing about the transformation as they do so. In the ceremony, they dance sideways, from north to south. The rock at Kunajarrayi has a big hole in it.

Verse 12 (traveling)

A *Nyarla kurarra rdangka*
B *Nyarla jurrparna janji*

A The seeds are hanging down from the dead finish tree.
B Collecting them as they hang down.

nyarla *noun.* hanging down (Rice and Egan 2008)
kurarra *noun.* dead finish tree (Laughren et al. 2007)
rdangka *preverb.* apart from, away from, separate (Laughren et al. 2007)
kurarra *noun.* edible seeds from tree (Rice and Egan 2008)
rdangka *preverb.* apart from, away from, separate from (Laughren et al. 2007)
jurrnarpa *noun.* entity used as a tool (Laughren et al. 2007)
-rna *noun suffix.* first-person singular subject suffix (Laughren et al. 2007)
janji *preverb.* searching (Laughren et al. 2007)

The ancestral women leave Kunajarrayi and travel east. This is a traveling song. They collect the edible seeds hanging off the *kurarra* tree. In the ceremony, they dance from side to side, north to south, in a loose style.

Verse 13 (traveling)

A *Ngapirlirli marraya*
B *Ngatulampa kurraya*

A The sweet sugar is swaying
B Dripping down

ngapirli *noun*. the sweet sugar on the mulga tree (like kunpu but on the mulga tree) (Rice and Egan 2008)
*ngapiri *noun*. red river gum (Laughren et al. 2007)
marraya *verb*. swaying in the wind (Laughren et al. 2007)
*marrara *noun*. tree species (Laughren et al. 2007)
ngatulampa *verb*. dripping to the ground (Rice and Egan 2008)
kurrara *noun*. dead finish (Laughren et al. 2007)

In this verse, the mulga trees are swaying in the wind and the sweet sugar is dripping to the ground. On the branches of the mulga tree there are red lumps with white sugar on top. When it gets hot, it drips to the ground. Warlpiri people collect it, gathering it in a coolamon and mixing it with water. When it dries, you can suck on it like a lollipop. Each tree has a different sugary substance, and they all have a different taste. Warlpiri people put the substance in a soft grass, called *yilyirri*, covered with bark to keep it from melting.

Verse 14 (place)

A *Yalkiri rapawala pawala*
B *Yalkiri jawirri jawala*

A The sky is all in the cracks in the ground
B Only sky in the cracks in the ground

jawirri jawala *noun*. water running all over the place (Rice and Egan 2008)
jawirri *noun*. no more than, only, simply, just, and nothing more, nothing else, leaving, desisting
jawala (perhaps play on pawala?)
yalkiri *noun*. sky (Laughren et al. 2007)
pawala *noun*. watering hole, swamp, depression, lake (Laughren et al. 2007), a crack in ground typically caused by a tuber growing below (Laughren et al. 2007)

Fresh water is flowing everywhere. The women look around at it. At Miyikirlangu (lit: delicacy food–belonging), the bush plums grow in abundance.

Verse 15 (place)

A *Yanjiwarrarra rdaku*
B *Yanjata patarrpala*

A There is a hole in the flat rock
B The kangaroos are stretching their limbs

Yanjiwarra *proper noun*. place name, a rockhole, a large flat rock (Rice and Egan 2008)
rdaku *noun*. hole in ground, hollow, cavity (Laughren et al. 2007)
yanjata *noun*. kangaroo [syn. *marlu* (Rice and Egan 2008)]
patarrpala *noun*. stretching their limbs around showing off (Rice and Egan 2008)
*palapala *noun*. stiff ([leg] muscles from walking), tired, tight (muscles), paining, aching, weary (Laughren et al. 2007)

The two kangaroos sing this verse. They are drinking from the rockhole and stretching out their legs. They are showing off, trying to get the women's attention. They look at them sideways while they're having a drink. They are traveling from the north (in Gurinji country) to the south when they cross paths with the women.

Verse 16 (place)

A *Mulyurna wilypiri*
B *Yajanpurrukarri yajanpurrukarri*

A I am a nose with a big hole
B Enticing further and further

yajarni *verb*. invite, entice, ask for, solicit, fetch, round up, get to go with, enlist, ask along, get to accompany (Laughren et al. 2007)
karri *verb*. stand (Laughren et al. 2007)
mulyu *noun*. nose (Laughren et al. 2007)
-rna *pronoun suffix*. first-person singular suffix (Laughren et al. 2007)
wilypiri *noun*. hollow in something, cavity (Laughren et al. 2007)

The kangaroos are singing that their noses have big holes for nosepegs. The two kangaroos are singing themselves. They are trying to win the affection of the women by singing about their nose pegs—a symbol of their ritual importance. Yanjiwarra is a big rockhole where the two kangaroos and the ancestral women meet.

Verse 17 (place)

A *Wawirrirna parnkaparnka*
B *Yilimirntirrirna karri*

A I am a kangaroo, running
B I am two legs going farther and farther

yilimirntirri. two legs (Rice and Egan 2008)

-rna *pronoun suffix.* first-person singular
karri *interj.* farther and farther, on and on (Laughren et al. 2007)
wawirri *noun.* red kangaroo, plains kangaroo (Laughren et al. 2007)
parnka (-mi) *verb.* run, fly, dart (Laughren et al. 2007)

The two kangaroos are leaving Yanjiwarra. They sing about their two legs as they run off to the south.

Verse 18 (place)

A *Wujuju wangkaja*
B *Wujuju wangkaja yatingangakarrarra*

A Called out in complaint
B Called out in complaint, calling out from the nest in the tree.

wujuju *preverb.* complaining, protesting (Laughren et al. 2007)
wangka *verb.* speak, talk, say, tell (Laughren et al. 2007)
-ja *verb suffix.* past tense (Laughren et al. 2007)
yardi *noun.* scar, scarification, gash(es), cut(s), cicatrice
ngangkarrarra *noun.* nest (a hole in the side of the tree) (Laughren et al. 2007)
*ngangangamani *preverb.* yak-yak-yak, yakity-yakity-yak, blah-blah- blah (Laughren et al. 2007)
*karrarrarra *preverb.* special call made by mothers at the *Kankarlu* rituals when the initiates are brought out into public view (Laughren et al. 2007)

This is *Kakalyalya Jukurrpa* (Major Mitchell's Cockatoo Dreaming). The ancestral women start their travels on the western side of Pikilyi and then fly to Yumurrpa and then to Tanami. They are at Japangardirranyi on the northern side of Pikilyi.

Verse 19 (traveling)

A *Yarlkinjirrpa*
B *Yurrupa yurrku*

A Up high
B The fat people

yurrupa yurrku *noun.* fat people (Rice and Egan 2008)
*yulyupardi *noun.* fat women (Rice and Egan 2008)
yarlkinjirrpa *noun.* on top, up high (Rice and Egan 2008)

The young ones are helping the fat old women to climb to the top of Pikilyi. They really want to get to the top. They do not want to walk around the hill. This verse is sung when they are climbing other places too.

Verse 20 (place)

A *Yimirta nyarrurrangka nyarrurrangka*
B *Yapata nyarrurrangka nyarrurrangka*

A Tired with aching legs
B Groaning with weakness

yimirta *noun.* veins are throbbing and sticking out from exertion (Rice and Egan 2008)
nyarrurr-wangka *verb.* groan in pain (Laughren et al. 2007)
yapata *adjective.* tired (Laughren et al. 2007)
*yapaja *noun.* expression of pain (Laughren et al. 2007)
nyarrurrangka *noun.* tired (Rice and Egan 2008)
*narrunarru *noun.* weak, hungry, starving (Laughren et al. 2007)

The women are on top of Pikilyi. Their legs are sore from walking, so they sit down by the fire to massage them. There is a big rockhole on top of Pikilyi. The women are placing all the seeds on top. The *warnayarra* snake is underneath—they cannot see it, but it can be heard and felt under the ground. When Rice was working as a stockman, he used to camp there and could hear it moving underneath the ground—it is like thunder.

Verse 21 (place)

A *Minyi ngapangaparla parrakurra kujurnu*
B *Warlu yintiyintirla parrakurra kujurnu*

A Threw the black Acacia seeds in the water toward the sun
B Threw into the heat toward the sun

warlu *noun.* fire, heat (Laughren et al. 2007)
yintiyinti *noun.* heat (Rice and Egan 2008)
-rla *noun suffix.* at, in, on, near (Laughren et al. 2007)
minyi *noun.* little black seeds from an Acacia (Rice and Egan 2008)
*minyi *noun.* wattle, Acacia species (Laughren et al. 2007)
parra *noun.* sunlight, daylight, daytime, day, sun, sunshine (Laughren et al. 2007)
-kurra *noun suffix.* toward, to, into, onto, against (Laughren et al. 2007)
kujurnu *verb.* threw [past tense of *kijirni*] (Rice and Egan 2008)

*kijirni *verb*. throw, propel, toss, project, hurl, pitch, chuck, topple, knock down (Laughren et al. 2007)

ngapa *noun*. water, rain, humidity, raincloud, water source (Laughren et al. 2007)

The women throw all the seeds in the sun to dry, then they mix them with water to make damper. They make little seedcakes called *pirdijirri*. These seeds have a strong smell (*warrkaripiya*). The women are still at Pikilyi.

Verse 22 (place)

A *Ngurrapalangurlu kaninju rdatirla*
B *Yangungu kurrangka yangungu kurrangka*

A Sitting quietly inside the cave at Ngurrapala
B Echoing around, echoing around

Ngurrapalangu *proper noun*. place on top of Pikilyi (lit. "bed-two," two grooves in the rock where the kangaroos sleep) (Rice and Egan 2008)
kaninju *noun*. deep inside (Rice and Egan 2008)
*kaninjarra *noun*. inside and under, down under, below, within (Laughren et al. 2007)
rdatirla *noun*. sitting around (Rice and Egan 2008)
*rdatu *noun*. quiet, well behaved, not causing trouble, not instigating a fight, retiring (Laughren et al. 2007)
-rla *noun suffix*. at, in, on, near (Laughren et al. 2007)
yangungu *noun*. echo (Rice and Egan 2008)
-kurra *noun suffix*. while, when, as (Rice and Egan 2008)
-ngka *noun suffix*. while, when, then, at (time) (Laughren et al. 2007)

The women are inside the cave at Ngurrapalangu on top of Pikilyi, eating seeds, talking, and dancing.

Verse 23 (place)

A *Ngurrangurra punju*
B *Kujarrala*

A Two camps at the rockhole
B Two kangaroos

ngurra *noun*. camp, home, residence (Laughren et al. 2007)
Ngurrangurrapunju *proper noun*. big rockhole on top of Pikilyi (Rice and Egan 2008)

ngurrangurrapunju *noun.* when they hollow out a bit of soil to sleep in (like in the old days when there were no swags) (Rice and Egan 2008)
kujarrala (kuyujarra in spoken Warlpiri) *noun.* the two kangaroos

The women leave the two kangaroos where they lie at Ngurrapalangu. The women are leaving Pikilyi now. This is a sacred site. There are two grooves in the rock where the kangaroos slept.

Verse 24 (traveling)

A *Walyarna pinaru wapa*
B *Jurrmarlinjirna*

A I am throwing up the soil as I move
B I am dancing shake-a-leg style

walya *noun.* ground, earth, land (Laughren et al. 2007)
-rna *suffix.* first-person singular subject suffix (Laughren et al. 2007)
pinaru *verb.* throwing up soil (Rice and Egan 2008)
wapa *verb.* move, slither, crawl (Laughren et al. 2007); shuffle feet along the soil without lifting them (Rice and Egan 2008)
jurrmalinji- *noun.* shake-a-leg style dancing (Rice and Egan 2008)
*jurrmurl-jurrmurl(pa) *preverb.* convulsing, shaking, in a fit, in a spasm (Laughren et al. 2007)
*-nji *noun suffix.* characteristic: having the property, quality denoted by a noun; associated with or effected by the event, state, or process denoted by infinitive (Laughren et al. 2007)
-rna *suffix.* first-person singular subject suffix

The women alternate their dance style, first throwing up soil as they shuffle their feet along the ground, then dancing shake-a-leg style. They leave Pikilyi, coming down the hill.

Verse 25 (traveling)

A *Talkinji tarritarri warra*
B *Turlpanji tarritarri warra*

A The tall women are dancing around
B Red ochred legs moving around

talkinji *noun.* tall (Rice and Egan 2008)
turlpanji [yurlpa-nji] *noun.* having red ochre (Rice and Egan 2008)
tarritarri *noun.* long legs (Rice and Egan 2008)
warra [wapa] *verb.* move (Laughren et al. 2007)

All the tall women are putting *yurlpa* on themselves and on their *waluwarnu*, etc. They are singing about themselves, their long legs moving as they dance. They are still at Pikilyi, but now at the bottom on the eastern side.

Verse 26 (traveling)

A *Watijiyimarurla (ya)*
B *Ngaru wilyiwilyi (ya)*

A In the dense mulga scrub
B Ripe Bush tomatoes growing everywhere

wardiji *noun.* mulga (Laughren et al. 2007)
maru *noun.* ripe, really green, lush (cannot see things clearly because of the overgrowth (Rice and Egan 2008)
*maru *noun.* black, dark color of (Laughren et al. 2007); ripe, really green, dark green and lush, can't really see things very well because it's so green
-rla *noun suffix.* at, on, with (Laughren et al. 2007)
ngaru *noun.* Bush tomato, Wild tomato (Laughren et al. 2007)
wilyiwilyi *noun.* abundant (Rice and Egan 2008)
*wilyirrki *noun.* visible, able to be seen, exposed, revealed, not hidden, uncovered, bare
(ya). added for an extra syllable when they are singing (Rice and Egan 2008)

There are bush tomatoes everywhere, like at a farm. There are different ways of singing this verse. Thomas sang it like this:

A Watijarntakurlka (ya)– can see through a little bit
B Ngaru wilyiwilyi (ya)–ripe *warnakiji*

A *kajalarra* (scoop, scraper) is used to clean the black seeds from bush tomatoes (*wanakiji*). If you eat them, you can go blind. The women are traveling between Pikilyi and Yurnmaji.

Verse 27 (traveling)
Version 1
A *Ngiji juturrungkarni*
B *Juturrungkarni*

A The firesticks in a row pushing up the soil
B In a row pushing up the soil

Version 2
A *Jangiyi juturrungkarni*
B *Juturrungkarni*

ngiji *noun*. firestick, piece of burning wood, flaming stick, torch (Pintupi word) (Laughren et al. 2007)
jangiyi *noun*. firestick, piece of burning word, flaming stick, torch (Warlpiri word) (Laughren et al. 2007)
juturrungkarni *verb*. pushing up the soil as they dance in a row (Rice and Egan 2008)
jangiyi *noun*. firestick (Rice and Egan 2008)

The women are all dressed up. They have *ngamirdangamirdi* (circular combs), and they have put *yininti* (bean seeds) in their hair, as well as hanging *waluwarnu* (headbands) and *jinjirla* (white tips of bilby tails that women once wore in their headbands). In the *Jukurrpa*, everyone had firesticks, and they danced in a big line with others behind them. The mothers-in-law, fathers' sisters and mothers danced with firesticks in lines in the middle. The women behind them held their waists. The *rdiliwarnu* (cousins), sisters, and both grandmothers (father's mother and mother's mother) dance on the sides with no firesticks. The mothers-in-law who dance with the firesticks are promising their daughters to the boy whose firestick they are holding. They are at Yurnmaji.

Verse 28 (place)

A *Wakurlunjarri wilyarri wulya (ya)*
B *Wakurlunjarri linjalja (ya)*

A They have long hair.
B They have short hair.

wakurlu *noun*. head hair (Laughren et al. 2007)
-njarri *pluralizer*. denotes lots (Laughren et al. 2007)
wilyarri wulya *noun*. long hair (Rice and Egan 2008)
linjalja *noun*. short (Rice and Egan 2008)

This verse is about the women combing their (long or short) hair (with a *ngamirdingamirdi* or a *pimirdipimirdi*) and making themselves pretty. Anmatyerre people perform this verse too. Men also used to have long hair, which they would tie in a *pukardi*. They would wear a headband made of emu feathers at the hairline. The women throw their hands alternately behind their head when they dance for this verse. They are at Yurnmaji (although they also sing this verse at Yinintiwarrkuwarrku).

Verse 29 (traveling)

A *Karntawurrurlparna parlintirri*
B *Yati nganjalalyanganja*

A I am a woman dancing low in defense
B A long spear with hairstring

yatinganjalyanganja *noun.* long spear with hairstring wound around it and feathers hanging from the end [syn. *wirriji*] (Rice and Egan 2008)
parlintirri *noun.* the way they are standing holding the spears out in front of them to stop from being hit (Rice and Egan 2008)
*parlintirri *noun.* club, in a defensive position (Laughren et al. 2007)
karnta *noun.* woman (Laughren et al. 2007)
wurrurl(pa) *preverb.* low, out of sight (Laughren et al. 2007)
-rna *noun suffix.* first-person singular subject suffix

At *Kirrirdikirrawarnu* in the morning, there is a spear with *wirriji* (hairstring). The mothers give food to the boys to take into the bush. The boys give their mothers-in-law the *wirriji* (or *purduru*). At the end of the all-night section of *Marnakurrawarnu*, the *juka* put it in the middle of the group until morning and then the mothers-in-law give it to the fathers. Nowadays, they do not do this because they do not have *Kirrardikirrawarnu* anymore. They just give it straight to the fathers. All the mothers and fathers' sisters dance in a line while holding a *karlangu* (digging stick) in front of them for this verse.

Verse 30 (traveling/business)

Version 1
A *Wurrumpu parntirninya*
B *Ngarnampu parntirninya*

A There it is hidden
B Desired to come up

Version 2
A *Wurrumpu partirninya*
B *Lanji marramarra lungkarrungka*

wurrumpu *noun.* lance, stabbing spear (Laughren et al. 2007); hidden (it is light but cannot see the sun yet) (Rice and Egan 2008)
pantirni *verb.* pierce, stick into, prick, jab, stab, poke, spear, sting, puncture, peck (Laughren et al. 2007)
ngarnampu *verb.* wanting (Rice and Egan 2008)
*ngarnungarnu *noun.* desired
marramarra *noun.* wings, flapping wings (Laughren et al. 2007)

This verse is sung to make the daylight come more quickly. When singers get tired, they sing this verse to bring the sun up. All the women click their fingers and point to the east while they dance. They are at Yurnmaji (although they also sing this verse at Yuluwurru).

Verse 31 (place)

A *Wirangkurlurla rdanjiwirnparanya*
B *Yanangkurlurlu rdanjiwirnparanya*

A Hanging off their bodies at Wirangkurlu
B The old women are hanging down

Wirangkurlu *proper noun.* place [lit. hanging down] (Rice and Egan 2008)
-rla *noun suffix.* in, at, on, with (Laughren et al. 2007)
yanangkurlurlu *noun.* old women (*muturna*) (Rice and Egan 2008)
*yangarlu *noun.* alone, by oneself (Laughren et al. 2007)
rdanjiwirnpa *preverb.* stomachs, breasts, sagging skin is hanging down off the bodies of the old women (Rice and Egan 2008)
*rdanjarrpa *preverb.* loaded, amassed, laden, large quantity, big load (Laughren et al. 2007)

At Wirangkurlurla the ancestral women leave the oldest members of their group. The old women's bodies are weighing them down such that they cannot continue to travel or dance.

Verse 32 (traveling)

A *Wirangkurlu nampunampu*
B *Wirangkurlu wintijarna*

A The thud of Wirangkurlu
B I danced at Wirangkurlu

Wirangkurlu *proper noun.* place [hanging down] (Rice and Egan 2008)
wirntija *verb.* danced (*wirnti+ja*) (Laughren et al. 2007)
-rna *noun suffix.* first-person singular subject suffix (Laughren et al. 2007)
nampunampu *noun.* heavy thud on the ground as they dance (Rice and Egan 2008)
*ngampungampu *noun.* sprightly, lively, brisk (Laughren et al. 2007)

The old women are too heavy to dance properly. As they attempt to dance in a row they lean on their *karlangu*, which they place in the ground in front of them to support their bodies. They try to dance, but the others hold them down. Nowadays, old women who are too fat are ashamed to dance, but in the *Jukurrpa* they were not. They are at Wirangkurlu.

Verse 33 (place)

A *Ngipiri ngarnungarnu*
B *Warapija*

A Desiring the eggs
B Moving around

ngipiri *noun*. egg (Laughren et al. 2007)
ngarnungarnu *noun*. highly desirable, craved for, lusted after, highly prized, an entity that people fight and kill in order to possess (Laughren et al. 2007)
warapija *verb*. move around (Rice and Egan 2008)

A python from Yarliyumpu came to Ngipiri and ate all the little snake eggs. Little rockholes on a flat rock appear there today (*panma*). Then the python went north to Palkurda before returning to Yarliyumpu. This is an Anmatyerre story. When the mother snakes came back and found their eggs missing, they began to fight with each other.

Verse 34 (place)

A *Ngurra jangiyi pirlirli*
B *Wari jangiyi manta*

A At home, the rock has a firestick
B Get on it, without the firestick

wari *noun*. fire, firestick (possibly Pintupi) (Laughren et al. 2007)
jangiyi *noun*. firestick (Rice and Egan 2008)
manta *preverb*. absent (Laughren et al. 2007)
ngurra *noun*. home (it was a swamp) (Laughren et al. 2007)
pirli *noun*. stone, rock, pebble, mountain, hill (Laughren et al. 2007)
-rli *case suffix*. ergative case suffix (Laughren et al. 2007

Wirdangurla is singing again. He leaves the group of women at Warnayurlpa and travels to a big rockhole just north of Wanayurlpa where he sings this verse. He dances with a firestick, copying the women. From here, he goes north through Wijilpa and Warnpirrki to Wakurlpa. At Ngarnawilpiri, all the Napaljarris and Nungarrayis from Wakurlpa kill him with their digging sticks because he is trying to rape them as they urinate. Warijangiyi is also the name of the place where this happens. A Palkurda there is a white rock.

Verse 35 (place)

A *Ngapiyataka yataparrkara*
B *Waraparrpa karrinya*

A Standing with crossed legs at the red river gums
B Farther and farther into the bump

ngapiri *noun*. red river gum (Laughren et al. 2007)
yataparrkara *noun*. two crossed legs (the way the women stand when they get *yipilanji*) (Rice and Egan 2008)
waraparrpa *noun*. the bump that the *yipilanji* make under the bark, there is a hole inside where the *yipilanji* sits—it eats the bark away to form the hole and turns the wood yellow (Rice and Egan 2008)
*wara-paarr-paarr(pa) *preverb*. restricting, restraining, keeping for oneself (Laughren et al. 2007)
karri-. farther and farther, on and on (Laughren et al. 2007)
-nya *verb suffix*. presentative suffix

The ancestral women are singing about the witchetty grubs that live in a hole in the side of the Ngapiri tree. They are called *yipilanji* and are pink and white. The women rush to get them with their *karlangu* and *narngu* (a stick with a small hook on it). They stand with their legs crossed when they collect them.

Verse 36 (place)

A *Yanakirri jantarra*
B *Nyarla panturru*

A Searching for frogs
B Escaping downward

yanakirri *noun*. estivating frog (Laughren et al. 2007); big, fat, edible frogs (Rice and Egan 2008)
nyarla *noun*. downward (Rice and Egan 2008)
panturru *verb*. the frogs are burrowing down (getting away from the women), making a hole downward (Rice and Egan 2008)
*panturni *verb*. extract, pull out, extricate, take out from, remove from, get out of, gut (Laughren et al. 2007)
*parntu-pinyi *verb*. get the better of, win, conquer (Laughren et al. 2007)
jantarra *verb*. kneeling down (Laughren et al. 2007)
janta *preverb*. sharing, distributing, lending (Laughren et al. 2007)

The *yanakirri* frogs are everywhere. They go down into the ground in the sandhills, sometimes one meter deep. The women are getting them with their digging sticks. This verse is tricky to sing. The place is called Jarlji.

Verse 37 (traveling)

A *Waparlaku karrimarnkarra*
B *Karrimarnkarrimarnkarra*

A Dancing in a line, holding on to each other from behind
B Holding on to each other from behind

waparlaku *verb.* holding on to waist or shoulders (Rice and Egan 2008)
*waparla *noun.* disappeared (Laughren et al. 2007)
karrimarnkarra *verb.* standing behind each other in a line (Rice and Egan 2008)

The old women are standing in the front of the line, and the younger ones are behind them. They are at Pangkunaparnta, at the bottom of Pikilyi.

Verse 38 (traveling)

A *Yinirnti jilpirri jilpi (ya)*
B *Yinirnti nanparri nanparrirna (ya)*

A Cupped hands full of *yinirnti*
B The *yinirnti* seeds are making a noise

yinirnti *noun.* bean tree, bat's wing coral tree, seeds of bean tree (Laughren et al. 2007)
jilpirri *verb.* dancing with cupped hands with big handfuls of *yinirnti* necklaces shaking up and down (Rice and Egan 2008)
*jilypirri *verb.* crowded into, fill up, fill to capacity (Laughren et al. 2007)
nanparri *noun.* sound made by necklaces (Rice and Egan 2008)
-rna *noun suffix.* first-person singular subject suffix (Laughren et al. 2007)

The women are dancing with *yinirnti* everywhere—on their waists, hands, necks, and head. They are cupping their hands so that the *yinirnti* gather to make a sound as they hit against each other. The *yinirnti* are strung together on hairstring (*yinirnti larlka*). They are at Pangkunaparnta.

Verse 39 (traveling)

A *Yarrilkinjirrpa*
B *Yurrpayurrku*

A Climbing up high
B The old women

yurrpayurrku *noun*. old women (Rice and Egan 2008)
yarrilkinjirrpa *noun*. up high, on top (Rice and Egan 2008)

The big women are keen to climb up—they really want to go up instead of walking around. They are climbing up Warnipiyi.

Verse 40 (place)

A *Wipiya wipiya rdijipiya*
B *Ngarnkirrinya kutakuta rduluya*

A Stretching out as set alight
B Struggling toward the hole near the creek's edge.

wipiya *verb*. extend out, stretch out, radiate, go out from (Laughren et al. 2007)
rdiji *preverb*. firing, setting fire to, lighting, igniting (Laughren et al. 2007)
ngarnkirri *noun*. brow, deep washout, gorge, steep gully, sharp edge, ridge, steep bank, steep slope (Laughren et al. 2007)
kutakuta [rdakukurra] *noun*. hole + toward (*noun suffix*) (Laughren et al. 2007)
rduluya *verb*. struggling (Rice and Egan 2008)
*rdultu *preverb*. display of anger (Laughren et al. 2007)

This verse is about Japanangka, the crow, being burned. First the ancestral women sing about him sitting on the hill watching the ceremony. But the crow is captured by a Jampijinpa and a Jangala from Warnipiyi who had joined up with the Kunajarrayi women to travel east, and they blindfold Japanangka. They take him to the creek and dig a hole where they light a fire. They throw him in the fire as he is so evil. As Japanangka burns, a swarm of crows comes out of the fire. All the crows today come from the creek near Wangala.

Verse 41 (place)

A *Wangalarlanjirringirli nyina jarlarra pata*
B *Yanurrupungurlu nyina jarlarra pata*

A Coming from the place of the crow, sitting down
B Getting things, sitting down

Wangala *noun*. crow, place name (Laughren et al. 2007)
-rla *noun suffix*. on, at, in

-ngirli/-ngurlu *noun suffix.* from, away from (Laughren et al. 2007)
nyina *verb.* sit (Laughren et al. 2007)
*yanurrpu *noun.* coolamon, water carrier (Laughren et al. 2007)
*jarlardapu *noun.* hot-tempered person, bossy, overbearing, speechless with anger (Laughren et al. 2007)

Japanangka is sitting on top of the hill at Wangala watching all the women doing *Kurdiji*. Japangardi from Mount Theo passes the crow, but he doesn't stop because he is too focused on finding Nungarrayi. Japanangka is the owner of this country, so they bring him lots of food as payment for having the ceremony there. He watches a Napaljarri, stretching around and showing off as crows do so that she will notice him. She is getting shamed in front of the group because he keeps looking at her. He sits up at the ceremony like Anmatyerr and Papunya do, facing the women a bit so he can watch Napaljarri. He has one hand over his head so no one can tell that he is watching her. When they finish, everyone walks off. Japanangka holds on to Napaljarri's dog and pretends to tell it to go even though he knows it can't because he is holding it. When Napaljarri comes back to get the dog, Japanangka grabs her and sleeps with her.

Verse 42 (place)

A *Larnkatipi kanpirriya*
B *Larnkajarra pajurrima*

A Two crossed legs with emu fat
B Two legs, two knees

larnka *noun.* long legs (Rice and Egan 2008)
-jarra *noun suffix.* dual (Laughren et al. 2007)
kanpi *noun.* animal fat, emu fat (Laughren et al. 2007)
tipi *noun.* crossed legs (so they can get up and run really fast) (Rice and Egan 2008)
pajurrima *noun.* two knees crossed over (Rice and Egan 2008)

The ancestral women are singing about how the emus are standing at Rdukirri with their legs crossed over. All women and men performing the ceremony are on one side, and the emus are standing around in a semicircle watching them as they travel past. These emus are from Ngarna and Rdukirri. They also watch the fire from the Warlukurlangu Jukurrpa. They are at Mirdirdijarra (west from Ngarna).

Verse 43 (place)

A *Mirdijirijirirla*
B *Malantakurra lantirni japa*

A At Mirdirdijarra
B Sharp nails scratch as they move along

mirdi *noun*. knee (Laughren et al. 2007); rough leatherlike skin (Rice and Egan 2007)
-jarra *noun suffix*. dual (Laughren et al. 2007)
Mirdijirijiri (Mirdirdijarra) *proper noun*. place name; the Emu Dreaming travels through here (Rice and Egan 2008)
-rla *noun suffix*. locative case suffix (Laughren et al. 2007)
malanta *noun*. sharp nails of emu's foot (Rice and Egan 2008)
*malantarrpa *noun*. Sandhill wattle (Laughren et al. 2007)
lantirni japa *verb*. scratching the ground while moving (Rice and Egan 2008)
*larrjirni *verb*. claw, scratch, maul, rip into (Laughren et al. 2007)
*wapa *verb*. move (Laughren et al. 2007)

They emus' nails are sharp, and their legs have rough skin. The ancestral women sing about the skin on the legs and the sharp nails of the emus. They have traveled from Wawurrwawurrpa in the east through Yarliyumu.

Verse 44 (place)

A *Mirdijintilyiyirna*
B *Parrarna yangkurrngurla*

A I am two legs
B I am the daylight in the green vegetation

parra *noun*. daytime, sunlight, day, sun, sunshine (Laughren et al. 2007)
yangkurrngu [from mungkurrmungkurrpa] *noun*. green vegetation (Rice and Egan 2008)
mungkurrmungkurrpa *noun*. bush fan flower (Laughren et al. 2007)
*yangkurl(pa) *noun*. habitat, nest, burrow, hole, perch, place, resting place (Laughren et al. 2007)
-rla *noun suffix*. locative case suffix (Laughren et al. 2008)
mirdi *noun*. knee (Laughren et al. 2007); rough skin (Rice and Egan 2008)
mirriji *noun*. legs (Laughren et al. 2007)
-rna *noun suffix*. first-person subject singular suffix (Laughren et al. 2008)

The ancestral women go into a jungle with a lot of grass. Here they can only see the rough legs of the emus. *Mungkurrmungkurrpa* is the green food that the emus eat. The emus walk around looking for this food and eat it when they find it.

Verse 45 (traveling)

A *Yarrajipirli*
B *Yarrajipirli ngipipurla ngara*

A At Yarranjipirli
B A dense forest of mulga trees

Yarranjipirli *proper name*. place name, country with lots of *yalpilyardu* trees (broadleaf variety of *Mulga Acacia aneura*, similar to the scrub to at Yuwalinji) (Rice and Egan 2008)
*yarrajipi *noun*. edible grass seed (Laughren et al. 2007)
ngipipu *noun*. (syn. *yuwurrku*) thick trees (Rice and Egan 2008)
-rla *noun suffix*. at, on, in, with (Laughren et al. 2007)

The ancestral women are singing about the scrub around Yarranjirrpirli. It is country with lots of *yalpiyaru* trees (a type of mulga). This place has the same scrub as Yuwalinji. Rice said they can sing this verse for Yuwalinji too, like this:

Yuwalinjirli
Yuwalinjirli ngipipurla ngara

Verse 46 (place)

A *Ngapakurla jurarri jurarri ngunanya*
B *Ngapakurla parla wamu-ngunanya*

A There in the water, streams lying around
B There in the water, leafy branches lying around

ngapa *noun*. water (Laughren et al. 2007)
-ku *noun suffix*. for (Laughren et al. 2007)
-rla *noun suffix*. dative pronoun enclitic (Laughren et al. 2007)
jurarri *verb*. making tracks, running along, streams (Rice and Egan 2008)
*jurajura *preverb*. drag along the ground (Laughren et al. 2007)
nguna *verb*. lie (Laughren et al. 2007)
-nya *verb suffix*. presentative suffix (Laughren et al. 2007)

parla *noun.* leaf, foliage, leafy branches, small plant, bush (Laughren et al. 2007)

wamu-ngunanya *verb.* lying dark

The *Ngapa Jukurrpa* from Wardalpunyu comes through here. It travels alongside the *Karntakarnta* mob for awhile. They are also going to Yurnkuru.

Verse 47 (place)

A *Walyaramarrirla marrirla*
B *Walyara jangijirna ngurla*

A At Walyaramarri
B I am belonging to the ground

Walyaramarri *proper noun.* place name (Rice and Egan 2008)
-rla *noun suffix.* locative suffix (Laughren et al. 2007); *jangiji* belonging to (Rice and Egan 2008)

The ancestral women are dancing just before Yurnkuru. This is now Anmatyerr country. They are at a place called Walyaramarri, just west of Yurnkuru

Verse 48 (place)

Version 1
A *Yuluwurru rdajiwarnpungu*
B *Rdajiwarnpungu*

A Getting tired at Yuluwurru
B Tiredness

Version 2
A *Wirriwirri rdajiwarnpungu*
B *Rdajiwarnpungu*

A Slumping down with tiredness
B Tiredness

Yuluwurru *proper noun.* place name, salt lake (Lake Lewis) (Rice and Egan 2008)
wirriwirri *noun.* tired, slumping down (Rice and Egan 2008)
*wirri *preverb.* escaping, breaking away from (Laughren et al. 2007)
rdajiwarnpungu *noun.* tired, headachy, weak (*rdalinpardalinirli nyina*) (Rice and Egan 2008)

The ancestral women are getting tired at Yuluwurru.

Verse 49 (traveling)

A *Walarakuraku walarakuraku wirnpirla*
B *Wakumintirrirla wakumintirrirla wirnpirla*

A Dancing low down in the soft sand
B Dancing low down, arms joined

walarra *noun.* soft sand, loose earth (Laughren et al. 2007)
waku *noun.* arm (Rice and Egan 2008)
wirnpirla *noun.* low dance with heads down (Rice and Egan 2008)
wiirnpirnpa *preverb.* shaking, vibrating, to and fro, jiggling, moving, swaying (Laughren et al. 2007)

The ancestral women are dancing with their fingers hooked to each other. Some of them dance like this and some dance with a coolamon or a dancing board. They are dancing in no order, mixed up. At times they dance like this in Mount Allan.

Glossary

jaja: maternal grandmother (mother's mother), granduncle (mother's mother's brother), or grandchild (daughter's child)

Jakamarra: male subsection name

jamirdikipungu: mother's father

Jampijinpa: male subsection name

Jangala: male subsection name

Japanangka: male subsection name

Japangardi: male subsection name

Japaljarri: male subsection name

Jardiwanpa: name of a conflict-resolution ceremony

Jarnamiljarnpa: generation moiety of speaker's parents or children

jarrardili: elder brothers of an initiand, Northern Warlpiri word for

jarrawarnu: Australian magpie-lark, mud lark; *name for elder brothers of an initiand or the elder siblings of a deceased person

jilkaja: initiation travel, initiation travelers, "business mob"

jinpurrmanu: the high-pitched sound made by mothers, fathers' sisters, and mothers-in-law while they dance during a *Kurdiji* ceremony, also refers to the group of women who are in the opposite generation moiety to the initiand

juka: ritual guardian, initiates brother-in-law (sister's husband)

jukana: (female) cross-cousin (father's sister's daughter, mother's brother's daughter)

Jukurrpa: Dreaming, dream, creational moment

Jupurrurla: male subsection term

juyurdu: powerful incantation, evil spell, murderer's song

Jungarrayi: male subsection term

Kajirri: a ceremony associated with initiation in northern Warlpiri regions

kana: digging stick, yam stick

kaninjarra: inside, down, underneath, downward, way down in

kankarlu: high, up, upper, top, outer

Kankarlu: religious festivals in the past held as part of initiatory rites

kardiya: non-Aboriginal, European, white person

karlangu: digging stick

karnta: woman

karntakurlangu: belonging to women

karntamipa: exclusively for women

kirda: father, paternal uncle, father's brother, father's sister, paternal aunt (used in this book mainly to refer to the people who have inherited ownership of Dreamings, country and ceremonies from their father's side)

Kirrirdikirrawarnu: initiation ceremony, in the past held on the second night after *Kurdiji*

kumunjayi: no-name, taboo, name used for those whose name is the same or similar to that of someone who has recently deceased

Kunapipi: ceremonial name for an initiatory rite held in Arnhem Land (described by Berndt 1951)

Kura-kurra: name of a conflict-resolution ceremony

kurdaitcha: spooky being, monster, revenge killer

Kurdiji: ceremonial name for initiatory rites

kurdungurlu: maternal kin, *used in this book mainly to refer to the people who inherit managerial rites to Dreamings, country, and ceremonies

kuyukirda: Dreaming of father's mother and her patriline

kuyuwapirra: Dreaming of father's father and his patriline

kuyuwurruru: Dreaming of mother's mother and her patriline

kuyuyarriki: Dreaming of mother's father and his patriline

lampanilyka: maternal uncle, maternal nephew

Malamala: "Sorry business," "Sorry meeting," bereavement ceremony, mourning rite

Marnakurrawarnu: part of initiation ground, ceremonial name

marrkarilyka: co-initiate in brother-in-law's (wife's brother's) subsection

milarlpa: sprites, spirit people

Nakamarra: female subsection term

Nangala: female subsection term

Nampijinpa: female subsection term

Napaljarri: female subsection term

Napanangka: female subsection term

Napangardi: female subsection term

Napurrurla: female subsection term

Ngaliya: Southern Warlpiri

Ngajakula: conflict-resolution ceremony

Ngapa Jukurrpa: Rain Dreaming

ngarnarntarrka: own generation moiety

ngarrmarilyka: cross-cousin

ngarrmirni: increase ceremony (directed at a specific circumstance)

ngunjungunju: white ochre

ngurlu: seeds, grain

Nungarrayi: female subsection term

nyurnukurlangu: a type of *yawulyu* sung for healing

pardinjalpa: plant species used to make a strong-scented tea for healing colds

parnpa: increase ceremony, men's corroboree, Dreaming rituals

parraja: coolamon, shallow dish

pukurdi: pointed headdress

Puluwanti: name of conflict-resolution ceremony, barn owl

purlapa: corroboree, dance, ritual performance, song, singing

purrpu-pakarni: clap (at crotch), beat time on lap, beat rhythm on lap

purunyungu: hidden away, concealed, used to refer to initiands when they are secluded in the bush

rdiliwarnu: senior brother, senior sister

wajamirnilyka: co-initiate in subsection of uncle-in-law (wife's mother's brother), great-grandfather (mother's mother's father), or great-grand-nephew (sister's daughter's daughter's son)

wampana: spectacled hare-wallaby

wapirralyka: co-initiate in father's subsection

Warawata: ceremony held directly prior to the circumcision of the initiates

Warlukurlangu: Fire Dreaming (literally: fire+belonging)

Warnayaka: Northern Warlpiri

warringiyi: paternal grandfather, paternal grand aunt, father's father, father's father's brother, father's father's sister, grandchild (man's son's child), grandnephew (brother's

son's son), grandniece (brother's son's daughter)

warungka: deaf, hard of hearing, *senile, *mad, crazy, *ignorant

watikirlangu: belonging to men

watimipa: exclusively for men

wati-rirri-rirri: person in authority, person able to commence ceremonies, ceremonial boss, respected person, leader, boss, knowledgeable (especially for ceremonies) person

wirikirlangu: belonging to businesspeople

wirntimi: dance, hover

Yalpari: particular group of Warlpiri people

yankirri: emu

yapa: Aboriginal people

yarlpurru: co-initiates, age mates, people of same age

yarlpurru-kurlangu: belonging to initiates

yarripiri: inland Taipan snake

yawulyu: women's ritual, women's ceremonies, women's songs, women's ritual performances, women's ritual designs, women's dancing

yilpinji: love songs, love charms, love magic

yinirnti: bean tree, a small bean used to make necklaces for ceremonial dancing

yinjakurrku: firestick, burning torch

yulpurru: parents and great-grandparents of the initiates

yunparni: sing

yurlpa: red ochre

yurrampi: honey ant

References

Austin J. L. 1975 [1962]. *How to Do Things with Words*. Cambridge, MA: Harvard University Press.
Australian Bureau of Statistics. 2006. Community Profile Series: Indigenous Profile, Yuendumu (CGC) (IARE 22007). Catalogue No. 2002.0. Canberra: Commonwealth of Australia.
Barwick L. 1989. "Creative (Ir)regularities: The Intermeshing of Text and Melody in Performance of Central Australian Song." *Australian Aboriginal Studies* 1: 12–28.
Barwick L., A. Marett, and G. Tunstill, eds. 1995. *The Essence of Singing and the Substance of Song*. Sydney: University of Sydney.
Barwick L., and A. Marett. 1995. "Introduction." In *The Essence of Singing and the Substance of Song*, edited by L. Barwick, A. Marett, and G. Tunstill, 1–10. Sydney: University of Sydney.
Bateson, G. 1972. *Steps to an Ecology of Mind: Collected Essays in Anthropology, Psychiatry, Evolution, and Epistemology*. Chicago: University of Chicago Press.
Bauman, R. 1975. "Verbal Art as Performance." *American Anthropologist*, New Series 77: 290–311.
Bell D. 1983. *Daughters of the Dreaming*. Sydney: McPhee Gribble/George Allen Unwin.
Bern J., and J. Larbalestier. 1985. "Rival Constructions of Traditional Aboriginal Ownership in the Limmen Bight Land Claim." *Oceania* 56: 56–76.
Berndt, C. 1950. "Women's Changing Ceremonies in Northern Australia." *L'homme* 1: 1–87.
Berndt, R. M. 1951. *Kunapipi: A Study of an Australian Aboriginal Religious Cult*. Melbourne: Cheshire.
———. 1952. *Djanggawul: An Aboriginal Religious Cult of North-Eastern Arnhem Land*. Melbourne. Cheshire.
Biddle, J. 2019. "Milpirri: Activating the At-Risk." In *Energies in the Arts*, edited by D. Kahn. Cambridge: MIT Press.
Birdsell, J. B. 1993. *Microevolutionary Patterns in Aboriginal Australia: A Gradient Analysis of Clines*. Oxford: Oxford University Press.

Bloch, M. 1974. "Symbols, Song, Dance and Features of Articulation: Is Religion an Extreme form of Traditional Authority?" *European Journal of Sociology* 15: 55–81.

Bourdieu, P. 1977. *Outline of a Theory of Practice*. Cambridge: Cambridge University Press.

Briggs, C. L., and R. Bauman. 1992. "Genre, Intertextuality and Social Power." *Journal of Linguistic Anthropology* 2(2): 131–72.

Burke P. 2018. *An Australian Indigenous Diaspora: Warlpiri Matriarchs and the Refashioning of Tradition*. New York: Berghahn Books.

Clunies Ross, M. 1982. "The Song Series Djambidj." In *Djambidj: An Aboriginal Song Series from Northern Australia*, edited by M. Clunies Ross and S. A. Wild. Canberra: Australian Institute of Aboriginal Studies.

Clunies Ross, M. 1983. "Modes of Formal Performance in Societies without Writing: The Case of Aboriginal Australia." *Australian Aboriginal Studies* 1: 18–26.

———. 1987. "Research into Aboriginal Songs: The State of the Art." In *Songs of Aboriginal Australia*, edited by M. Clunies Ross, T. Donaldson, S. A. Wild, 1–13. Sydney: University of Sydney Press.

Clunies Ross M., T. Donaldson, and S. A. Wild (eds.). 1987. *Songs of Aboriginal Australia*. Sydney: University of Sydney Press.

Curran, G. 2010. "Linguistic Imagery in Warlpiri Songs: Some Examples of Metaphor, Metonymy and Image-Schema in Minamina Yawulyu." *Australian Journal of Linguistics* 30: 105–15.

———. 2013. "The Dynamics of Collaborative Research Relationships: Examples from the Warlpiri Songlines Project." *Collaborative Anthropologies* 6: 353–72.

———. 2016. "Travelling Ancestral Women: Connecting Warlpiri People and Places through Songs." In *Language, Land and Story: Essays in Honour of Luise Hercus*, edited by P. Austin, J. Simpson, and H. Koch. London: EL Publishing.

———. 2019. "'Waiting for Jardiwanpa': History and Mediation in Warlpiri Fire Ceremonies." *Oceania* 89(1): 20–35.

Curran, G., M. Turpin, L. Barwick, and F. Walsh. 2019. "Central Australia Aboriginal Songs and Ecological Knowledge: Evidence from Women's Ceremonies Relating to Edible Seeds." *Journal for Ethnobiology* 39(3): 354–370.

Dail-Jones, M. 1982. "Movements to Live by for the Warlpiri Women of Central Australia." Paper presented to the Australian Anthropological Society annual meeting, Canberra.

———. 1984. "A Culture in Motion: A Study of the Interrelationship of Dancing, Sorrowing, Hunting, and Fighting as Performed by the Warlpiri Women of Central Australia." MA thesis. Honolulu: University of Hawaii.

Dixon, R. M. W., and M. Duwell (eds.). 1990. *The Honeyant Men's Love Song and Other Aboriginal Song Poems*. St. Lucia: University of Queensland Press.

Donaldson, T. 1979. "Translating Oral Literature: Aboriginal Song Texts." *Aboriginal History* 3: 62–83.

———. 1984. "Kids That Got Lost: Variation in the Words of Ngiyampaa Songs." In *Problems and Solutions: Occasional Essays in Musicology presented to Alice M. Moyle*, edited by J. C. Kassler and J. Stubbington, 229–53. Sydney: Hale and Iremonger Pty. Ltd.

Donaldson T. 1995. "Mixes of English and Ancestral Language Words in Southeast Australian Aboriginal Songs of Traditional and Introduced Origin." In *The Essence of Singing and the Substance of Song*, edited by L. Barwick, A. Marett, G. Tunstill, 143–58. Sydney: University of Sydney.

Dussart, F. 2000. *The Politics of Ritual in an Aboriginal Settlement: Kinship, Gender and the Currency of Knowledge*. Washington, DC: Smithsonian Institution Press.

———. 2003. "The Engendering of Ceremonial Knowledge between (and among) Warlpiri Women and Men in the Australian Central Desert." In *Values and Valuables: From the Sacred to the Symbolic*, edited by C. Werner, D. Bell, 49–63. Washington, DC: American Anthropological Association and Altamira Press.

———. 2004. "Shown but Not Shared, Presented but Not Preferred: Redefining Ritual Identity among Warlpiri Ritual Performers, 1990–2000." *Australian Journal of Anthropology* 15(3): 253–67.

Elkin, A. 1970. "The Aborigines of Australia: One in Word, Thought and Deed." In *Pacific Linguistics Studies in Honour of Arthur Capell*, edited by S. A. Wurm and D. C. Laycock, 697–718. Canberra: Pacific Linguistics.

Ellis, C. 1963. "Ornamentation in Australian Vocal Music." *Ethnomusicology* 7(2): 88–95.

———. 1966. "Central and South Australian Song Styles." *Anthropological Society of South Australia* 4: 2–11.

———. 1968. "Rhythmic Analysis of Aboriginal Syllabic Songs." *Miscellanea Musicologica* 3: 21–49.

———. 1983. "When Is a Song Not a Song? A Study from Northern South Australia." *Bikmaus* 4: 136–44.

———. 1984. "Time Consciousness of Aboriginal Performers." In *Problems and Solutions: Occasional Essays in Musicology Presented to Alice M. Moyle*, edited by J. Kassler and J. Stubington, 149–85. Sydney: Hale and Iremonger Pty. Ltd.

———. 1985. *Aboriginal Music, Education for Living: Cross-Cultural Experiences from South Australia*. St. Lucia: University of Queensland Press.

———. 1997. "Understanding the Profound Structural Knowledge of Central Australian Performers from the Perspective of T. G. H. Strehlow." *Strehlow Research Centre Occasional Papers* 1: 57–78.

———. 1998. "Traditional Australian Music: Central Australia." In *The Garland Encyclopedia of World Music. Australia and the Pacific Islands*, edited by A. L. Kaeppler and J. W. Love, 432–38. New York: Garland Publishing.

Ellis, C. and L. Barwick. 1987. "Musical Syntax and the Problem of Meaning in a Central Australian Songline." *Musicology Australia* 10(1): 41–57.

Foley, W. 1997. *Anthropological Linguistics: An Introduction*. Oxford: Blackwell Publishers.

Gallagher, C., P. Brown, G. Curran, and B. Martin. 2014. *Jardiwanpa Yawulyu: Warlpiri Women's Songs from Yuendumu* (including audio CD). Batchelor, NT: Batchelor Press.

Giles, E. 1875. *Geographic Travels in Central Australia from 1872–1874*. Melbourne: M'Carron, Bird.
Glowczewski, B. 1983. "Death, Women, and 'Value Production': The Circulation of Hair Strings among the Warlpiri of the Central Australian Desert." *Ethnology* 22(3): 225–39.
———. 1991. *Du rêve à la loi chez les Aborigènes: mythes, rites et organisation sociale en Australie*. Paris: Presses Universitaires de France.
———. 2001. *Dream Trackers: Yapa Art and Knowledge of the Australian Desert* [CD ROM]. Lajamanu: Warnayaka Art Centre.
———. 2016. *Desert Dreamers*. Minneapolis: Univocal Publishing.
Goffman, E. 1974. *Frame Analysis*. New York: Harper Colophon.
Grant, C. 2014. *Music Endangerment: How Language Maintenance Can Help*. Oxford: Oxford University Press.
Green J. 2001. "'Both Sides of the Bitumen': Ken Hale Remembering 1959." In *Forty Years On: Ken Hale and Australian Languages*, edited by J. Simpson, D. Nash, M. Laughren, P. Austin, and B. Alpher, 29–43. Canberra: Pacific Linguistics.
Gosse, W. C. 1874. "W. C. Gosse's Explorations, 1873." *Parliamentary Paper, South Australia* 48. Adelaide: Government Printer.
Gummow, M. 1994. "The Power of the Past in the Present: Singers and Songs from Northern New South Wales." *The World of Music* 36(1): 42–65.
———. 1995. "Songs and Sites Moving Mountains: A Study of One Song from Northern NSW." In *The Essence of Singing and the Substance of Song*, edited by L. Barwick, A. Marett, and G. Tunstill, 121–31. Sydney: University of Sydney.
Hale, K. 1971. "A Note on a Warbiri Tradition of Antonymy." In *Semantics: An Interdisciplinary Reader in Philosophy, Linguistics and Psychology*, edited by D. D. Steinberg and L. A. Jakobovits, 472–482. Cambridge: Cambridge University Press.
———. 1984. "Remarks on Creativity in Aboriginal Verse." In *Problems and Solutions: Occasional Essays in Musicology Presented to Alice M. Moyle*, edited by J. C. Kassler and J. Stubington, 254–62. Sydney: Hale and Iremonger Pty. Ltd.
———. 1986. "Notes of World View and Semantic Categories: Some Warlpiri Examples." In *Features and Projections*, edited by P. Muysken and H. van Riemsdijk, 233–54. Dordrecht: Foris.
Hansen, I. V. 1954. "An Account of the Ngalia Initiation Ceremonies at Yuendumu, Central Australia, January 1953." *Transactions of the Royal Society of South Australia* 77: 175–81.
Hartwig, M. C. 1960. The Coniston Killings. BA (Hons) thesis. University of Adelaide, Adelaide.
Hercus L., and G. Koch. 1995. "Song Styles from Near Poeppel's Corner." In *The Essence of Singing and the Substance of Song*, edited by L. Barwick, A. Marett, and G. Tunstill, 106–20. Sydney: University of Sydney.
———. 1997. "Old yet Always New: Song Traditions of Southern Central Australia." Strehlow Research Centre Occasional Papers 1: 83–106.
———. 1999. "'Wire Yard': A Song from Near Lake Eyre." *Aboriginal History* 23: 72–82.

Hill, B. 2002. *Broken Song: T. G. H. Strehlow and Aboriginal Possession.* Milsons Point, NSW: Random House Australia.
Hinkson, M. J. 1999. "Warlpiri Connections: New Technology, New Enterprise and Emergent Social Forms at Yuendumu." PhD thesis. La Trobe University, Melbourne.
———. 2017. *Remembering the Future: Warlpiri Life through the Prism of Drawing.* Canberra: Aboriginal Studies Press.
Jackson, M. 1983. "Knowledge of the Body." *Man* 18(2): 327–45.
Kaberry, P. M. 1939. *Aboriginal Woman Sacred and Profane.* London: George Routledge and Sons Ltd.
Kapferer, B. 1979. "Introduction: Ritual Process and the Transformation of Context." *Social Analysis* 1: 3–19.
Kassler, J. C., and J. Stubington (eds.). 1984. *Problems and Solutions: Occasional Essays in Musicology Presented to Alice M. Moyle.* Sydney: Hale and Iremonger Pty. Ltd.
Keats, B. 1977. "Genetic Structure of Indigenous Populations in Australia and New Guinea." *Journal of Human Evolution* 6(4): 319–39.
Keen, I. 1994. *Knowledge and Secrecy in an Aboriginal Religion: Yolngu of North-east Arnhem Land.* Oxford: Oxford University Press.
Keys, C. 1999. "The Architectural Implications of Warlpiri Jilimi." PhD thesis. University of Queensland, St. Lucia.
Kolig, E. 1981. *The Silent Revolution: The Effects of Modernization on Australian Aboriginal Religion.* Philadelphia: The Institute for the Study of Human Issues.
Lander, N., and R. Perkins [producers]. 1993. *Jardiwarnpa–A Warlpiri Fire Ceremony* [videorecording]. Blood Brothers series part 1. Sydney: Australian Film Finance Corporation, City Pictures.
Laughren, M. 1981. *Religious Movements at Yuendumu 1975–1981.* Canberra: Australian Institute for Aboriginal Studies.
———. 1982. "Warlpiri Kinship Structure." *Oceania Linguistic Monographs* 24: 72–85.
———. 1984. "Warlpiri Baby Talk." *Australian Journal of Linguistics* 4(1): 73–88.
———. 2010. "Warlpiri Women's Songs and Ceremonies: Types, Themes, Form and Functions." Presented to the ANU Seminar Series, 9 March 2010, Australian National University, Canberra.
Laughren, M., Kenneth Hale, and The Warlpiri Lexicography Group. 2007. *Warlpiri-English Encyclopaedic Dictionary.* St. Lucia: University of Queensland.
Leach, E. 1976. *Culture and Communication: The Logic by Which Symbols Are Connected.* Cambridge: Cambridge University Press.
Lewis. J. L. 1999. "Sex and Violence in Brazil: 'Carnaval, Capoeira,' and the Problem of Everyday Life." *American Ethnologist* 26(3): 539–57.
Mackinlay, E. 2000. "Blurring Boundaries between Restricted and Unrestricted Performance: A Case Study of the Ngardirdi of Yanyuwa Women in Borroloola." *Perfect Beat* 4: 73–84.
Magowan, F., and K. Neuenfeldt (eds.). 2005. *Landscapes of Indigenous Performance: Music, Song and Dance of the Torres Strait and Arnhem Land.* Canberra: Australian Institute for Aboriginal and Torres Strait Islander Studies.

Marett, A. 1994. "Wangga: Socially Powerful Songs?" *The World of Music* 36: 67–81.
———. 2005. *Songs, Dreamings and Ghosts*. Middletown, CT: Wesleyan University Press.
Marett, A., and L. Barwick (eds.). 2007. "Studies in Aboriginal Song." Special issue, *Australian Aboriginal Studies* 2.
Mauss, M. 1973. "Techniques of the Body." *Economy and Society* 2(1): 70–88.
McConvell, P. 1985. "The Origin of Subsection in Northern Australia." *Oceania* 56(1): 1–33.
———. 1996. "Backtracking to Babel: The Chronology of Pama-Nyungan Expansion in Australia." *Archaeology in Oceania* 31: 125–44.
McConvell, P., and M. Laughren. 2004. "The Ngumpin-Yapa Subgroup." In *Australian Languages: Classification and the Comparative Method*, edited by C. Bowern and H. Koch, 151–77. Philadelphia: John Benjamins Publishing Company.
McKenzie K. [producer, editor]. 1977. *A Warlbiri Fire Ceremony, Ngatjakula* [motion picture]. Canberra: Australian Institute of Aboriginal Studies.
Meggitt, M. 1962. *Desert People*. Sydney: Angus and Robertson Publishers.
———. 1966. "The Gadjiri among the Warlpiri Aborigines of Central Australia." In *The Oceanic Monographs*, no. 14, edited by A. P. Elkin. Sydney: University of Sydney.
———. 1984. "Initiation among the Warlbiri." In *Religion in Aboriginal Australia: An Anthology*, edited by M. Charlesworth, H. Morphy, D. Bell, K. Maddock, 241–66. St. Lucia: University of Queensland Press.
Merlan, F. 1987. "Catfish and Alligator: Totemic Songs of the Western Roper River, Northern Territory." In *Songs of Aboriginal Australia*, edited by M. Clunies Ross, T. Donaldson, S. Wild, 142–67. Sydney: University of Sydney Press.
Merleau-Ponty, M. 2002. *Phenomenology of Perception* [English edition first published 1962 by Routledge and Kegan Paul]. New York: Routledge Classics.
Merriam, A. P. 1964. *The Anthropology of Music*. Evanston, IL: Northwestern University Press.
Middleton, M. R. and S. H. Frances. 1976. *Yuendumu and Its Children: Life and Health on an Aboriginal Settlement*. Canberra: Australian Government Publishing Service.
Moore, S. F. 1978. *Law as Process: An Anthropological Approach*. London: Routledge and Kegan Paul.
Moore, B., A. Laugesen, M. Gwynn, and J. Robinson. 2016. *The Australian National Dictionary: Australian Words and Their Origins*. 2nd edition. Oxford: Oxford University Press.
Moyle, A. M. 1973. "Songs by Young Aborigines: An Introduction to North Australian Aboriginal Music." In *The Australian Aboriginal Heritage*, edited by R. M. Berndt and E. S. Phillips. Sydney: Australian Society for Education through the Arts.
———. 1974. "North Australia Music: A Taxonomic Approach to the Study of Aboriginal Song Performance." PhD thesis. Monash University, Clayton, Victoria.
———. 1984. "Aboriginal Music and Dance: Reflections and Projections." In *Problems and Solutions: Occasional Essays in Musicology Presented to Alice M. Moyle*, edited by J. C. Kassler and J. Stubington, 15–30. Sydney: Hale and Iremonger Pty. Ltd.

———(ed.). 1992. *Music and Dance of Aboriginal Australia and the South Pacific: The Effects of Documentation on the Living Tradition.* Sydney: University of Sydney.
Moyle, R. 1979. *Songs of the Pintupi: Musical Life in a Central Australian Society.* Canberra: Australian Institute of Aboriginal Studies.
———. 1986. *Alyawarra Music.* Canberra: Australian Institute of Aboriginal Studies.
Munn, N. 1973. *Warlbiri Iconography: Graphic Representation and Cultural Symbolism in a Central Australian Society.* Chicago: University of Chicago Press.
Musharbash, Y. 2003. "Warlpiri Spaciality: An Ethnography of the Spacial and Temporal Dimensions of Everyday Life in a Central Australia Aboriginal Settlement." PhD thesis. Australian National University, Canberra.
———. 2008a. *Yuendumu Everyday: Contemporary Life in Remote Aboriginal Australia.* Canberra: Aboriginal Studies Press.
———. 2008b. "Sorry Business Is Yapa Way: Warlpiri Mortuary Rituals as Embodied Practice." In *Mortality, Mourning and Mortuary Practices in Aboriginal Australia,* edited by K. Glaskin, M. Tonkinson, Y. Musharbash, V. Burbank, 21–36. Ashgate: Aldershot.
Myers, F. 1986. *Pintupi Country, Pintupi Self.* Berkeley. University of California Press.
Nettl, B. 1983. *The Study of Ethnomusicology: Twenty-Nine Issues and Concepts.* Urbana: University of Illinois Press.
Nicholls, C. 1995. "Warlpiri Nicknaming: A Personal Memoir." *International Journal of the Sociology of Language* 113(1): 137–46.
O'Grady, F. 1977. *Francis of Central Australia.* Sydney: Wentworth Books.
O'Grady, G. 1960. "Comments on 'More on Lexicostatistics.'" *Current Anthropology* 1: 338–39.
O'Grady G., C. F. Voegelin, and F. M. Voegelin. 1966. "Languages and the World: Indo-Pacific Fascicle Six." *Anthropological Linguistics* 8(2): 1–197.
Ortner, S. B. 1978. *Sherpas through Their Rituals.* Cambridge: Cambridge University Press.
———. 2006. *Anthropology and Social Theory: Culture, Power, and the Acting Subject.* Durham, NC: Duke University Press.
Peterson, N. 1970. "Buluwandi: A Central Australian Ceremony for the Resolution of Conflict." In *Australian Aboriginal Anthropology: Modern Studies in the Social Anthropology of Australian Aborigines,* edited by R. M. Berndt, 200–215. Nedland: University of Western Australia Press.
———. 1972. "Totemism Yesterday: Sentiment and Local Organisation among the Australian Aborigines." *Man* 7(1): 12–32.
———. 2000. "An Expanding Domain: Mobility and the Initiation Journey." *Oceania* 70: 205–18.
———. 2006. "How Literally Should Warlpiri Metaphors Be Taken?" Paper presented to Critical Intersections, Ethnographic Analyses and Theoretical Influence: In Honour of Nancy Munn. American Anthropological Associations Annual Meetings 15–19 November 2006. San Jose, California.
———. 2008. "Just Humming: The Consequences of the Decline of Learning Contexts amongst the Warlpiri." In *Cultural Styles of Knowledge Transmission: Essays in*

Honour of Ad Borsboom, edited by J. Kommers and E. Venbrux, 114–18. Amsterdam: Askant.

———. 2010. "Other People's Lives: Secular Assimilation, Culture and Ungovernability." In *Culture Crisis: Anthropology and Politics in Aboriginal Australia*, edited by J. Altman and M. Hinkson, 248–58. Sydney: UNSW Press.

———. 2017. "Is There a Role for Anthropology in Cultural Reproduction? Maps, Mining, and the 'Cultural Future' in Central Australia." In *Entangled Territorialities: Negotiating Indigenous Lands in Australia and Canada*, edited by F. Dussart and S. Poirier. Toronto: University of Toronto Press.

Peterson, N., P. McConvell, S. Wild, and R. Hagen. 1978. *Claim to Areas of Tradition Land by the Warlpiri, Kartangarurru–Kurintji*. Alice Springs: Central Land Council.

Poirier, S. 2005. *A World of Relationships: Itineraries, Dreams and Events in the Australian Western Desert*. Toronto: University of Toronto Press.

Roheim, G. 1945. *The Eternal Ones of the Dream: A Psychoanalytic Interpretation of Australian Myth and Ritual*. New York: International Universities Press

Sadie, S. (ed.). 1980. *The New Grove Dictionary of Music and Musicians*. London: Macmillan.

Sahlins, M. 1985. *Islands of History*. Chicago: University of Chicago Press.

Sandall, R., and N. Peterson. 1977 [1967]. *A Warlbiri Fire Ceremony, Ngatjakula* [motion picture]. Canberra: Australian Institute of Aboriginal Studies.

Sanders, W. 1986. "Access, Administration and Politics: The Australian Social Security System and Aborigines." PhD thesis. Canberra, Australian National University.

Schieffelin, E. 1985. "Performance and the Cultural Construction of Reality." *American Ethnologist* 12: 707–24.

Seeger, A. 1987. *Why Suya Sing: A Musical Anthropology of an Amazonian People*. Cambridge: Cambridge University Press.

Shannon, C. 1971. "Warlpiri Women's Music: A Preliminary Study." BA (Hons) thesis. Monash University, Melbourne.

Smith, M. A., B. Fankhauser, and M. Jercher. 1998. "The Changing Provenance of Red Ochre at Puritjarra Rock Shelter, Central Australia: Late Pleistocene to Present." *Proceedings of the Preshistoric Society* 64: 275–92.

Spencer, B., and F. Gillen (ed.). 1899. *The Native Tribes of Central Australia*. London: Macmillan and Co., Ltd.

Stanner, W. E. H. 1966. *On Aboriginal Religion*. Oceania Monograph II. Sydney: University of Sydney.

———. 1979. *White Man Got No Dreaming: Essays 1938–1973*. Canberra: Australian National University Press.

Steer, P. J. 1996. *It Happened at Yuendumu*. Baxter: Phillip J Steer.

Strehlow, T. G. H. 1971. *Songs of Central Australia*. Sydney: Angus & Robertson.

Stuart, J. M. 1865. *The Journals of John McDougall Stuart*. Edited by William Hardman. 2nd edition. London: Saunders, Otley.

Sturzenhofecker, G. 1998. *Times Enmeshed: Gender, Space and History among the Duna of Papua New Guinea*. Stanford, CA: Stanford University Press.

Sutton, P. 1987. "Mystery and Change." In *Songs of Aboriginal Australia*, edited by M. Clunies Ross, T. Donaldson, and S. A. Wild, 77–96. Sydney: University of Sydney Press.

Tambiah, S. J. 1985. *Culture, Thought and Social Action*. Cambridge, MA: Harvard University.

Terry M. 1931. *Hidden Wealth and Hiding People*. New York: Putnam.

Toner P. 2001. "When the Echoes Are Gone: A Yolngu Musical Anthropology." PhD thesis. Australian National University, Canberra.

———. 2003. "Melody and the Musical Articulation of Yolngu Identities." *Yearbook for Traditional Music* 35: 69–95.

———. 2007. "Sing a Country of the Mind: The Articulation of Place in Dhalwangu Song." In *The Soundscapes of Australia: Music, Place and Spirituality*, edited by F. Richards, 165–84. Aldershot: Ashgate.

———. 2015. "Bakhtin's Theory of the Utterance and Dhalwangu *Manikay*." In *Strings of Connectedness: Essays in Honour of Ian Keen*, edited by P. Toner, 161–86. Canberra: ANU Press.

Turpin, M. 2005. "Form and Meaning of Akwelye: A Katyetye Women's Song Series from Central Australia." PhD Thesis. University of Sydney.

Turpin, M., and M. Laughren. 2013. "Edge Effects in Warlpiri Yawulyu Songs: Resyllabification, Epenthesis and Final Vowel Modification." *Australian Journal of Linguistics* 33(4): 399–425.

Turpin, M., T. Stebbins, and S. Morey (eds.). 2010. "The Language of Song." Special issue, *Australian Journal of Linguistics* 30(1).

Turpin, M., and T. Stebbins. 2010. "The Language of Song: Some Recent Approaches in Description and Analysis." *Australian Journal of Linguistics* 30(1): 1–18.

Turner, V. 1967. *The Forest of Symbols: Aspects of Ndembu Ritual*. Ithaca, NY: Cornell University Press.

van Gennep, A. 1960. *The Rites of Passage*. Chicago: University of Chicago Press.

Warburton, P. E. 1875. *Journey across the Western Interior of Australia*. Edited by H. W. Bates. London: Sampson Low, Marston Low and Searle.

Warlpiri women from Yuendumu (edited by G. Curran). 2017a. *Yurntumu-wardingki juju-ngaliya-kurlangu yawulyu:* Warlpiri women's songs from Yuendumu (including DVD). Batchelor, NT: Batchelor Press.

——— (produced by G. Curran). 2017b. *Yurntumu-wardingki juju-ngaliya-kurlangu yawulyu:* Warlpiri women's songs from Yuendumu (set of 4 CDs). Batchelor, NT: Batchelor Press.

Wild, R., and P. Anderson. 2007. *Ampe Akelyernemane Meke Mekarle "Little Children are Sacred": Report of the Northern Territory Board of Inquiry into the Protection of Aboriginal Children from Sexual Abuse*. Darwin: Northern Territory Government.

Wild, S. 1971. "The Role of Katjiri (Gadjiri) among the Warlpiri in Transition." Centre for Research into Aboriginal Affairs. Monash: Monash University.

———. 1975. "Warlbiri Music and Dance in their Social and Cultural Nexus." PhD thesis. Bloomington: Indiana University.

———. 1977/78. "Men as Women: Female Dance Symbolism in Warlpiri Men's Rituals [Based on Work at Hooker Creek, NT]." *Dance Research Journal* 10: 14–22.

———. 1981. "Contemporary Aboriginal Religious Movements of the Western Desert (Lajamanu)." Canberra: Australian Institute of Aboriginal Studies.

———. 1984. "Warlbiri Music and Culture: Meaning in a Central Australian Song Series." In *Problems and Solutions: Occasional Essays in Musicology Presented to Alice M. Moyle*, edited by J. C. Kassler and J. Stubington, 186–201. Sydney: Hale and Iremonger Pty. Ltd.

———. 1987. "Recreating the Jukurrpa: Adaptation and Innovation of Songs and Ceremonies in Warlpiri Society." In *Songs of Aboriginal Australia*, edited by M. Clunies Ross, T. Donaldson, S. A. Wild, 97–120. Sydney: University of Sydney Press.

———. 1990. "A Central Australian Men's Love Song." In *The Honeyant Men's Love Song and Other Aboriginal Song Poems*, edited by R. M. W. Dixon and M. Duwell, 49–69. St. Lucia: University of Queensland Press.

Young, E. 1981a. "Balgo Business at Yuendumu." Canberra: Australian Institute of Aboriginal Studies.

———. 1981b. "Tribal Communities in Rural Areas." Canberra: Australian National University.

Index

A
Aboriginal Land Rights (Northern Territory) Act 1976, 17
Adelaide, 34
Alekarenge (Ali Curung), 33, 72, 78
Anmatyerr (language), 2, 23, 27, 29, 35, 58, 67, 76, 80, 106, 107, 114, 128, 132, 147, 159, 162, 166, 169
Arnhem Land, 15, 61
Arrernte (language), 27, 58, 60
Assembly of God church, 37, 39
Austin, John, 18–19
Australian Institute for Aboriginal and Torres Strait Islander Studies (AIATSIS), 24, 70

B
Baarda, Frank and Wendy, 32
"baby talk," 36
Balgo, 15, 34, 40
"Balgo business," 52–53, 141
Baptist church, 36, 37, 39, 72
Baptist Union of Australia, 31
Baptist Union of South Australia, 29
Barwick, Linda, 55
Bateson, Gregory, 54
Bauman, Richard, 21, 59, 65
Bern, John, 50
Biddle, Jennifer, 125
Birdsell, J. B., 27
Bloch, Maurice, 19
Borroloola, 17

Bourdieu, Pierre, 16
Braitling, W., 29
Briggs, Charles, 59, 65
Brooks, Frederick, 29
Brooks Well, 29
Brown, Peggy Nampijinpa, 88
Bundaberg, 34

C
Central Land Council, 36, 37, 76
Clunies Ross, Margaret, 54, 60
co-initiates (*yarlpurru*), 84
coming back from the bush, 119–121
Community Development Employment Program, 36
Coniston, 28, 29
cosmological beliefs, 11, 14, 44–47, 122
cultural maintenance, 12, 13

D
Dail-Jones (Morais), Megan, 21, 63–64, 97–98, 114
Daly region, 61, 126
dancing, 5, 16, 19, 25, 49, 50, 55, 58, 63–64, 65, 68, 71, 72, 75, 76, 78, 125, 128, 130, 131, 132, 136, 139
for *Kurdiji*, 85, 86, 91, 93, 94, 95, 97–99, 101, 102, 104, 106, 107, 108, 111, 112, 113, 114, 116, 118, 119
in song texts, 144–176

185

Darwin, 28, 34
demography, 33, 80
Donaldson, Tamsin, 61, 142
Dussart, Françoise, 2, 15, 17, 22, 30, 31, 39, 40, 47–49, 51, 65, 66, 68, 70, 71, 75, 76, 85, 130, 132

E
Eastern Kimberley, 34
Egan, Jeannie Nungarrayi, 22–24, 57, 63, 78, 128, 144
Elkin, A. P., 35
Ellis, Catherine, 58, 61, 142
endangerment, 13, 122, 136

F
feuding (inter-family), 30, 38, 40, 79
firestick (for dancing), 6, 68, 86, 95, 99, 104, 105, 107, 112, 116, 118, 128, 134, 148, 155, 159, 162
Fleming, Reverend T. J., 31
Foley, William, 54

G
gender
  ceremonial roles, 17, 129–132
  ceremonial contexts, 47, 49, 139
genres of song, 65–66, 75
getting "caught," 1, 4, 6, 23, 80, 81, 82, 83–87, 105
Gillen, Francis, 26
Glowczewski, Barbara, 45, 49, 84, 101, 129
Goffman, Irvine, 54
Gosse, W. C., 28
Granites, Rex Japanangka, 18, 25
Granites, the (mine), xii, xiii, 18, 25, 28, 30, 102, 150
Grant, Catherine, 122
Gulf of Carpentaria, 17, 50

H
Hale, Kenneth, 8, 15, 58, 61, 132
Hansen, I. V., 78

Hermannsberg, 28
Hinkson, Melinda, 31, 42
Hooker Creek. *See* Lajamanu

J
Jackson, Michael, 16
Jardiwanpa (ceremony), 40, 65, 68–70, 77
jarrawarnu (elder brother), 85. *See also rdiliwarnu*
Jaru Pirrjirdi, 13
jilkaja (initiatory travels), 41, 52, 74–75, 80, 133–134
jinpurrmanu (undulating ritual call, women in opposite generation moiety), 86
juka (brother-in-law/guardian), 81, 84, 85, 91, 93, 94, 115, 116, 117, 118, 119, 120, 128, 133, 160, 171
Jukurrpa (Dreaming), x, xi, 18, 20, 24, 28, 36, 41, 43, 59, 60, 71, 73, 76, 77, 124, 129, 132, 135, 139
  cosmology, 44–47, 48, 140
  designs, 85, 91
  rights, 48–54, 93
  songs and stories, 59, 68, 69, 88, 89, 90, 95, 96, 97, 99, 100, 101, 115, 121, 133, 159

K
Kajirri (ceremony), 59, 67, 68, 131
Kakalyalya Jukurrpa (Major Mitchel Cockatoo Dreaming), 103, 133
Kaninjarra (*kaninju*), 48, 101, 104, 144, 145, 156
Kankarlu, 41, 48, 66, 71, 86, 101, 121, 139, 141, 154
Karntakarnta (traveling women)
  stories and songs, 51, 60, 67, 86, 96, 100, 107, 116, 127, 128, 131, 169
Katherine, xiii, 28, 34
Katyetye (language), 61
Keen, Ian, 15, 16
Kennedy, Lucy Napaljarri, 15

kirda (ownership rights), 48–53, 77, 88–89
Kirrirdikirrawarnu (ceremony), 52, 67, 98, 160
knee quiver, 64, 69, 109, 112
Kolig, Erich, 124, 140, 141
Kunajarrayi (Mount Nicker), 51, 67, 100, 101–102, 108, 109, 111, 112, 113, 149, 150, 151, 165
Kunapipi (ceremony), 67
Kura-kurra (ceremony), 68
Kurdiji (ceremony), 66–68
  ceremony in February 2007, 79–121
  song verses, 144–170
kurdungurlu (manager rights), 48–53, 77, 88–90, 114

L
Lajamanu (Hooker Creek), 13, 28, 30, 33, 40, 64, 67, 68, 77, 78, 123, 125, 126, 133
Larbalestier, Jan, 50
large-scale ceremonies, 40, 65, 79, 132, 141
Laughren, Mary, 25, 27, 42, 52, 68, 69, 77, 84, 143
Leach, Edmund, 16
Lewis, J. Lowell, 53
liminal states, 125, 126–128, 136
Luritja (language), 23, 27, 35, 58, 67, 106

M
Mackinlay, Elizabeth, 17
Malamala, 52, 53, 141. *See also* mortuary rituals; "Sorry business"
manager rights. See *kurdungurlu*
Marett, Allan, 18, 60, 61, 126, 142
Marnakurrawarnu, 52, 66–67, 74, 123, 134, 144, 160
  daytime, 85–92
  after sunset, 92–94
  sunset–sunrise, 95–116
McConvell, Patrick, 27

McGarry, Francis, 30
Meggitt, Mervyn, 22, 28, 29, 30, 45, 59, 67, 71, 73, 80, 84, 85, 101, 123, 135
Melbourne, 34
Merriam, Allan, 17
Merlan, Francesca, 15, 61, 141
milarlpa (spirits), 15, 44, 48
Milpirri, 13, 125, 126
Minamina *yawulyu*, 59, 67, 77, 78
Mornington Island, 27
mortuary rituals, 38, 41, 52, 73, 85, 130, 141. *See also malamala*; "Sorry business"
Mount Allan Aboriginal Settlement (also Wariyiwariyi and Yuelamu), 2–3, 43, 51, 67, 79–80, 87, 113, 132, 138, 143, 170
Mount Denison, 28, 29, 91, 99
Mount Doreen, 29
Mount Wedge, 43
Moyle, Alice, 55
Moyle, Richard, 55, 56, 63
Mt Theo program (now WYDAC), 13, 37
Munn, Nancy, 37, 45, 53, 65, 70, 73
Murray, Constable George, 29
Musharbash, Yasmine, 2, 32, 52, 53, 134
musical change, 24, 30, 31, 33, 79, 93, 152, 155
musical features, 58, 61–63
Myers, Fred, 14, 52, 53, 121, 132, 133

N
Napperby, 28, 67
Native Affairs Branch, 30
Nelson, Harry, 68
Nettl, Bruno, 14
nicknames, 36
Ngajakula (ceremony), 68–69
Ngapa *Jukurrpa*, 107, 169
Ngiyampaa, 61
Nyirrpi, 30, 33
nyurnu-kurlangu (healing songs), 75, 89

O

ochre, 5, 26, 64, 84, 88, 89, 90, 118, 120, 128, 129
  ngunjungunju (white ochre), 4, 5
  yurlpa (red ochre), 4, 59, 137, 157, 158, 162
O'Grady, Geoff, 15, 26, 27
Oldfield, Ruth Napaljarri, 90
outstations, 32–33
ownership. *See kirda*

P

painting up, 4, 5, 50, 54, 55, 58, 64, 65, 70, 75, 85, 86, 87, 88, 91
Pama-Nyungan, 26, 27
Papunya Aboriginal settlement, 168
parnpa (men's restricted songs), 51, 66, 67, 70–71, 74, 78, 85, 86, 90–95, 129, 130, 132
patricouples, 36, 48, 49, 50, 68, 77, 100
patrimoieties, 36, 48, 50, 68
Pentecostal church, 37, 39
Peterson, Nicolas, 12, 19, 27, 32, 33, 41, 42, 52, 53, 68, 69, 71, 78, 80, 124, 128, 133, 141, 142
Pikilyi, 29, 101, 104, 112, 114, 133, 154, 155, 156, 157, 158, 164
Pintupi (language), 14, 52–53, 55, 57, 67, 121, 133, 159, 162
Pitjantjatjara (language), 27, 61, 129
Poirier, Sylvie, 15, 45–46
Port Augusta, 34
pukurdi, 84
Puluwanti (ceremony), 68–69
purlapa (men's public songs), 17, 62, 66, 70, 71–72, 76, 78

R

rdiliwarnu (elder brother), 81, 85, 94, 95, 99, 116, 119, 120, 148, 159, 173
Reece, Laurie, 31
rhythmic texts, 61, 77–80
Rice, Thomas Jangala, 22, 52, 73, 97, 101, 106, 110, 112, 114, 116, 130, 142, 144

Ringer's Soak (Yaruman), 34
rite of passage, 22, 126
Roper River, 61

S

Sahlins, Marshall, 16
Seeger, Anthony, 17
self-determination, 20, 31, 32, 42
Shannon, Cynthia, 64, 67, 78
Sims, Otto Jungarrayi, x–xi (foreword), 18
social organization, 35
song language, xi, 58–61
"Sorry business," 38, 39, 52, 53, 73. *See also malamala*; mortuary rituals
Spencer, Baldwin, 26
sports weekends, 38, 40, 42, 76
Stanner, W. E. H., 14
Steer, Phillip, 30, 31
Strehlow, Carl, 28
Strehlow, T. G. H., 14, 28, 55, 58, 60
Stuart, J. M., 28
subsection system, 35–36, 49, 51, 82, 84, 85, 101, 118, 135
Sutton, Peter, 58, 60

T

Tanami, the (mine), 26
Tanami Network, the, 32
Terry, Michael
Ti-Tree Aboriginal settlement, 28, 108, 146, 164, 168
Toner, Peter, 61, 100
Turpin, Myfany, 55, 58, 61, 64, 78

U

United Nations Education, Scientific and Cultural Organisation, 122

V

Voegelin, C. F. and F. M., 27

W

Wapurtarli yawulyu, 57, 63

Warawata, 52–53, 67, 117–119
Warburton, P. E., 28
Warlmanpa, 26
Warlpiri Media Association (now PAW Media & Communications), 24, 32, 37, 78
Warlukurlangu Artists, 32
Warlukurlangu Jukurrpa (Belonging to Fire Dreaming), 106, 166
Warnipiyi, 99, 106, 165
wati-rirri-rirri (ritual boss), 86, 92–95, 115, 117, 118, 121
Watiyawarnu yawulyu (Acacia tenuissima songs), 88–89
Wild, Stephen, 21, 40, 52, 57, 68, 71, 78, 80, 129, 131, 140
Willowra, 7, 30, 33, 63, 69, 87–89, 97, 114, 121
Whitlam Labor government, 32

Y

Yanyuwa, 17
Yapurnu (Lake Mackay), 67, 78, 100, 144, 145
yawulyu (women's songs), 4, 5, 24, 51, 57, 59, 63–64, 67, 70, 73, 75–78, 85–86, 87–90, 91, 92, 114, 121, 126, 130, 131, 137
yilpinji (love songs)
  men's, 70, 73
  women's, 74, 75, 76–77, 78
Yolngu, 15
Young, Elspeth, 31, 32, 33, 52, 53
Yuendumu Aboriginal Reserve, 30
Yuendumu Aboriginal Settlement
  history, 26–33
  daily life, 33–35
Yuendumu Clinic, 37
Yuendumu Council, 30, 32, 36, 37
Yuendumu Mining Company, 32
Yuendumu Women's Centre, 32
Yujutuyungu, 43, 48
yulpurru (fathers and uncles), 86, 94, 95, 116, 120
Yurrampi Craft, 32
Yurrampi *Jukurrpa*, 30, 43, 48

www.ingramcontent.com/pod-product-compliance
Lightning Source LLC
Chambersburg PA
CBHW051545020426
42333CB00016B/2111